PRINCIPLES OF GERMAN CRIMINAL LAW

German criminal law doctrine, as one of the more influential doctrines over time
and on a global scale, takes rather different approaches to many of the problems of
substantive law from those of the common law family of countries like the United
Kingdom, the United States, Canada, New Zealand, Australia, etc. It also differs
markedly from the system which is most often used in Anglophone writing as a
civil law comparison, the French law. German criminal law is a code-based model
and has been for centuries. The influence of academic writing on its development
has been far greater than in the judge-oriented common law models. This book
will serve as a useful aid to debates about codification efforts in countries that are
mostly based on a case law system, but which wish to re-structure their law in one
or several criminal codes. The comparison will show that similar problems occur
in all legal systems regardless of their provenance, and the attempts of individual
systems at solving them, their successes and their failures, can provide a rich
experience on which other countries can draw and on which they can build.

This book provides an outline of the principles of German criminal law, mainly
the so-called 'General Part' (eg *actus reus*, *mens rea*, defences, participation) and
the core offence categories (homicide, offences against property, sexual offences).
It sets out the principles, their development under the influence of academic
writing and judicial decisions. The book is not meant as a textbook of German
criminal law, but is a selection of interrelated in-depth essays on the central
problems. Wherever it is apposite and feasible, comparison is offered to the
approaches of English criminal law and the legal systems of other common and
civil law countries in order to allow common lawyers to draw the pertinent
parallels to their own jurisdictions.

Studies in International and Comparative Criminal Law: Volume 2

Studies in International and Comparative Criminal Law

General Editor: Michael Bohlander

Criminal law had long been regarded as the preserve of national legal systems, and comparative research in criminal law for a long time had something of an academic ivory tower quality. However, in the past 15 years it has been transformed into an increasingly, and moreover practically, relevant subject of study for international and comparative lawyers. This can be attributed to numerous factors, such as the establishment of ad hoc international criminal tribunals and the International Criminal Court, as well as developments within the European Union, the United Nations and other international organisations. There is a myriad of initiatives related to tackling terrorism, money laundering, organised crime, people trafficking and the drugs trade, and the international 'war' on terror. Criminal law is being used to address global or regional problems, often across the borders of fundamentally different legal systems, only one of which is the traditional divide between common and civil law approaches. It is therefore no longer solely a matter for domestic lawyers. The need exists for a global approach which encompasses comparative and international law.

Responding to this development, this new series will include books on a wide range of topics, including studies of international law, EU law, the work of specific international tribunals and comparative studies of national systems of criminal law. Given that the different systems to a large extent operate based on the idiosyncrasies of the peoples and states that have created them, the series will also welcome pertinent historical, criminological and socio-legal research into these issues.

Editorial Committee:

Mohammed Ayat (ICTR, Kigali)
Robert Cryer (Birmingham)
Caroline Fournet (Exeter)
Kaiyan Kaikobad (Brunel)
Alex Obote-Odora (ICTR, Arusha)
Dawn Rothe (Old Dominion University, VA)
Silvia Tellenbach (Freiburg)
Helen Xanthaki (IALS, London)
Liling Yue (Beijing)

Volume 1: The German Criminal Code: A Modern English Translation
Michael Bohlander

Volume 2: Principles of German Criminal Law
Michael Bohlander

Principles of German Criminal Law

Michael Bohlander

·H A R T·
PUBLISHING

OXFORD AND PORTLAND, OREGON
2009

Published in North America (US and Canada) by
Hart Publishing
c/o International Specialized Book Services
920 NE 58th Avenue, Suite 300
Portland, OR 97213-3786
USA
Tel: +1 503 287 3093 or toll-free: (1) 800 944 6190
Fax: +1 503 280 8832
E-mail: orders@isbs.com
Website: http://www.isbs.com

Hart Publishing Ltd, 16C Worcester Place, OX1 2JW
Telephone: +44 (0)1865 517530 Fax: +44 (0)1865 510710
E-mail: mail@hartpub.co.uk
Website: http://www.hartpub.co.uk

British Library Cataloguing in Publication Data
Data Available

ISBN: 978-1-84113-630-1

Typeset by Hope Services, Abingdon
Printed and bound in Great Britain by
CPI Antony Rowe Ltd, Chippenham

To my parents

Ruth Emmi Bohlander and Heinrich Benjamin Bohlander

God could not be everywhere and therefore he made mothers.
Jewish Proverb

One father is more than a hundred schoolmasters.
George Herbert, Outlandish Proverbs, 1640

PREFACE

This book is meant as a companion to my translation of the German Criminal Code, recently published by Hart. Despite the fact that there are many publications that deal with individual comparative aspects of German criminal law, a coherent presentation of the main principles in English has been missing so far. I hope that the book together with the Criminal Code translation will give readers a reliable first impression of the German law.

Principles of German Criminal Law has been long in the making and I must first of all thank Richard Hart for his patience in waiting for the manuscript, due date after due date, and all the staff at Hart Publishing for their professional and diligent support, also with the previous Criminal Code translation. The writing of the final chapters was greatly aided by a six-week sabbatical which I spent in the United States in March and April 2008 at the invitation of the Department of Sociology, Anthropology and Criminology of the University of Northern Iowa. I thank its Head of Department, Professor Kent Sandstrom, and the Dean of the College of Behavioral and Social Sciences, Professor John W Johnson, for the exemplary hospitality and generosity that was extended to me during my stay. I am furthermore indebted to the Department of Law at the University of Durham for its generous research leave policy. A former student of mine, Ms Anna Fingerit, graciously assisted me in gathering Anglophone materials in the preparatory phase. Professor Clare McGlynn kindly gave helpful comments on the sexual offences chapter.

A big thank you must again go to Chris Newman, Senior Lecturer, of Sunderland University, who read the entire text and made sure that the offence to native speaker sensibilities was kept to a minimum. Stefan Kirsch, criminal defence attorney from Frankfurt, Germany, and advisory board member of the Durham Centre for Criminal Law and Criminal Justice, read the chapters and commented on the substance from the German point of view; to him I also owe a debt of deep gratitude.

Most of all, I am immensely grateful to my dear friend and colleague, Professor Dawn L Rothe, now at Old Dominion University in Virginia, for taking me into her home during my stay in Iowa, for looking after me so well and making me feel like family, at a time when she herself was going through a very difficult patch fighting a serious disease. Without her, my stay would not nearly have been half as rewarding. Thanks also to the family Husky, Tasha Rae, for being such a considerate, civilised and cuddly canine.

Christine and Laura, thank you for letting me go away yet again for such a long time, and for your continuous understanding and support. You both are a blessing in my life.

Durham, June 2008   Michael Bohlander

TABLE OF CONTENTS

Table of Contents

LIST OF ABBREVIATIONS

§, §§	Section, sections
AG	*Amtsgericht* = County Court
BayObLG	*Bayerisches Oberstes Landesgericht* = Bavarian Supreme Court
BBG	*Bundebeamtengesetz*
BGB	*Bürgerliches Gesetzbuch* = Civil Code
BGH	*Bundesgerichtshof* = Federal Court of Justice
BGHR	*BGH-Rechtsprechung Strafsachen*, cited by section, keyword and number
BGHSt	*Amtliche Sammlung der Entscheidungen des Bundesgerichtshofes in Strafsachen* = Official Gazette of the Decisions of the Federal Court of Justice in Criminal Matters, cited by volume and page
BGHZ	*Amtliche Sammlung der Entscheidungen des Bundesgerichtshofes in Zivilsachen* = Official Gazette of the Decisions of the Federal Court of Justice in Civil Matters, cited by volume and page
BSG	*Bundessozialgericht* = Federal Social Welfare Tribunal
BVerfG	*Bundesverfassungsgericht* = Federal Constitutional Court
BVerfGE	*Amtliche Sammlung der Entscheidungen des Bundesverfassungsgerichts* = Official Gazette of the Decisions of the Federal Constitutional Court, cited by volume and page
DAR	*Deutsches Autorecht*, cited by year and page
DRiZ	*Deutsche Richterzeitung*, cited by year and page
EzSt	Lemke (ed), *Entscheidungssammlung zum Straf- und Ordnungswidrigkeitenrecht*, cited by section and marginal number
ff	Forth-following
GA	*Goltdammers Archiv für Strafrecht*, cited by year and page after 1953; prior to that by volume and page
GDR	German Democratic Republic
JR	*Juristische Rundschau*, cited by year and page
JW	*Juristische Wochenschrift*, cited by year and page
JZ	*Juristenzeitung*, cited by year and page
KG	*Kammergericht* = State Supreme Court of Berlin
LG	*Landgericht* = District Court
LK-contributor	*Leipziger Kommentar zum Strafgesetzbuch* (11th edn, de Gruyter, 1992–2004), cited by section and marginal number
MDR	*Monatsschrift für Deutsches Recht*, cited by year and page
Mn	Marginal number
NJW	*Neue Juristische Wochenschrift*, cited by year and page

NStZ	*Neue Zeitschrift für Strafrecht*, cited by year and page
NStZ-RR	*Neue Zeitschrift für Strafrecht Rechtsprechungs-Report*, cited by year and page
OGHSt	*Entscheidungen des Obersten Gerichtshofes der Britischen Zone in Strafsachen* = Decisions of the Supreme Court of the British Zone in Criminal Matters, cited by volume and page
OLG	*Oberlandesgericht* = State Supreme Court
OLGSt	*Entscheidungen der Oberlandesgerichte zum Straf- und Strafverfahrensrecht*, cited by section and para or page
RG	*Reichsgericht* = Supreme Court of the Reich
RGSt	*Amtliche Sammlung der Entscheidungen des Reichsgerichts in Strafsachen* = Official Gazette of the Decisions of the Supreme Court of the Reich in Criminal Matters, cited by volume and page
ROW	*Recht in Ost und West*, cited by year and page
Roxin AT I & AT II	Claus Roxin, *Strafrecht Allgemeiner Teil*, Band I (4th edn, Munich, CH Beck, 2006); Band II (Munich, CH Beck, 2003)
Sch/Sch-contributor	Schönke and Schröder, *Strafgesetzbuch, Kommentar* (27th edn, Munich, CH Beck, 2006), cited by § and marginal number
Smith & Hogan	David Ormerod, *Smith & Hogan, Criminal Law* (Oxford, Oxford University Press, 2005)
SoldatenG	*Soldatengesetz*
StGB	*Strafgesetzbuch* = Criminal Code
StV	*Strafverteidiger*, cited by year and page
StVollzG	*Strafvollzugsgesetz*
Tröndle/Fischer	Herbert Tröndle and Thomas Fischer, *Strafgesetzbuch und Nebengesetze* (54th edn, Munich, CH Beck, 2007), cited by section and marginal number
UZwG	*Gesetz über den unmittelbaren Zwang*
Vorbem.	*Vorbemerkung*
VRS	*Verkehrsrechtssammlung*, cited by volume and page
Wessels/Beulke, AT	Johannes Wessels and Werner Beulke, *Strafrecht Allgemeiner Teil* (34th edn, Heidelberg, CF Müller, 2004)
Wistra	*Zeitschrift für Wirtschaft, Steuer, Strafrecht*, cited by year and page
WStG	*Wehrstrafgesetz*
ZDG	*Zivildienstgesetz*
ZStW	*Zeitschrift für die gesamte Strafrechtswissenschaft*, cited by year, volume and page

1

Introduction

Purpose of the Book

This book is meant to present what its title says: principles. It is not a traditional textbook of German criminal law in the way that German academics would understand it. My German colleagues will probably say that I left out too much, emphasised the wrong things and indulged in oversimplification, not to mention the mistakes I may have made. While I do not feel that I should immediately plead guilty to that charge in its entirety, a plea of *nolo contendere* to the first three may be unavoidable, but I will leave that to the judgement of the reader. My intention is to present the salient features of the German substantive criminal law to an Anglophone legal audience in order to allow them to understand the fundamental differences and similarities between a system that is said to be based on a top-down model of deductive logical reasoning, and the inductive, case-by-case pragmatic approach behind the common law. However, as I point out in the chapter on basic concepts (chapter two), this distinction has become much more blurred in recent times than it had been before.

Some difficult choices had to be made to keep the task manageable within the space confines of the book. I have concentrated on the principles found in the so-called 'General Part', and less on individual offences, because the General Part usually tells us more about the genetic code, as it were, of a legal system than individual offences. It also informs the application of all specific offences and the latter can therefore not be understood without the knowledge of the principles of the former. Yet even within the General Part, I have left out one major section, namely the law and practice of sentencing, not to mention procedural issues such as the statute of limitations, jurisdiction, conditions of prosecution, etc. While the last three are not immediately necessary for the understanding of the material principles governing criminal liability, the section on penalties and sentencing would merit a book in its own right, because it has wide ramifications regarding criminal procedure and juvenile criminal law. For the moment, the reader is referred to the Criminal Code to gather information on the principles of sentencing and the arsenal of available sanctions. The presentation will touch upon these in individual places where necessary for the understanding of a certain general issue. The offence categories I selected for closer attention were homicide, and sexual and property offences. Apart from the fact that they represent what one might call core concepts of any criminal legal system, major reforms have recently been or are still ongoing in the United Kingdom in these areas. The chapters on the offences are in themselves mere introductions and cannot describe the wide ambits of judicial casuistic interpretations of individual problems. I hope that the reader will nevertheless get an idea of their basic structure.

While I have endeavoured to include comparative aspects, especially with regard to the law of England and Wales which I had the opportunity of teaching and studying more closely since my move to Durham in 2004, this is not a comparative law book. Not every principle received a comparative treatment, but some of them presented themselves as worthy of that attention, be it because of a recent development in legislation or in the case law. To a lesser degree I have included references to legal systems other than that of England and Wales. The terminology used to describe German concepts is meant to imitate the English usage to the closest approximation; however, I trust that readers more familiar with the terminology employed in other Commonwealth jurisdictions or the United States will have no difficulty in adapting. Some German concepts are difficult to express with the vocabulary available in English law, a fact that forced me either to use approximate English concepts such as conspiracy, that have no material counterpart in German theory, or to coin new phrases in the hope that they will catch on, as, for example, the principle of limited dependence as describing the specific doctrine of limited accomplice liability.

History and Development

The criminal law of Germany, originally codified in 1871, in its present form is mainly based on a major reform in the 1970s and several less fundamental but still major subsequent reforms. However, academic doctrine and judicial practice still rely to some extent on commentary and case law from before that time. While it is true that analysing the historical environment at any given time is a necessary tool in order to understand fully the development and status quo of a legal system, I have decided not to include a separate, general chapter on the development before the 1970s and have only looked at specific issues in reform since then. The major issues that had an impact apart from the 1970s reform were, of course, the period of the Nazi regime from 1933–45, German re-unification in 1990 and the transitional phase since then. Where historical developments were conducive to the description of principles addressed in this book, they were considered in the relevant context.

German Materials Used

Returning to what I said at the beginning of this chapter, the introductory overview character of the book also had an impact on the German sources I used in the footnotes and other references. While I emphasise that academic commentary and doctrine still play a larger role in the German system than, for example, in the law of the United Kingdom, the fact is nevertheless that in practice the law is what the courts say it is. The presentation thus follows in principle the views of the courts, with pertinent references to academic literature on certain contentious matters. Thus, the footnotes contain a large number of case law citations; among those I have tried to restrict myself to quoting decisions of the Federal Court of Justice (*Bundesgerichtshof*—BGH), the Federal Constitutional Court (*Bundesverfassungsgericht*—BVerfG) and of the *Reichsgericht*—RG, the Supreme Court of the German Reich until 1945. In some instances, decisions by state courts of appeal (*Oberlandesgerichte*—OLG), district courts (*Landgerichte*—LG) and county courts (*Amtsgerichte*—AG) were also included.

References to academic commentary have been restricted to a few easily accessible sources, and among those mostly to the standard one-volume commentary founded in 1942 by Adolf Schönke and Horst Schröder, now in its 27th edition of 2006. This commentary, written by a number of Germany's foremost criminal law academics, has the necessary academic depth of analysis and scope of further references in order to function as this main base of citation. While it would be a serious mistake for a German first-year law student to use only one commentary as a source for his or her course assignments, I felt justified in relying mainly on this commentary for our purposes: apart from the much shorter commentary by *Fischer*, which is moreover a practitioner commentary, it is the most up-to-date (and affordable) overall work available that has the necessary depth. The large multi-volume commentaries (for example, the *Leipziger Kommentar* and the *Münchener Kommentar*) are prohibitively expensive for individual academics and are in part several years behind the actual status quo due to their cumbersome publication process. It is a banal insight that any further study of a legal system other than one's own demands foreign language skills commensurate with the requirements of understanding the legal terminology. Any reader with a sufficient command of the German language desiring to gain a deeper insight will already find a wealth of additional information in the more than 2,800 pages of *Schönke/ Schröder*. The nature of a commentary is that it contains references to specific treatises and articles on individual problems for further study, and the *Schönke/ Schröder* commentary does that in an exemplary fashion; in fact, a German lawyer looking for materials on a certain problem would follow exactly the same route, namely, start with one commentary. In sum, I am convinced that no significant additional gain was to be derived from citing those other commentaries (or even the specialist writings) in the footnotes (although the library of Durham University stocks them).

A Note on Citation

As in my translation of the Criminal Code, from which this section is actually taken, I have kept to the German method of law citation. To keep the text as short and uncluttered as possible, I have used the German symbol for 'section', which is '§'. After that, the subdivisions are 'subsection' ('(1)', or '(2) to (7)'), 'sentence' ('1st sentence'), 'number' ('No 1', or 'Nos 2 to 5') and letters ('(a)'), 'alternatives', etc. This is not necessarily an exclusive hierarchical sequence, as, depending on the length of individual provisions, numbers could have several sentences, etc.

Thus, for example, the following citation '§ 211(2) 3rd alt' would read: 'Section 211, subsection (2), third alternative' and would denote killing a person out of greed.

The double '§§' means 'sections' and has normally been used here, other than in the German practice, to denote an uninterrupted sequence of sections, such as '§§ 176 to 177'. Unless another law is mentioned, all §§ are those of the Criminal Code.

Chapter Overview

Finally, an overview of how the study of this book's object is meant to progress. It moves from the general to the particular, beginning with the chapter on basic concepts.[1] This lays out the ideology behind the approach of German criminal law, explain the sources of law and their hierarchy, principles of interpretation and the role of precedent, the fundamentally important tripartite structure of offences, basic material tenets of German criminal policy, rule-of-law principles as well as the basic definitional dichotomy between felonies (*Verbrechen*) and misdemeanours (*Vergehen*) and its consequences.

The second chapter looks at the *objektiver Tatbestand*, the equivalent of the *actus reus*, as the bottom rung of the tripartite offence structure, and covers issues such as types and functions of the *actus reus*, acts and omissions, causation and objective negligence.

This is followed by the third chapter on the subjective side of the *Tatbestand*, comparable to *mens rea*. It deals with matters of intent and its delineation from advertent negligence, mistakes of fact in the *actus reus* and the facts underlying generally recognised defences as well as transferred malice scenarios.

Chapter four, the longest chapter, deals with the justificatory defences on the second tier of the tripartite ladder. It first addresses general common issues such as their conceptual basis and the cumulation of defences, the criterion of a sub-

[1] Excerpts of the chapter on Basic Concepts have been used in the Brief Introduction to *The German Criminal Code: A Modern English Translation* (Hart Publishing, 2008).

jective element, provocation of defence situations and rule-of-law aspects such as retro-activity. The individual defences examined are consent and presumed consent, official authorisation, official power or instructions and superior orders, collision of duties, exercise of justified interests, citizen's arrest, self-defence and necessity.

Chapter five examines the third tier of guilt and particularly in that context the requirements of subjective negligence, as well as the excusatory defences of mistake of law, excessive self-defence, duress and supra-legal duress, insanity and diminished responsibility.

Chapter six attempts to explain the requirements for liability, short of the full commission of an offence. It examines the definition of attempt, impossible attempts and imaginary offences as well as the withdrawal from an attempt and its effects on the offender's liability.

Chapter seven investigates the liability of accomplices under different forms of participation, namely, principals by proxy using another person as an instrument or agent, joint principals, abetting and aiding and how to distinguish between them. The principle of limited dependence (*limitierte Akzessorietät*) under §§ 28 and 29 is explained, as are the effects of errors by the individual participants. Finally, attention is given to the German principle corresponding to conspiracy and withdrawal from a conspiracy.

Chapters eight, nine and 10 contain introductions to the law of homicide, and sexual and property offences.

2

Basic Concepts and Terminology:
An Overview

The Ideology of German Criminal Law

German criminal law is heavily doctrine-driven, much more so than is the case under the approach taken, for example, by English criminal law, or for that matter, the criminal law of many common law systems. While it is true that parliamentary law-making has gained a lot of ground especially in recent decades, the latter have traditionally relied on a judge-based development on a case-by-case basis. Because their law had to be tailored for use by lay people as fact-finders in the criminal process, be they jurors or lay magistrates, a high emphasis was put on remaining as close as possible to what judges like to call 'common sense'. The following quote from a well-known English case[1] on the effects of voluntary intoxication on the *mens rea* of the accused, *DPP v Majewski*, is a good example of this attitude:

> A number of distinguished academic writers support this contention on the ground of logic. As I understand it, the argument runs like this. Intention, whether special or basic (or whatever fancy name you choose to give it), is still intention. If voluntary intoxication by drink or drugs can, as it admittedly can, negative the special or specific intention necessary for the commission of crimes such as murder and theft, how can you justify in strict logic the view that it cannot negative a basic intention, eg the intention to commit offences such as assault and unlawful wounding? *The answer is that in strict logic this view cannot be justified. But this is the view that has been adopted by the common law of England, which is founded on common sense and experience rather than strict logic.* There is no case in the 19th century when the courts were relaxing the harshness of the law in relation to the effect of drunkenness on criminal liability in which the courts ever went so far as to suggest that drunkenness, short of drunkenness producing insanity, could ever exculpate a man from any offence other than one which required some special or specific intent to be proved. [Emphasis added.]

A similar argument with a view to the importance of procedural rules was made on the international level by the Australian judge David Hunt, who had previously been the Chief Judge at Common Law at the Supreme Court of New South Wales,

---

[1] *DPP v Majewski* (1977) AC 443, repeated in *R v Powell and another; R v English* (1999) AC 1.

at the International Criminal Tribunal for the Former Yugoslavia (ICTY) in the case against Milan Milutinovic[2] and others, when he said in relation to the prosecution's contention that he no longer had jurisdiction to decide on the request of the accused:

> The Rules of Procedure and Evidence were intended to be the servants and not the masters of the Tribunal's procedures.[3]

Nothing could in principle be further from the truth under German law. As we will see, German law has widely subscribed to the use of historical and teleological interpretation, which includes the application of public policy arguments like the one used by the court in the Majewski case, but such a bare-faced rejection of the appeal of logic would be an alien thought to any German judge, let alone academic. Despite the fact that the development of German criminal law has also increasingly come under the influence of judicial reasoning about legal principles, especially if it happens at the levels of the BGH or BVerfG, or as far as much of the procedural law is concerned, the ECtHR, there is still a discernible impact of and reliance on academic writing, mainly based on the German legal commentary culture. German academics and practitioners have over the centuries produced large and intricate commentaries on the different codified laws, and handbooks on practice and procedure. Only the latter can be equated with common law publications such as Archbold or Stone's Justice Manual. Large multi-volume commentaries on specific codes, such as, for example, the *Leipziger Kommentar zum Strafgesetzbuch* or the *Löwe-Rosenberg* on the Criminal Procedure Code, as much as one-volume works such as the '*Schönke/Schröder*' or '*Fischer*' on the Criminal Code, as well as the '*Meyer-Goßner*' or the *Karlsruher Kommentar* on the procedural code, the *Strafprozeßordnung*, written by respected academics, seasoned judges and practitioners through many editions, do not just digest the development of literature and jurisprudence, but they also analyse them and criticise the arguments put forward by the writers and judges and if they happen to disagree with them, set out their own view of how things should be done,

---

[2] *Prosecutor v Milan Milutinovic et al*, Case No II-99-37-I, Decision on Application by Dragoljub Ojdanic for Disclosure of ex parte Submissions, of 8 November 2002, at para 14. He had previously made the same argument in the case of *Prosecutor v Dario Kordic & Mario Cerkez*, Case No IT-95-14/2, Decision Authorising Appellant's Briefs to Exceed the Limit Imposed by the Practice Direction on the Length of Briefs and Motions, of 8 August 2001, at para 6, and in *Prosecutor v Zoran Kupreskic et al*, Case No IT-95-16-A, Separate Opinion of Judge David Hunt on Appeal by Dragan Papic against Ruling to Proceed by Deposition, of 15 July 1999, at para 18. He was right to the extent that the Rules of Procedure and Evidence at the ICTY were judge-made in the first instance and ranked below the Statute in the hierarchy of norms. However, in systems where the rules are not made by judges, this statement is questionable.

[3] Citing as authority in the decisions mentioned above merely two English civil law cases from 1897 and 1907: *Kendall v Hamilton* (1879) 4 App Cas 504 at 525, 530–1; and *In the Matter of an Arbitration between Coles and Ravenshear* [1907] 1 KB 1. In the latter, Sir Richard Henn Collins, the Master of the Rolls, said in the Court of Appeal (at 4): 'Although I agree that a Court cannot conduct its business without a code of procedure, I think that the relation of rules of practice to the work of justice is intended to be that of handmaid rather than mistress, and the Court ought not to be so far bound and tied by rules, which are after all only intended as general rules of procedure, as to be compelled to do what will cause injustice in the particular case.'

something hardly ever found, for example, in Archbold. It is no rarity to find a court changing its long-standing jurisprudence on a certain topic because the logic behind the arguments of renowned academic writers, often made in such commentaries, convinces the judges that their previous views were wrong.

The fact that German law is to a large extent based on the more or less strict application of logic and well-developed methods of interpretation is also a function of the German academics' attitude to the judicial process: they do not see academia as the mere handmaiden of the judges, but as the guiding light. To their minds, judicial practice should follow abstract reasoning rather than adhere to a casuistic approach that favours justice in the individual case over systemic coherence to the major and overarching legal principles across the board.[4] The German approach, to use a simplistic description, is thus deductive in nature, as opposed to the more inductive one of the common law,[5] and it runs counter to the inclination of laymen who have been said to be 'likely to prefer warm confusion to cool consistency'.[6] I hasten to add that in some areas of German law, notably labour and employment law, large sections are almost wholly judge-made because the government has for some reason or other not taken up the burden of providing for proper codification. Very often, Parliament will in its acts codify a long-standing and proven judicial tradition and to that extent there is, of course, a judicial influence on codified law-making, too.

The BVerfG has indeed reclaimed for itself the power to order the government to provide for a codified law, often in the criminal sphere, within a certain time frame and sometimes even with a direction as to its possible substance; otherwise the court threatened to regulate the area judicially or quash any future decision based on the unchanged law as unconstitutional. The most famous of these decisions was the 1975 judgment on the criminal law of abortion,[7] when the BVerfG struck down an act of Parliament that had advocated a pure time-lapse-based solution, allowing for an abortion within the first three months of a pregnancy without requiring serious reasons for the abortion. The court went on to state in the disposition of the judgment that an abortion was acceptable if otherwise the life or the health of the mother were in grave danger, and that the legislator *was free to add other cases of a similar gravity.*[8] The court was in effect telling the legislature the parameters it had to abide by when drafting its next version of the act. It expressly did so to establish a basis for the criminal courts to decide pending abortion charges and to provide for legal certainty until the legislature had amended the law as requested.[9] Many at the time, including the dissenting judges, saw that

---

[4] This is another typical area of divergence between common and civil law systems, as has been shown by Mirjan Damaska in his seminal work *The Faces of Justice and State Authority, A Comparative Approach to the Legal Process* (New Haven and London, Yale University Press, 1986).

[5] See also Radbruch, *Der Geist des englischen Rechts und die Anglo-Amerikanische Jurisprudenz, Aufsätze herausgegeben und eingeführt von Heinrich Scholler* (Berlin, Lit-Verlag, 2006).

[6] Damaska, fn 4; 28.

[7] BverfGE 39, 1.

[8] *Ibid*, fn 7, at no 5 of the disposition and para 204 of the reasons.

[9] *Ibid*, fn 7, at para 204.

as a usurpation of legislative functions and as a violation of the separation of powers,[10] but the court has since employed that approach in other circumstances. However, these instances are few and far between.[11]

The function and view of the trial and its effect on legal reasoning in the sphere of substantive law are markedly different. This begins with the nature and structure of the German criminal process, on which a few words must be said. German criminal proceedings are by their nature not a contest between parties, but an objective, judge-led inquiry into the material truth of the facts underlying a criminal charge. Equality of arms is not a principle that would apply to a similar extent as it does in adversarial systems. From the German point of view, the prosecution, on the one hand, has no individual rights of fair trial; it has powers and duties, with the consequence that the prosecution cannot argue a violation of the right to equality of arms because the system is not adversarial, but the court *itself* is under a duty to find the truth. The defence, on the other hand, has no duties, only rights, yet it may suffer if it does not exercise them properly, as is the case under the well-known common law 'save-it-or-waive-it' principle relating to grounds of appeal, which appears to find more and more favour with German courts, too, especially in connection with § 238 II StPO. The defence is seen as being by definition inferior in power and facilities to the prosecution, so from a German point of view, equality of arms is a principle that protects the defence, but not the prosecution. Any idea of changing the law, for example, by introducing probative burdens of proof on the defence or reading down the requirements the prosecution has to prove (see, for example, the Sexual Offences Act 2003 with regard to requiring only proof of absence of *reasonable* belief in consent as opposed to the *honest* belief standard still applicable to all other offences under *DPP v Morgan*[12]) in order to make it easier for the prosecution to bring its case, would have no equivalent in German doctrine, and indeed would be seen as constitutionally questionable. Difficulties of the prosecution to prove its case cannot lead to an abridgement of the defence's position by interpreting down the threshold of certain offence requirements.

Sources of Criminal Law and Hierarchy of Norms

German law follows, in principle, the strict application of the maxim *nullum crimen, nulla poena sine lege*. As far as the criminal liability of a person is concerned, the maxim is augmented by the adjective *scripta*, namely, the law must be a written law, and article 103(2) of the *Grundgesetz* (Basic Law—hereinafter: GG)

---

[10] See the references in Sch/Sch-Eser, Vorbem. §§ 218 *ff*, Mn. 3.
[11] See Hartmut Maurer, *Staatsrecht I* (4th edn, Munich, CH Beck, 2005) 681, with examples of further instances and academic commentary.
[12] [1976] AC 182.

makes it clear that criminal liability must be based on a full Act of Parliament; mere secondary governmental instruments and regulations will not usually suffice, unless the Act of Parliament refers to those in order to demarcate the conduct which it criminalises. Such laws are called *Blankettgesetze*, or 'blanket Acts', because they themselves do not contain (all) the elements of the offence, but refer to other legislation for that purpose.

Yet, recent German history after the Second World War and the 1990 Unification Treaty appears to have accepted one category of law that would stand outside the requirements of article 103(2) GG: the demands of natural justice or natural law. After the abject failure of the post-war German judiciary to address the gross abuse of the formal legal process from 1933 to 1945, this issue arose again when the courts of the unified Germany after 1990 had to deal with the murders committed by GDR border guards, and with the orders given by their superiors in the military and political chain of command.[13] This time, everyone was bent on not repeating the mistakes made after the Third Reich. The thinking behind this approach is based on the so-called 'Radbruch formula',[14] after the German philosopher Gustav Radbruch (1878–1949), who analysed the relationship between positive law and natural law at the example of the Nazi regime's legislation. The formula states that formally valid positive law usually prevails over substantive concepts of justice, even if it is unjust and irrational. This primacy ends when there are breaches of principles of justice, of intolerable proportions, which are in turn defined as instances where the positive law explicitly and systematically neglects its goal of pursuing the aims of justice, and when the principle of equality is ignored on purpose. In short, the German courts held that former East German soldiers and judges were bound to interpret the socialist law in the light of the liberal spirit of fundamental concepts of human rights[15] over the commands of the written law. This approach was upheld by the European Court of Human Rights (ECtHR) in the cases of *Streletz, Kessler and Krenz*,[16] members of the

---

[13] See, eg Peter E Quint, 'Judging the Past: The Prosecution of East German Border Guards and the GDR Chain of Command' (1999) *The Review of Politics* 303.

[14] German original text in (1946) *Süddeutsche Juristenzeitung*, 105, at 107: '*Der Konflikt zwischen der Gerechtigkeit und der Rechtssicherheit dürfte dahin zu lösen sein, daß das positive, durch Satzung und Macht gesicherte Recht auch dann den Vorrang hat, wenn es inhaltlich ungerecht und unzweckmäßig ist, es sei denn, daß der Widerspruch des positiven Gesetzes zur Gerechtigkeit ein so unerträgliches Maß erreicht, daß das Gesetz als unrichtiges "Recht" der Gerechtigkeit zu weichen hat. Es ist unmöglich, eine schärfere Linie zu ziehen zwischen den Fällen des gesetzlichen Unrechts und den trotz unrichtigen Inhalts dennoch geltenden Gesetzen; eine andere Grenzziehung aber kann mit aller Schärfe vorgenommen werden: wo Gerechtigkeit nicht einmal erstrebt wird, wo die Gleichheit, die den Kern der Gerechtigkeit ausmacht, bei der Setzung positiven Rechts bewußt verleugnet wurde, da ist das Gesetz nicht etwa nur "unrichtiges" Recht, vielmehr entbehrt es überhaupt der Rechtsnatur. Denn man kann Recht, auch positives Recht, gar nicht anders definieren als eine Ordnung und Satzung, die ihrem Sinne nach bestimmt ist, der Gerechtigkeit zu dienen.*'

[15] See for examples of cases BVerfGE 23, 98; BGHZ 3, 94 (shooting of a deserter by members of the *Volkssturm* in the last days of the war); BGHSt 39, 1 and BGHSt 41, 101 (GDR border killings); and BGHSt 41, 157 and BGHSt 41, 247 (perverting the course of justice by GDR judges and prosecutors).

[16] *Streletz, Kessler and Krenz v Germany* [GC], case nos 34044/96, 35532/97, 44801/98; judgment of 22 March 2001.

political ruling class, and *K-H.W*, a border guard.[17] In *Streletz et al*, the ECtHR stated:[18]

> Indeed, the Court reiterates that for the purposes of Article 7 § 1, however clearly drafted a provision of criminal law may be, in any legal system, there is an inevitable element of judicial interpretation. There will always be a need for elucidation of doubtful points and for adaptation to changing circumstances . . .
>
> Contrary reasoning would run counter to the very principles on which the system of protection put in place by the Convention is built. The framers of the Convention referred to those principles in the preamble to the Convention when they reaffirmed 'their profound belief in those fundamental freedoms which are the foundation of justice and peace in the world and are best maintained, on the one hand, by an effective political democracy and, on the other, by a common understanding and observance of the human rights upon which they depend' and declared that they were 'like-minded' and had 'a common heritage of political traditions, ideals, freedom and the rule of law'. . . .
>
> Moreover, regard being had to the pre-eminence of the right to life in all international instruments on the protection of human rights . . . including the Convention itself, in which the right to life is guaranteed by Article 2, the Court considers that the German courts' strict interpretation of the GDR's legislation in the present case was compatible with Article 7 § 1 of the Convention.
>
> The Court notes in that connection that the first sentence of Article 2 § 1 of the Convention enjoins States to take appropriate steps to safeguard the lives of those within their jurisdiction. That implies a primary duty to secure the right to life by putting in place effective criminal-law provisions to deter the commission of offences which endanger life, backed up by law-enforcement machinery for the prevention, suppression and sanctioning of breaches of such provisions . . .
>
> The Court considers that a State practice such as the GDR's border-policing policy, which flagrantly infringes human rights and above all the right to life, the supreme value in the international hierarchy of human rights, cannot be covered by the protection of Article 7 § 1 of the Convention. That practice, which emptied of its substance the legislation on which it was supposed to be based, and which was imposed on all organs of the GDR, including its judicial bodies, cannot be described as 'law' within the meaning of Article 7 of the Convention.
>
> The Court, accordingly, takes the view that the applicants, who, as leaders of the GDR, had created the appearance of legality emanating from the GDR's legal system but then implemented or continued a practice which flagrantly disregarded the very principles of that system, cannot plead the protection of Article 7 § 1 of the Convention. To reason otherwise would run counter to the object and purpose of that provision, which is to ensure that no one is subjected to arbitrary prosecution, conviction or punishment . . .

Interestingly, the courts in these cases used considerations of natural justice to establish the liability of the defendants by debunking positivistic rules of justifica-

---

[17] *K-HW v Germany* [GC], case no 37201/97; judgment of 22 March 2001. There were dissents by Judges Pellonpää, Zupancic and Cabral-Barreto, who thought that art 7(1) ECHR had been violated in the case of a mere border guard as opposed to members of the government.

[18] At paras 82–9.

tion based on GDR law, whereas the much more common application of these ideas occurs in arguments which are to the benefit of the accused. This beneficial approach to the primacy of natural justice over positive law had been taken in the last century with the famous decision by the *Reichsgericht* in the 'Abortion Case',[19] when the Supreme Court of the German Reich accepted in 1927 that a pregnancy could be terminated if otherwise there would be a grave danger to the mother's health or life. At the time, German law had no provision to this effect, and the *Reichsgericht* 'invented' the so-called '*übergesetzlicher Notstand*' (supra-legal state of necessity) from the commands of natural justice. The decision was the basis on which § 34 on necessity was finally modelled, although § 34 goes further in its ambit, as we will see when discussing justificatory defences below. For the offence of abortion, it can also be found explicitly in § 218 a (2).

Natural justice, from the German point of view, should be seen as a kind of safety-valve in a legal system tending towards a positivistic approach, as far as the usual primacy of the written law is concerned. One might compare it to the function that the principles of equity jurisprudence as a corrective to the stricter rules of the common law have had in English legal history. It is difficult to place natural justice firmly into a hierarchy of laws, as it applies in different shapes and forms at any level of the German legal system. It permeates the law as a guiding principle of interpretation. It would, however, not be unfair to say that the principle of natural justice has the force of influencing the application even of the highest-ranking legal rules on the constitutional level. Looking at it that way, one can make the statement that it represents the top tier in the hierarchy of laws.

The more tangible sources of criminal law begin with the next rung down on the ladder, the constitution (*Grundgesetz*—Basic Law) and international law. We must mention these two together because at least in some cases there is an overlap or exchange of hierarchical position between them. The ground rule is that the constitution is the supreme law of the land; international law must be ratified and implemented by a domestic act of legislation and normally takes the rank of simple federal law, except for generally accepted rules of international law, which under article 25 GG rank between the *Grundgesetz* and simple federal law and do not, as a matter of principle, require domestic implementation. Yet, care should be taken not to interpret article 25 GG as meaning that criminal liability can be established on the basis of international customary law, even if it has the quality of *jus cogens erga omnes*. The tension between article 25 GG and the above-mentioned article 103(2) GG must be resolved in favour of the latter, meaning that criminal liability always requires implementation by domestic law.[20] This has been severely

---

[19] RGSt 61, 252; 62, 137.

[20] Sch/Sch-Eser, Vorbem § 1 Mn 22. For a similar approach in the Netherlands despite the further-reaching wording of art 94 of the Dutch Constitution (*Grondwet*), see de Hullu, *Materieel Strafrecht* (2nd edn, 2003) 86–7; and for an argument to the effect that Kosovo courts under UNMIK administration could not apply international criminal law directly, see Bohlander, 'The Direct Application of International Criminal Law in Kosovo' (2001) *Kosovo Legal Studies* 7.

criticised by some[21] who wish to see a greater and more direct influence of international criminal law, especially in the wake of the establishment of the war crimes tribunals for Yugoslavia, Rwanda, Sierra Leone, Cambodia, etc, as well as the International Criminal Court. However, the way in which law is made in these institutions should make us wary of adopting the principles reached on the international level too easily.[22]

The *Grundgesetz* and international law can trade places in the hierarchy when we examine the supranational effect of European law, as was made clear by the European Court of Justice (ECJ) in the seminal case of *Costa v ENEL*:[23] Even the lowest category of self-executing and binding European law takes precedence over the constitution. This had, however, been disputed by the BVerfG[24] in the so-called '*Solange*' ('as long as') cases where the court at first claimed the final word on the applicability of EC legislation as long as it conflicted with German constitutional law and especially the fundamental civil rights therein, but then moved on to accepting that the European law had reached a level of protection that made such control superfluous unless the complainant showed good cause that and why the degree of protection on the European level had slipped below that of the *Grundgesetz*. Similar problems arise when Germany has to abide by resolutions of the UN Security Council adopted under the powers of Chapter VII of the UN Charter.

At the next level down, we have the simple federal legislation, both parliamentary and to some extent derivative governmental instruments, as long as there is an Act of Parliament authorising the government to fill in the conditions of criminal liability. Federal law, which these days contains the vast bulk of criminal law applicable in all Member States of the Federation, outranks the law of those states, even their constitutional law. At the very bottom there is the municipal law, which may in restricted cases be made the basis of minor regulatory offences, *Ordnungswidrigkeiten*, which no longer count as proper criminal offences.[25]

Judicial case law, as should have become clear by now, can never be the basis of creating new criminal offences; in this respect, the laws in Germany and England and Wales have converged substantially after the 2006 decision by the House of Lords in *Jones*,[26] where the justices held that the courts could no longer create new offences based on their traditional common law powers, and that it was for Parliament to do so.[27]

---

[21] Ferdinandusse, *Direct Application of International Criminal Law in National Courts* (Asser Press, 2006).

[22] See Bohlander, 'The General Part: Judicial Developments' in Bassiouni (ed), *International Criminal Law* (3rd edn, Brill Publishers, 2008) (forthcoming).

[23] [1964] ECR 585, 593.

[24] See BVerfGE 37, 271; 73, 339. This was reaffirmed in the so-called 'Solange-III' decision of 7 June 2000, 2 BvL 1/97; English version online at <http://www.bundesverfassungsgericht.de/entscheidungen/ls20000607_2bvl000197en.html> accessed 26 June 2008.

[25] For further explanation, see Sch/Sch-Eser, Vorbem § 1, Mn. 36–57.

[26] [2006] UKHL 16.

[27] Interestingly enough, classic Islamic Shari'ah law, for example, allows for the judicial creation of offences and sanctions by analogy in the so-called Ta'zir category, if and when the high evidential threshold for the most serious class, the Hudud crimes based directly in the Qur'an, is not reached. However, this mechanism, in the eyes of Islamic legal scholars, is meant as a safety-valve against too

Principles of Interpretation and the Role of Precedent

German criminal law, as any area of German law, knows of and applies five methods of interpretation, which to some extent vary from the approach taken in England and Wales. They are, in their supposed order of application:

a) literal;
b) grammatical;
c) systematic;
d) historical; and
e) teleological.

Courts will usually start by interpreting any provision literally. If that does not result in a clear picture, the expression in question will be looked at in its grammatical context. Should the exercise remain unsatisfactory, the rule will then be placed in its systematic context, namely, how does it fit together with other rules or provisions using the same wording. The next step is the question of what problem the law was meant to address in its historical development; this is akin to the English 'mischief rule'. Finally, and more or less anathema for many common lawyers of the old school, the court will ask what aim the legislator intended to achieve by making that particular rule, what was the *telos* of the law-giver, hence the name teleological. This sequence is, of course, only a sequence in theory, as German courts will regularly base their decisions on a combination of these arguments, each corroborating the others.

German courts are not bound by a doctrine of *stare decisis*, such as is, for example, found in the United Kingdom. However, for pragmatic reasons, lower level courts will not, as a rule, deviate from the settled jurisprudence of the superior courts of their districts and the federal courts. This is done to avoid pushing the parties into an appeal the outcome of which is practically clear. Yet any judge at the lowest court is free to disregard the jurisprudence of the highest courts of the land, even that of the BVerfG, unless the decision in question has the force of an Act of parliament under § 31 BVerfGG or is binding because it determines an appeal in a specific case—yet in the next, even identical case, the judge is no longer bound.

wide an application of Hudud crimes which carry draconic penalties (capital punishment, amputation of limbs and flogging), if otherwise the unpalatable alternative would be an acquittal although the conduct clearly appears deserving of a criminal sanction. Moderate states such as the United Arab Emirates have chosen a middle path by restricting the use of Ta'zir offences unless they have been laid down previously by law, thus moving towards a Western understanding of the legality principle. Generally, however, it must be noted that only very few Islamic countries apply the criminal law of the Shari'ah in its pure form; most have enacted Criminal Codes, not all of which adhere to the principles of Shari'ah themselves. See generally on the Ta'zir offences, An Na'im, *Toward an Islamic Reformation* (New York, Syracuse University Press, 1996) 118–20; Ibrahim and Mehemeed, 'Basic Principles of Criminal Procedure under Islamic Shari'ah' in Haleem, Sherif and Daniels (eds), *Criminal Justice in Islam* (London/New York, IB Tauris, 2003) 20–1.

The Tripartite Structure of Offences—an Overview

In this overview of basic concepts, we need to take a brief look at the tripartite structure of German criminal law, because that structure will determine the course of our examination. The StGB is divided into a General Part (*Allgemeiner Teil*) applicable to all offences, and a Special Part (*Besonderer Teil*), containing the individual offences. Further offences can be found in special legislation, but as a rule the General Part applies to these, too. Each offence, based on this twofold division, is subject to three stages of examination, hence the name 'tripartite structure' (*dreistufiger Verbrechensaufbau*):

a) *Tatbestand*: offence description or (loosely translated) *actus reus* (*objektiver Tatbestand*) plus *mens rea* (*subjektiver Tatbestand*);
b) *Rechtswidrigkeit*: the general element of unlawfulness and the absence of justificatory defences; and
c) *Schuld*: the general element of blameworthiness or guilt and the absence of excusatory defences.

The *objektiver Tatbestand* contains the objective elements of offences, similar to the *actus reus* as understood in the common law. The element of unlawfulness is not a general element of the *actus reus*, but a separate and distinct category; its absence, unlike under English law in some cases, does not, therefore, negate the *objektiver Tatbestand*. In connection with offences requiring intention, the *objektiver Tatbestand* is made out if and when the elements listed in it have been fulfilled. With offences based on negligence, the general elements of the *objektiver Tatbestand* are augmented by the requirement of a violation of a duty of care and the foreseeability of the result, both by a reasonable man standard. Negligence is only a basis of liability if the law expressly provides for it (§ 15). Simple negligence, unlike in English law, can be sufficient, unless the law requires a higher degree of negligence.

The *subjektiver Tatbestand* only refers to forms of intent; subjective, individualised negligence is usually a question of the third tier, *Schuld*. An honest mistake of fact eliminates intent. The *subjektiver Tatbestand* does not normally encompass such issues as intoxication or insanity; these belong to the general element of *Schuld*.

The general element of unlawfulness, *Rechtswidrigkeit*, is in the normal course of events made out if the *Tatbestand* has been infringed (*Tatbestandsmäßigkeit indiziert Rechtswidrigkeit*), unless a justificatory defence eliminates it. Potential justificatory defences are self-defence, necessity, duress, superior orders, citizen's arrest, etc. One needs to be aware that some defences that apply in this tier can apply in the *Tatbestand* as well, if the *actus reus* or *mens rea* require absence, for example, of consent, as in theft under § 242. They are then not defences, but positive or negative elements of the *Tatbestand*.

As stated above, the law assumes *Schuld* with young adult and adult offenders and requires the court to establish the individual maturity of juveniles. The law requires the court to establish the individual maturity of young adults in order to decide whether juvenile law is applied. Potential excusatory defences include insanity, diminished responsibility, duress, excessive self-defence, provocation and crimes of passion, unavoidable mistake of law and, depending on which theory one follows, errors about facts underlying a recognised justificatory defence; some put these errors into the subjective *Tatbestand*.

The law finally recognises categories outside the tripartite structure, such as *Strafausschließungsgründe*, namely, reasons that eliminate the need for punishment (for example, withdrawal from attempts) and o*bjektive Bedingungen der Strafbarkeit*, namely, factors that must be present before liability is triggered, but that do not form part of the tripartite structure and are thus not subject to the *mens rea* requirements. In both cases, mistakes are usually irrelevant. The above may be (roughly) illustrated by the flowchart in Figure I:

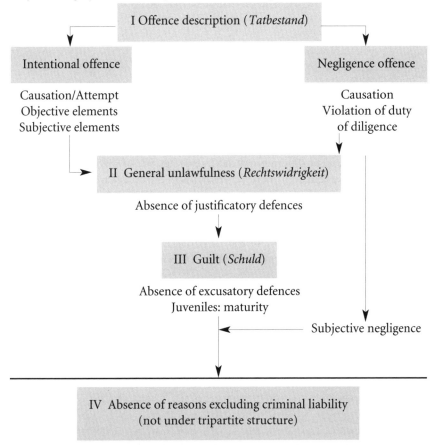

Figure I—Schematic Examination Sequence Tripartite Structure—Simplified Overview

Basic Tenets of German Criminal Policy

In this section, we will take a very cursory look at some of the most important foundations of criminal policy that support the German approach.[28] Many of the aspects will return when we consider the individual concepts one by one. However, it is useful to have a summary that sets the scene for the following chapters.

Nullum Crimen Sine Lege Scripta

As we have seen, German law does not know of the establishment of criminal offences by common or customary, judge-made law; it does recognise the judicial creation of substantive law principles in favour of the accused. Jefferson[29] has pointed out, for the English system, that there may be a sort of residual function of law-making, namely, when courts apply old law to new situations not originally envisaged, as was the case, for example, in England with the acceptance of biological and psychological harm as falling under the provisions of the Offences Against the Person Act (OAPA) 1861.[30] From a socio-legal point of view, that may be an apt observation, yet strictly legally speaking all the courts are doing is interpreting existing law until they reach the limits set by the ban on the use of analogy to the detriment of the defendant. Any law by its very nature as a general injunction for a multitude of unspecified situations now and in the future is prone to face new and not-envisaged scenarios based on the development of society. This development may also lead to differing judicial interpretations of identical norms over time. It may thus lead to a more severe application of a law after a period of leniency, without changing the wording of the law. This is especially evident in sentencing law, where the spirit of the age inevitably influences judges in their approach to the interpretation of general aspects of punishment. In times of heightened crime rates and rising fear of crime, it is only natural for judges to resort to a harsher employment of the arsenal of sanctions they have had at their disposal for some time.

Rechtsgüterlehre and Schutzzweck der Norm

German criminal law academics and practitioners, when dealing with the interpretation of the StGB's provisions, defining their objects and interrelation with other norms, in their majority subscribe to the so-called *Rechtsgüterlehre* (doctrine of protected legal interests) and the concept of the *Schutzzweck der Norm*, namely,

---

[28] For an overview of the development and a deeper analysis, see Zipf, *Kriminalpolitik* (1980).

[29] See his textbook on *Criminal Law* (8th edn, Harlow, Pearson/Longman, 2007) 23–5.

[30] See, eg *Ireland and Burstow* [1998] AC 147; *Dica* [2004] 3 WLR 213; and *Konzani* [2005] EWCA Crim 706.

the specific protective purpose of a law. The former looks at defining the legal interest (*Rechtsgut*) a law is meant to protect, namely, to give a simple example, the law on theft is meant to protect property from appropriation by taking away; the law on deception offences protects property from being appropriated by false pretences. This division would, in theory, prevent conceptual amalgamations such as happened in English law with theft and obtaining by deception in *Hinks*.[31] The determination of the *Rechtsgut* may also have an impact on the questions of how to deal with offenders who have by one and the same act violated several provisions of the StGB, namely, how to deal with multiple offences. The *Schutzzweck* defines whether a certain act or behaviour of the defendant, whilst possibly falling under the wording of a law, is actually meant to be sanctioned under it. According to Roxin,[32] this must not be confused with questions of hypothetical causation, for example, when an act causes a result which would have been caused anyway, even if the defendant had employed all necessary diligence. He questions the value of the idea and prefers to call our version of the *Schutzzweck*: '*Reichweite des Tatbestandes*' (scope of the offence). In this, he combines issues such as participation in the conscious self-endangerment of another, some areas of consent to risk, shifting spheres of risk and responsibility, and the so-called damage or injury arising from shock or as a consequence of the offender's action, but where the link is found to be too tenuous.[33] The first category relates to *Kennedy*-type[34] scenarios. The second encompasses cases such as that of a man who wishes to be ferried over a river in a severe storm; the ferryman strongly counsels against it, but at the insistence of the man starts across with the consequence that the boat capsizes and the man drowns.[35] The third refers to situations such as that of a lorry driver who is stopped by the police in the dark because the tail lights of his vehicle do not work properly; the police put up a lamp to warn following traffic and in the meantime order the driver to proceed to the next service station with the police following behind him to warn the traffic. Before he drives off, a policeman removes the lamp and when the driver pulls into the road, the lorry crashes into a car whose driver did not see it; the car driver is killed.[36] Shock damage or injuries arise in cases where a mother watches her two-year-old son being driven over and killed by a car and as a consequence suffers a heart attack. The last category focuses on late-occurring injury as a consequence of an earlier action of the defendant, for example, a woman whose leg was seriously injured in an accident caused by D and who is now partially disabled, goes for a walk months later after being released from hospital; she stumbles because of the impairment and cannot steady herself; as a consequence she dies or is seriously injured. Shall we hold D liable for the result of the chains of events he undoubtedly set in motion under those categories in the

---

[31] [2000] 1 Cr App R 1.
[32] AT I, 391.
[33] Roxin, AT I, 401–21 and 1078–9.
[34] [2007] UKHL 38.
[35] RGSt 57, 172.
[36] BGHSt 4, 360.

physical, factual sense? In all of these cases, Roxin says, the law does *a priori* not intend to cover these scenarios, whereas one may easily say that English law would solve some of them under the heading of causation in the legal sense. The terminology is not uniform, but as we shall see when examining the equivalent to the common law concept of *actus reus*, the substance of the ideas is largely identical.

Schuldprinzip

One of the central tenets of the German approach is the *Schuldprinzip*, namely, the requirement of personal guilt and blameworthiness[37] as the determining parameters for liability and punishment. Combined with the lack of acceptance of any reverse burdens of proof in procedural law, the first obvious consequence is that German law rejects any idea of strict liability. The *Schuldprinzip* was famously established by the judgment of the Great Senate of the BGH in BGHSt 2, 194 of 18 March 1952. In this case, a defence counsel had taken on the case of a lady without first agreeing on a fee. He then approached his client on the morning of the trial and asked her to pay him 50 Deutsche Mark (DM) or he would decline to represent her, and when she paid him on the next day, he used the same threat to make her sign a fee note of 400 DM. He was convicted of an offence under § 240, *Nötigung*, which is akin to blackmail, but applies to any act or omission, not just financial or property transactions, to which the victim is coerced by the defendant under the use of threats or physical force. Apparently, his line of defence was that he thought he was entitled to ask that sum of her and thus did not know that he was acting unlawfully or *rechtswidrig*. The trial court convicted him based on the traditional Roman-law-based approach coined previously by the *Reichsgericht* that a mistake about the criminal law, as opposed to errors about civil law underlying an offence which it treated as a mistake of fact,[38] did not provide a defence. The term '*rechtswidrig*' in § 240 was not seen as an element of the *actus reus*, but as an expression of the general requirement of unlawfulness. The law at the time did only provide for mistakes of fact. Under the *Reichsgericht*'s jurisprudence, the defendant had no defence. The question which the BGH asked itself was whether this approach was still correct. The court decided it was not. Its judgment contains the following classic passage,[39] which in its almost philosophical and in places

---

[37] However, the debate about determinism and the findings of neurological science has reached the German literature, too. See Gunnar Spilgies, 'Zwischenruf: Die Debatte über "Hirnforschung und Willensfreiheit" im Strafrecht ist nicht falsch inszeniert!' <http://www.zis-online.com/dat/artikel/2007_4_129.pdf> accessed 26 June 2008.

[38] Much like the English law, see *Smith* [1974] QB 354 (CA); and Simester and Sullivan, *Criminal Law—Theory and Doctrine* (Oxford/Portland, Hart, 2007) 624–5 for a cautionary note on the equalisation of mistakes of civil law with mistakes of fact.

[39] At pp 201–2 (my translation). The German original text reads:

'*Strafe setzt Schuld voraus. Schuld ist Vorwerfbarkeit. Mit dem Unwerturteil der Schuld wird dem Täter vorgeworfen, daß er sich nicht rechtmäßig verhalten, daß er sich für das Unrecht entschieden hat, obwohl er sich rechtmäßig verhalten, sich für das Recht hätte entscheiden können. Der innere Grund des Schuldvorwurfes liegt darin, daß der Mensch auf freie, verantwortliche, sittliche*

rather convoluted diction typical of the time, is also a wonderful example of the cultural differences in the style of judicial reasoning:

> Punishment is premised on guilt. Guilt means blameworthiness. By finding a defendant guilty we blame him for not having acted lawfully, for having chosen to break the law, although he could have acted lawfully, could have chosen to abide by the law. The inner reason for the judgment of guilt lies in the fact that man's nature is grounded in the freedom and responsibility of moral self-determination, and that he is therefore capable to decide for the law and against injustice, to model his actions on the norms of the legal commands and to avoid that which is forbidden by law, as soon as he has gained moral maturity and as long as the natural capacity of moral self-determination is not temporarily paralysed or permanently destroyed by the illnesses mentioned in § 51 StGB. The pre-condition for a free and responsible human choice for the law, based on moral self-determination, is the knowledge of the law and of the forbidden. He who knows that what he chooses to do in freedom is unlawful, acts blameworthy if he does so despite this insight. That knowledge may be lacking because the defendant is unable, based on the illnesses mentioned in § 51 (1) StGB, to appreciate the unlawfulness of his actions. In such a case the lack of knowledge is the consequence of an unavoidable fate. He cannot be blamed for it and incurs no guilt. He lacks mental responsibility under the criminal law.

> *Selbstbestimmung angelegt und deshalb befähigt ist, sich für das Recht und gegen das Unrecht zu entscheiden, sein Verhalten nach den Normen des rechtlichen Sollens einzurichten und das rechtlich Verbotene zu vermeiden, sobald er die sittliche Reife erlangt hat und solange die Anlage zur freien sittlichen Selbstbestimmung nicht durch die in § 51 StGB genannten krankhaften Vorgänge vorübergehend gelähmt oder auf Dauer zerstört ist. Voraussetzung dafür, daß der Mensch sich in freier, verantwortlicher, sittlicher Selbstbestimmung für das Recht und gegen das Unrecht entscheidet, ist die Kenntnis von Recht und Unrecht. Wer weiß, daß das, wozu er sich in Freiheit entschließt, Unrecht ist, handelt schuldhaft, wenn er es gleichwohl tut. Die Kenntnis kann fehlen, weil der Täter infolge der in § 51 Abs 1 StGB aufgezählten krankhaften Vorgänge unfähig ist, das Unrechtmäßige seines Tuns einzusehen. Hier ist die Unkenntnis des Täters Folge eines unabwendbaren Schicksals. Sie kann ihm nicht zum Vorwurf gemacht und nicht zur Schuld zugerechnet werden. Er ist deshalb strafrechtlich unzurechnungsfähig. Das Bewußtsein, Unrecht zu tun, kann im einzelnen Falle auch beim zurechnungsfähigen Menschen fehlen, weil er die Verbotsnorm nicht kennt oder verkennt. Auch in diesem Falle des Verbotsirrtums ist der Täter nicht in der Lage, sich gegen das Unrecht zu entscheiden. Aber nicht jeder Verbotsirrtum schließt den Vorwurf der Schuld aus. Mängel im Wissen sind bis zu einem gewissen Grad behebbar. Der Mensch ist, weil er auf freie, sittliche Selbstbestimmung angelegt ist, auch jederzeit in die verantwortliche Entscheidung gerufen, sich als Teilhaber der Rechtsgemeinschaft rechtmäßig zu verhalten und das Unrecht zu vermeiden. Dieser Pflicht genügt er nicht, wenn er nur das nicht tut, was ihm als Unrecht klar vor Augen steht. Vielmehr hat er bei allem, was er zu tun im Begriff steht, sich bewußt zu machen, ob es mit den Sätzen des rechtlichen Sollens in Einklang steht. Zweifel hat er durch Nachdenken oder Erkundigung zu beseitigen. Hierzu bedarf es der Anspannung des Gewissens, ihr Maß richtet sich nach den Umständen des Falles und nach dem Lebens- und Berufskreis des Einzelnen. Wenn er trotz der ihm danach zuzumutenden Anspannung des Gewissens die Einsicht in das Unrechtmäßige seines Tuns nicht zu gewinnen vermochte, war der Irrtum unüberwindlich, die Tat für ihn nicht vermeidbar. In diesem Falle kann ein Schuldvorwurf gegen ihn nicht erhoben werden. Wenn dagegen bei gehöriger Anspannung des Gewissens der Täter das Unrechtmäßige seines Tuns hätte erkennen können, schließt der Verbotsirrtum die Schuld nicht aus. Je nach dem Maß, in dem es der Täter an der gehörigen Gewissensanspannung hat fehlen lassen, wird der Schuldvorwurf aber gemindert. Bewußtsein der Rechtswidrigkeit bedeutet überall weder die Kenntnis der Strafbarkeit, noch die Kenntnis der das Verbot enthaltenden gesetzlichen Vorschrift. Andererseits genügt es auch nicht, daß der Täter sich bewußt ist, sein Tun sei sittlich verwerflich. Vielmehr muß er, zwar nicht in rechtstechnischer Beurteilung, aber doch in einer seiner Gedankenwelt entsprechenden allgemeinen Wertung das Unrechtmäßige der Tat erkennen oder bei gehöriger Gewissensanspannung erkennen können.*'

The awareness of acting unlawfully may, in individual cases, also be absent in an otherwise mentally competent person, because he does not know or fully comprehend the law prohibiting his actions. In this case of a mistake of law, too, the defendant is not in a position to make a choice against what is forbidden. Yet, not every mistake of law excludes blameworthiness. Gaps in one's knowledge can to a certain extent be remedied. Because of his capacity for free moral self-determination, man must at all times make the responsible choice to act according to the law, as a participant in the legal community, and to avoid the unlawful. He does not live up to this obligation if he only abstains from doing that which he clearly perceives as unlawful. On the contrary, he must make himself aware in all of his plans whether they comply with the principles of what is required by the law. Doubts must be eradicated through reflection or consultation. What is required is a diligent effort of conscience, the measure of which depends on the circumstances of the case in question and the personal and professional background of each individual. If, despite having duly so exerted his conscience, he could not recognise the unlawfulness of his actions, the error was insuperable, the crime unavoidable. In such a case he cannot be found blameworthy. If, however, the offender could have realised the unlawfulness of his actions, had he but duly exerted his conscience, the mistake of law will not exclude blameworthiness. Yet, depending on the degree to which the offender lacked the due diligence to exert his consience, the degree of blame may be mitigated. Awareness of unlawfulness does, however, never require the knowledge of the fact that the action is punishable, nor the knowledge of the law that contains the prohibition. Moreover it is not sufficient that the offender is aware of the moral turpitude of his actions. Rather, he must recognise or be able to recognise with due diligence, the unlawfulness of his actions, not necessarily in the technical, juridical fashion, but in a general evaluation according to his intellectual abilities.

Capacity and the Treatment of Juveniles and Young Adults

The provision on the age of capacity, § 19, states that persons under the age of 14 cannot be held liable for criminal offences. However, according to § 29, this does not exclude the criminal liability of any accomplices to their actions. Any sanctions against them can only be adopted within the wider ambit of family law. They, and their parents, under § 832 BGB—without regard to the children's age so long as they are under age—may, however, be liable in tort for damages under civil law, because § 828(1) BGB reduces the age of civil capacity to seven years and—leaving aside some exceptions related to negligently caused traffic accidents, etc under § 828(2) BGB—§ 828(3) BGB only requires the court to determine whether the child or juvenile had the maturity to appreciate the consequences of their actions. Juveniles between 14 and 18 years, apart from being subject to being treated under family law, are criminally liable, according to § 3 JGG, if they have that maturity and are capable of recognising the unlawfulness of their conduct within the meaning of the judgment of the BGH explained above. Young adults (*Heranwachsende*) between the ages of 18 and 21 are criminally liable, but the court may choose to apply juvenile law under § 105 JGG if it finds that the defendant either is still in a juvenile state of maturity, or if the act committed has the character of a typically juvenile transgression. For adults over the age of 18, §§ 20 and 21 operate on the premise that any adult is presumed sane unless the court finds reasons for establishing reasonable doubt with regard to insanity or diminished responsibility. We will look at this more closely in a later chapter.

Corporate Criminal Liability

§ 14 makes provision for the liability of certain officers of companies, corporations, etc, yet this is nothing like the vicarious liability under English law;[40] otherwise only natural persons over 14 years of age (§ 19) can commit criminal offences under German law. It is generally thought that because of the stress on personal blameworthiness as the basis of liability, substantive criminalisation in the sense of direct criminal responsibility does not make sense vis-a-vis legal entities that cannot act for themselves, but are represented in the real world by human beings. However, certain criminal sanctions such as forfeiture of property, etc and of *instrumenta sceleris* can be taken against legal persons. There is also the possibility of fining them for *Ordnungswidrigkeiten* under § 30 OWiG, but that is not a criminal sanction. There appears to be a movement towards broadening the scope for corporate liability, not least on the basis of the European law. In one form or another, many European countries have laws that provide for genuine corporate criminal liability (the United Kingdom, Ireland, The Netherlands, Norway, Iceland, France, Finland, Denmark, Slovenia, Switzerland and Belgium) or they have adopted measures that possess similar effects (Sweden, Spain, Italy). There is a general trend in the post-communist Eastern European countries towards such liability, based on European and international legal principles.[41] Germany is lagging behind because the dogmatic problems of where to place such liability within the existing system are as yet unsolved. It is likely that a solution will be most easily found along the lines of introducing corporate-specific sanctions rather than substantive criminal liability.

Rule-of-law Principles in Substantive Criminal Law

The so-called *Allgemeiner Teil* or General Part of the StGB contains a number of fundamental principles of fairness and natural justice applicable to all offences

---

[40] See on the English position Simester and Sullivan, *Criminal Law—Theory and Doctrine* (Oxford/Portland, Hart, 2007) 247–68.
[41] See Sch/Sch-Cramer/Heine, Vorbem §§ 25 ff., Mn. 118–30.

that are maybe best qualified as emanations of the rule of law within the realm of criminal justice. Rule of law translates into German roughly as *Rechtsstaatsprinzip*, the concept of the state governed by the rule of law; its constitutional substance that is of relevance for criminal justice is mainly embodied in articles 20(3) GG,[42] 101 GG,[43] 102 GG,[44] 103 GG[45] and 104 GG.[46] Article 20(3) GG, which is a general principle and does not constitute an individual right, is, however, often cited by the courts together with a specific civil liberty when infringements of that specific liberty are said to violate the rule of law as well, and sometimes the very violation of that rule constitutes the infringement of the civil liberty. We shall not go into the mechanics and niceties of German constitutional law, but suffice it to say that the rule of law can be brought to bear in practice in criminal trials and appeals through the vehicles of the constitutional complaint (*Verfassungsbeschwerde*) or judicial requests for preliminary rulings (*konkrete Normenkontrolle*) before the BVerfG. Other than the situation in the United Kingdom under the Human Rights Act (HRA) 1998, the BVerfG has the power to strike down Acts of Parliament that it views as unconstitutional and to declare them null and void in whole or in part, and *any* German court is in principle free to disregard *any* law below the level of an Act of Parliament and even Acts of Parliament passed before the coming into force of the *Grundgesetz* (*vorkonstitutionelles Recht*) as unconstitutional in a specific case.

The StGB reiterates some of the constitutional rules and specifies others. The main principles of interest in this context are found in § 1, which is identical to article 103(2) GG and therefore in substance represents a constitutional principle in the shape of a simple federal law, and § 2:[47]

[42] 'The legislature shall be bound by the constitutional order, the executive and the judiciary by law and justice.'
[43] '(1) Extraordinary courts shall not be allowed. No one may be removed from the jurisdiction of his lawful judge. (2) Courts for particular fields of law may be established only by a law.'
[44] 'Capital punishment is abolished.'
[45] '(1) In the courts every person shall be entitled to a hearing in accordance with law.
(2) An act may be punished only if it was defined by a law as a criminal offense before the act was committed.
(3) No person may be punished for the same act more than once under the general criminal laws.'
[46] '(1) Freedom of the person may be restricted only pursuant to a formal law and only in compliance with the procedures prescribed therein. Persons in custody may not be subjected to mental or physical mistreatment.
(2) Only a judge may rule upon the permissibility or continuation of any deprivation of freedom. If such a deprivation is not based on a judicial order, a judicial decision shall be obtained without delay. The police may hold no one in custody on their own authority beyond the end of the day following the arrest. Details shall be regulated by a law.
(3) Any person provisionally detained on suspicion of having committed a criminal offense shall be brought before a judge no later than the day following his arrest; the judge shall inform him of the reasons for the arrest, examine him, and give him an opportunity to raise objections. The judge shall, without delay, either issue a written arrest warrant setting forth the reasons therefor or order his release.
(4) A relative or a person enjoying the confidence of the person in custody shall be notified without delay of any judicial decision imposing or continuing a deprivation of freedom.'
[47] See Bohlander, *The German Criminal Code: A Modern English Translation* (Oxford/Portland, Hart, 2008) for the full text.

§1 No punishment without law

An act may only be punished if criminal liability had been established by law before the act was committed.

§ 2 Jurisdiction ratione temporis; lex mitior

(1) The penalty and any ancillary measures shall be determined by the law which is in force at the time of the act.

(2) If the penalty is amended during the commission of the act, the law in force at the time the act is completed shall be applied.

(3) If the law in force at the time of the completion of the act is amended before judgment, the most lenient law shall be applied.

(4) A law intended to be in force only for a determinate time shall be continued to be applied to acts committed while it was in force even after it ceases to be in force, unless otherwise provided by law.

(5) Subsections (1) to (4) shall apply mutatis mutandis to confiscation, deprivation and destruction.

(6) Unless otherwise provided by law, measures of rehabilitation and incapacitation shall be determined according to the law in force at the time of the decision.

§ 1 contains the principle of *nullum crimen sine lege* (*Bestimmtheitsgrundsatz*— specifity of prescription); it requires the law to be as precise as possible in defining the prescribed conduct, which is similar to the principle of fair labelling. We have already seen that the German understanding of establishing liability requires a written law, which may be a blanket law, namely, a law that only provides for the penalty but not for the elements of offences which are to be found in another law to which the blanket law refers, under the conditions that both laws together must comply with the requirements of § 1.[48] So-called 'dynamic references', namely, laws merely referring to another law in its form 'as amended' at any given time, are problematic and face a high likelihood of being unconstitutional.[49] § 1 by necessary implication also contains the ban on the use of analogies to the detriment of the offender (*Analogieverbot*), although the line between mere extensive interpretation and analogy can be very thin, and a ban on retroactive penalisation and/or punishment (*Rückwirkungsverbot*). It is obvious that the German technique of using general terms in the definition of the elements of offences, as opposed to the more casuistic approach, for example, of UK legislation, inevitably leads to a wider impact of the judicial interpretation of these terms, but that has been consistently held to be acceptable as long as they form part of traditional criminal law norms and there is a consistent jurisprudence on their interpretation.[50] The retroactivity ban is subject to the exceptions outlined above when the concept of natural justice were addressed; natural justice will usually be infringed if the previous law contained grave and serious human rights violations when regulating the extent of state powers or justificatory defences, such as in the law of the

---

[48] See Tröndle/Fischer, § 1 Mn. 5 a.
[49] Tröndle/Fischer, § 1 Mn. 5 a.
[50] Tröndle/Fischer, § 1 Mn. 5 b–c.

Third Reich or the GDR.[51] The ban, according to the prevailing opinion, does not apply to procedural law, the law of limitation periods or a change in a merely consistent and long-standing judicial opinion.[52] It does not apply, either, to the categories of the most serious international crimes such as aggression, genocide, war crimes and crimes against humanity, as can be seen from article 7(2) of the European Convention on Human Rights (ECHR)[53] and Article 15(2) of the International Covenant on Civil and Political Rights (ICCPR), the so-called 'Nuremberg Clause'. However, Germany has chosen not to apply its Code of International Criminal Law (*Völkerstrafgesetzbuch*) of 2002 retroactively, as can be seen from its § 2, which refers to the law of the StGB, and thus also to § 1.

§ 2 is largely self-explanatory. It contains in § 2(3) the important principle of *lex mitior*, which commands the application of the most lenient law if the law has been changed between the commission of the offence and the final judgment. This may also be the case if the law was amended to a more lenient form and then amended again according to a harsher approach. According to the long-standing jurisprudence of the BGH and BVerfG,[54] the comparison between the old and the new law must be made on the basis of their application to the case in question, not in an abstract manner. In the view of the BVerfG, the *lex mitior* principle is not violated if a certain conduct was merely not punishable for a transitional, temporary period.[55] This is a questionable view;[56] it can, however, be explained by the fact that the BVerfG only examines any issues before it at the measure of the *Grundgesetz*, in this case article 103(2) GG, which does not have any reference to *lex mitior* as such, but not at the measure of simple federal law, such as § 2(3). Thus, the *lex mitior* rule may not have constitutional rank, but a court disregarding it would still violate § 2(3).[57]

---

[51] Tröndle/Fischer, § 1 Mn. 14–15 a.

[52] Tröndle/Fischer, § 1 Mn. 16–17.

[53] The fact that Germany had entered a reservation against art 7(2) ECHR to the effect that it would apply it only within the limits of art 103(2) GG is irrelevant: first, as it did not do so for the identical provision of art 15(2) ICCPR; and, secondly, because based on the recent jurisprudence of the BVerfG with regard to the GDR state crimes, the ambit of art 103(2) GG is restricted by interpretation so as not to include the most serious state-sponsored violations of human rights. See BVerfGE 95, 96 at 132. This interpretation in effect rests on and confirms the ethical and moral substance of the Nuremberg Clause. The reservation to art 7(2) ECHR was made because the official view of the German government regarding the Nuremberg trials was and still is that they constituted a violation of the ban on retroactivity at the time. That view is as such dogmatically correct, yet on the one hand the German war criminals would have faced summary execution under the international law at the time and were lucky to get a trial instead, however flawed it may have been, and on the other hand it is time that Germany faced up to the fact that it has for over a decade supported international tribunals and courts which do recognise the adoption of the Nuremberg Clause as one of the defining moments in the history of the global fight against impunity for mass atrocities. As was explained above, the ECtHR did not have to concern itself with the argument and in any case agreed with the interpretation of the BVerfG on the retroactivity ban. See on this Ahlbrecht, *Geschichte der völkerrechtlichen Strafgerichtsbarkeit im 20. Jahrhundert* (Baden-Baden, Nomos, 1999) 74.

[54] See references at Tröndle/Fischer, § 2 Mn. 8–11a.

[55] BVerfGE 81, 132 at 135.

[56] See the critical references at Sch/Sch-Eser, § 2 Mn. 16 and 29.

[57] However, one always needs to take great care to examine whether a law was merely suspended or was in effect amended or abolished. For a recent example from Iraq under the occupation of the

Verbrechen and *Vergehen*

A final important distinction[58] is the one between *Verbrechen* (equivalent to the old UK category of felonies) and *Vergehen* (akin to misdemeanours). The definition is provided by § 12, which states that a *Verbrechen* is any offence with a minimum sentence of one year's imprisonment, whereas a *Vergehen* is one punishable by fine or with a minimum sentence below one year's imprisonment. Note that the reference to minimum sentences is an abstract one, referring to the sentencing frames set by the provisions on the individual offences, and does not relate to the sentence in the case at hand. § 12(3) furthermore clarifies that the effects of any extenuating or aggravating circumstances arising from the General Part or specific sentencing provisions based on such circumstances are irrelevant for the purposes of the classification. For example, murder under § 212, with its minimum sentence of five years, is a *Verbrechen*, murder under mitigating circumstances (mainly provocation) according to the old[59] § 213 was punishable with imprisonment from six months to five years; in spite of this, it remained a *Verbrechen*, as it was a mere sentencing qualification to § 212. There is a third category, the lowest one, called *Ordnungswidrigkeiten*, which arose[60] out of the previous French classification of the *contraventions*; however, these are no longer considered criminal offences proper and are regulated by their own code, the *Ordnungswidrigkeitengesetz* or OWiG, which only refers to the StGB inasmuch as the OWiG does not make specific provision for general principles. We will, for reasons of space, not go into the separate dogmatic questions of the law on *Ordnungswidrigkeiten* unless the explanation under the individual chapters makes such reference necessary.

The most important consequences of the dichotomy between *Verbrechen* and *Vergehen* in the substantive criminal law lie in the treatment of attempts and of attempts at participation. § 23 provides that attempted *Verbrechen* always trigger criminal liability, whereas the same can be said for *Vergehen* only if the law

Coalition Provisional Authority (CPA) and the subsequent Iraqi law, in connection with the execution of Saddam Hussein, see Bohlander, 'Can the Iraqi Special Tribunal sentence Saddam Hussein to Death?' (2005) 3 *Journal of International Criminal Justice* 463–8. Whatever one may say on a moral level about Saddam Hussein being executed and getting his just deserts, what happened was, legally speaking, in my view murder by judgment because the correct interpretation of the *lex mitior* rule under Iraqi law, which is identical to the German law on the matter, made it clear that the tribunal did not have the power to sentence anyone to death. I took part, as an expert of the International Bar Association, in the training of the judges and prosecutors of the Iraqi High Tribunal that tried Hussein, and many of the judges asked for off-prints of that article long before the trial. The judgment of the Appeals Chamber addressed the issue in a very cursory and legally incorrect manner. I might after all have been wrong on the law, but the tribunal did not even bother to refute any of the substantive arguments and instead simply side-stepped the matter by blandly stating that the CPA law as the law of the occupiers was never really part of the Iraqi legal system, which was glaringly wrong under the 2004 and 2005 Iraqi constitutions. Obviously, political expediency and a desire to arrive at a certain result morally palatable to most of the Iraqi people may have played a part in the decision.

[58] See on the history and development from the French Code Pénal: Roxin, AT I, 272.

[59] The minimum sentence is now one year.

[60] See Roxin, AT I, 272.

expressly provides for this consequence. A good example in this context of how important it is to recognise the proper substance of and relationship between offences is § 216 (*Tötung auf Verlangen*), the offence of mercy killing or killing at the request of the victim: the sentencing frame is six months to five years and one might be tempted to say that it is a mere privileged qualification of § 212, and as such its attempt is always punishable. However, § 216(2) explicitly provides for attempt liability, which is an indicator that § 216 is a wholly separate and not a derivative offence. § 30 allows for punishment only in cases of incitement (namely, in the meaning of an attempted but fruitless act of abetting) or conspiracy[61] if the offence that is the object of that attempted participation or conspiracy is a *Verbrechen*.

---

[61] This is a loose utilisation of the common law concept, as the substance of the offence differs in common and civil law systems. However, *conspiracy* as a general term neatly catches the actual facts and actions of the offenders. As long as one bears that in mind, there is little harm in using the word in the German context.

3

The *Tatbestand*—Part One

The concept of the *Tatbestand* in German law encompasses such diverse issues as the definition of an act in the legal sense, causation, several categories of objective attribution—which in English law would be covered by the reference to causation in the legal sense—of a certain result, omissions liability, forms of intent and negligence, consent excluding a certain element of the objective *Tatbestand*, or *actus reus*. Especially in the area of causation, there is a wide field of problems where, on the one hand, things are far from cut and dried in the German debate, and on the other hand, some results differ from the approach of English law. In this chapter, we will be looking at some of the external or objective elements of the *Tatbestand*; the next chapter addresses the elements of the subjective side, such as intent, mistake, etc.

Types and Function of *Tatbestand*—*Deliktskategorien*

The *Tatbestand* is what defines a certain offence and has an impact on what elements the prosecution needs to prove,[1] or what must be established by the judges before the court can convict a defendant. In general, one can say that it consists of the written elements contained in the specific law, and of any unwritten factors that by necessity form a logical part of any offence, such as causation, quality as an act, etc, as stated above. In that respect, it is very similar in function to the English law concepts of *actus reus* and *mens rea*. When we talk about the concept of the *Tatbestand* from a German point of view, however, we first need to keep in mind the tripartite structure explained in chapter two; secondly, we encounter a typically Teutonic list that tries to establish more or less neat categories of *Tatbestand*.

---

[1] The approach to proving the *actus reus* advocated by David Ormerod in Smith and Hogan, *Criminal Law* (11th edn, Oxford University Press, 2005) 35 in the context of English law, namely that there is no need for the prosecution to prove each and every element of the offence to the jury in turn, but that it is more sensible to 'approach the crime as a whole' is unacceptable in a German context where each element of the offence as set out in the Criminal Code must be established by the court beyond reasonable doubt. It is also questionable whether his statement is ultimately helpful for the English context: of course, the prosecution does not have to follow a mechanical sequence in proving the elements of the offence, but at the end of the day, it *will* have to prove each and every one of them.

This list is not quite as dogmatic and removed from the necessities of real life as some might—perhaps with some justification—suspect in a German legal context. The purpose is to shed light on the function and object of protection of a given law which will aid in its interpretation and realising its interrelation with other norms in the overall context. It plays a role, for example, in deciding questions of the *concursus delictorum*, namely, the treatment of multiple charges, and in answering the question up until which point in time another can participate in the defendant's actions. Its function becomes even apparent in the shift of the wording when these categories are named: we do not, for example, speak of an *Erfolgstatbestand*, ie a result *Tatbestand*, but of an *Erfolgsdelikt*, ie a result *crime*. We shall see below what that means. The *Tatbestand* may be based on the kind of act committed by the offender, it may be based on the person of the offender, etc. Obviously, there is a lot of overlap between the different categories and, to that extent, the whole system loses some of its usefulness. At the end of the day, it is the substance, not the title, of a *Tatbestand* that matters. However, because these categories represent a kind of definitional shorthand for German lawyers and will re-appear in later chapters, it is indispensable that we familiarise ourselves at least with some of the terminology. I will spare the reader the debates and philosophical discussions that have been raging in German academia about the exact definitions and about the question of which offence belongs to which category; in the vast majority of cases the 'I know it when I see it' approach will be sufficient.[2]

The first distinction that is one of the most basic is the one between result- and conduct-based offences, namely, between *Erfolgsdelikte* and *Tätigkeitsdelikte*. The former category comprises offences where the offence is characterised by a result that needs to occur in addition, and mostly based on, the defendant's actions. Examples are murder (*Totschlag*, § 212), which requires the event of death based on an act or omission by the accused, or fraud, (*Betrug*, § 263), which requires the occurrence of damage to property based on the deception carried out by the defendant. The latter criminalises the mere conduct of the offender without the need for an additional extraneous result. Examples for this category are burglary (*Hausfriedensbruch*, § 123), which requires no more than that the defendant enters the house or other protected enclosure of another without the latter's consent, and perjury (*Meineid*, § 154), the only element of which is the taking of a false oath.

Another pair is the *Dauer-* and *Zustandsdelikte*. The former definition denotes that the commission of the offence lasts for a certain time after the first act by the accused, and again an example is burglary, which begins with entering the house and terminates only when the defendant leaves the house. The same applies to false imprisonment (*Freiheitsberaubung*, § 239) until the moment that the victim is released. The *Zustandsdelikte* require that, based on the actions of the accused, a certain state of affairs is established that violates the law. An example is bigamy (*Doppelehe*, § 172), which is completed when the marriage is contracted, but

---

[2] See on this and the following Roxin, AT I, § 10, from whom the sequence of the presentation has been partially borrowed.

endures as a state of affairs. Roxin also counts criminal damage, murder and actual bodily harm (ABH) in this category,[3] which shows the lack of a clear line between the categories and how questionable the over-dogmatisation can sometimes be: one could also classify them as *Erfolgsdelikte*, and it is a bit of a banality to say that once somebody is killed (result) they usually stay dead (state of affairs). The important effect of this distinction, however, occurs in the field of complicity: with *Dauerdelikte*, participation is possible until the principal terminates his or her action (D leaves the house); with *Zustandsdelikte*, any participation must happen before the end of the act that triggers the new state of affairs (until D says to his or her adored: 'I do').

A more substantial problem, both dogmatically and from the point of view of criminal policy, is posed by the so-called *erfolgsqualifizierte Delikte*, offence combinations where a basic offence has a further, extended consequence that is not an element of that basic offence. A very rough translation might be 'result-qualified offences'. This, at first glance, looks somewhat like the English law concept of constructive liability, for example, constructive manslaughter, although there is a major difference as regards the necessary *mens rea* for the extended result. Constructive liability in English law does not require a specific *mens rea* for the extended result, or at the most a greatly reduced one, whereas under § 18 at least negligence with regard to the extended result is required. German law resembled the English constructive liability approach until 1953,[4] based on the figure of *versari in res illicita*, which is at the bottom of the idea of constructive liability: if you commit an unlawful dangerous act, you are liable for any consequence flowing from it, intended or not. In 1953, § 18 was introduced because of the constitutional concerns caused by the prior practice.[5] Because of these concerns, the legislator has also increasingly taken to restricting the *mens rea* required for the extended result in *erfolgsqualifizierte Delikte* to gross negligence (*Leichtfertigkeit*). In effect, and despite the similarity of the combination of a basic offence and an extended result to the model of constructive manslaughter, the German system comes closer to the English concept applied, for example, in gross negligence manslaughter.

An illustration to explain the difference:[6] the German Federal Court (BGH) had to deal with the case of a mother who had forced her four-year-old daughter to eat a bowl of pudding to which the child had, in her mother's absence, added about 30 grammes of salt, thinking it was sugar. The accused became angry about what her daughter had done and forced her, despite the child's protests and obvious revulsion, to eat the whole bowl, including the 30 grammes of salt, recognising that this would cause the girl stomach upset, belly ache and that she might be sick. She

---

[3] Roxin, AT I, 331.

[4] See, eg very clearly, Reinhard Frank, *Das Strafgesetzbuch für das Deutsche Reich* (18th edn, 1931) § 59 at IV, with further references to the old law.

[5] Sch/Sch-Cramer/Sternberg-Lieben, § 18, Mn. 1–2.

[6] BGH, Judgment of 16 March 2006, Case No 4 StR 536/05 <http://www.bundesgerichtshof.de> accessed 26 June 2008.

did *not* know that eating an amount of 0.5 to 1 gramme of salt per kilogram of body weight will usually have lethal consequences. The girl at that time weighed 15 kg. Her condition immediately deteriorated and within about an hour, on her arrival at the hospital, the daughter had become comatose; within 35 hours the child was dead. The trial court found that the accused had had no foresight within the ambit of §§ 227, 18, the offence of assault occasioning death (*Körperverletzung mit Todesfolge*). The BGH, on appeal, held that the trial court had rightly refused to enter a conviction under § 227 for lack of the required *mens rea*. Under English law, committing the basic offence of assault or battery with the necessary *mens rea* for that offence is enough, for the consequence of death, foresight of any harm is sufficient; there is no need for the accused or a reasonable man or woman to have foreseen a likelihood of death. (We leave aside the matter of whether this might also have been a case of gross negligence manslaughter.)

This is not the case under the German approach. Any liability for a more serious result than that intended has to be based on negligence and foresight of that result, not just of any harm. As the offender is normally acting in violation of a duty of diligence by committing the basic offence, all that is usually needed for the serious result is the foreseeability of the latter. There can be exceptions if the violation of that basic duty of diligence did not actually cause the result. The standard for foreseeability, according to the decision, is as follows: could the offender at the relevant time with his or her abilities and knowledge foresee death as a potential *result* of his or her actions? It is not necessary that he or she has foresight of all the details of the causal chain. The jurisprudence allows for an exclusion of liability if the lethal danger was so far outside what could normally be expected that it can no longer be attributed to the offender. The test is thus in essence an objective one with subjective overtones, reminiscent of the provocation jurisprudence in England until *Holley*.[7] The BGH approved of the trial court's assessment that the accused had had no knowledge of the effect of her daughter's ingesting such a large amount of salt and that this knowledge was also not something that was widely known, even to experienced mothers. Even if this was not a case of a 'medical rarity', the BGH was satisfied that the trial court had not overstretched the requirements for the foreseeability of the lethal result. The gist of this reference betrays the fact that despite protestations in the literature and in the case law that the offender must have had cause to exercise his or her diligence according to *his or her* abilities,[8] the negligence criterion presumes that everyone will normally be aware of the potentially dangerous consequences of their actions unless an extraordinary subjective factor prevents this; subjective factors thus in effect provide a check on the basically objective test.[9]

---

[7] *Attorney General for Jersey v Holley Privy Council (Jersey)* [2005] UKPC 23; [2005] 2 AC 580; [2005] 3 WLR 29; [2005] 3 All ER 371; [2005] 2 Cr App R 36; [2005] Crim LR 966.

[8] See, eg Duttge in *Münchener Kommentar zum Strafgesetzbuch*, Vol I (2003), § 15, Mn. 104 *ff*, with further references.

[9] This example is a modified version of my case comment in (2006) 70 *Journal of Criminal Law* 482.

Erfolgsqualifizierte Delikte require, on the *actus reus* side, that the extended result must have been immediately, or directly (*unmittelbar*), caused by the commission of the basic offence. (One should bear in mind that even if the result-qualified offence option cannot be used for lack of that link, in many instances there may be a subsidiary liability based on a direct negligence offence, but with a lesser sentencing frame.) An intermediary cause may lead to extinction of liability, even if it is set by the victim him- or herself. However, there is no real clear line that would assist in determining when such an intervening event would break the link. The BGH has, for example, held that § 227 was not established for that reason when a woman, fleeing from the accused's maltreatment of her, fell from a balcony and died.[10] In a different case with a similar scenario, but where the victim threw herself out of the window after suffering severe physical abuse and being in a state of panic, the BGH accepted the link.[11] Other cases include arson occasioning death, if the death was not caused by the fire, but by the collapse of the building because of the explosion of the fuel used by the offender (no link);[12] robbery occasioning death, if the victim falls during the pursuit of the robber and dies as a consequence of the fall (no link);[13] if a third person acting in the interests of the offender hangs the victim while she was still alive, thus speeding up her demise which would have been inevitable anyway based on the offender's actions (link accepted);[14] if mistakes are made by a doctor in the medical treatment of the victim (link accepted);[15] if the offender uses a gun to hit the victim over the head and in the course of hitting a shot is loosed accidentally (link accepted).[16]

A special category of cases where the BGH routinely holds that there is no direct link are the scenarios where the offender hurts the victim without intent[17] to kill, thinks he or she killed him or her by mistake and then actually causes the death by destroying or hiding the supposed corpse. The BGH made it clear that it must be the particular danger immanent in the basic offence that causes the death, not a merely direct temporal link.[18] However, the court has accepted a link even in cases where the connection was tenuous and more or less explicitly rejected the 'direct link' element as being dispositive: § 227 was established in a case where the victim only suffered a non-lethal wound to his ankle and died because of serious medical mistakes during his treatment;[19] hostage-taking occasioning death under § 239 b(2) was accepted when the victim died of bullet wounds caused by gunfire from

---

[10] BGH NJW 1971, 152.

[11] BGH NStZ 1992, 335.

[12] BGHSt 20, 230.

[13] BGHSt 22, 362.

[14] BGH NStZ 1992, 333.

[15] BGH NStZ-RR 2000, 265.

[16] BGHSt 14, 110.

[17] These cases must be distinguished from those where D intends to kill V, but death occurs in a different manner than planned or envisaged by D. They are treated in the next chapter on the subjective side of the *Tatbestand*.

[18] BGHSt 10, 208; BGH StV 1993, 75 and especially BGH StV 1998, 203.

[19] BGHSt 31, 96.

the police who were trying to free her,[20] a situation that is strongly reminiscent of the *Pagett*[21] scenario. In the latter case, the BGH expressly stated that the 'direct link' criterion was of little conceptual assistance in a hostage situation.

This makes sense against the background of a systematic comparison: if the law, as in § 239 and § 239b, allows for an extended result qualification offence arising from a basic offence of false imprisonment or hostage-taking, where the basic offence as such has no direct lethal connotations, then the reasons for establishing the link to the lethal consequence cannot lie in the nature of the basic act, but must lie in the empirically known dangerous circumstances generally surrounding hostage situations—things tend to get out of hand in these scenarios and the offender has caused the general dangerous environment for the victim. The case of the abducted girl who jumps out of the assailant's car and is killed or injured as a consequence, as held in *Roberts*[22] based on issues of reasonable foreseeability, receives a similar treatment in German law based on judgments on the general dangerousness of the offender's behaviour.[23] The nature of the necessary link is thus best deduced from the specific danger created by the basic offence; the BGH is, however, certainly right to take a restrictive approach in general.

German law makes a further distinction between offences causing a definite harm to the *Rechtsgut* and acts that merely cause a danger (*Verletzungs-* versus *Gefährdungsdelikte*). The former to a large extent overlap with the category of the *Erfolgsdelikte*. The second category is sub-divided into *konkrete* and *abstrakte Gefährungsdelikte*. The first variety requires a concrete, actual danger to a certain person or object, such as, for example, dangerous driving under § 315 c, where the dangerous driving must cause a palpable danger for human life or objects of great value. The second sub-category is characterised by the fact that although there need not be an imminent danger, the conduct underlying the offence is generally highly dangerous and thus engaging in that conduct is deserving of punishment *eo ipso*. An example is § 316, driving whilst under the influence of alcohol or drugs. At an even less tangible level from the point of view of the harm principle, there are offences which penalise the mere preparation of a certain conduct, but instead of regulating this under the general law of attempts, the Special Part makes the act an offence in and of itself; this is in effect similar to the common law concept of a specific inchoate offence. They are called *Unternehmensdelikte*, because the activity in itself of endeavouring to bring about a certain result (*etwas zu tun unternehmen*) is the reason for liability. As in English law, a large percentage of these crimes is found in the context of political offences such as high treason and publication offences, etc. The reasons behind the separate criminalisation of purely preparatory acts lie in the great danger to the public good usually caused by such acts when successfully implemented, and in the fact that once started they tend to get out of control very easily. The debate as to how the general rules of

---

[20] BGHSt 33, 322.
[21] [1983] 76 Cr App R 279 (CA).
[22] (1971) 56 Cr App Rep 95; [1972] Crim LR 27; 115 Sol Jo 809.
[23] BGHSt 19, 382. See on the discussion in the literature Roxin, AT I, 334.

attempt and withdrawal apply to these offences is controversial and will be examined later in the chapter on attempt liability.

Some offences criminalise behaviour depending on certain qualities of the person who commits a crime: if anyone can commit them, as is the case for the vast majority of offences, they are called *Allgemeindelikte* (common offences); if they can only be committed by a certain class of persons, they are called *Sonderdelikte* (special offences). An example of the second type are those offences that can only be committed by state officials, such as accepting bribes or procuring the commission of an offence by a subordinate. Sometimes, the special quality of the offender is the basis for criminalising behaviour (such as perverting the course of justice—*Rechtsbeugung*, § 339); sometimes it merely increases the sentencing range, for example, in § 340, which penalises assault committed by a public official in the execution of his or her duty. This leads us to the last division that we need to examine for the purposes of our introduction: the distinction between basic offence (*Grunddelikt*), qualified offence (*qualifizierte Tatbestände*) and separate offence (*eigenständiges Delikt*), as well as sentencing provisions (*Strafzumessungsregeln*). The qualification can be based on aggravating or mitigating factors, as can be the sentencing provisions. The situation is further complicated by the additional category of the so-called *Regelbeispiele*, non-exhaustive sentencing factors that are mostly treated as if they were elements of a proper qualified offence and are enumerated in specific offences, for example, § 243, aggravated theft. There is no really uniform approach to deciding which is which in the case law and literature.

A good example of the potential for confusion is the relationship between *Mord* (§ 211), *Totschlag* (§ 212), *Totschlag im minderschweren Fall* (§ 213) and *Tötung auf Verlangen* (§ 216). § 211 covers intentional killing in several serious categories and threatens a mandatory life sentence; § 212 deals with intentional killing for persons who are not *Mörder* according to § 211 and provides for imprisonment from five to 15 years or a discretionary life sentence; § 213 covers cases of § 212 (not § 211!), which are, for some reason, mainly provocation scenarios, deemed less serious, and provides for imprisonment from one to 10 years. Finally, § 216 covers cases of mercy killings at the request of the victim and has a sentencing range from six months to five years. The sequence of the provisions would, under systematic and literal interpretation, indicate that § 211 is the basic offence, § 212 is a privileged qualification of § 211 and § 213 is a privileged sentencing provision to § 212, whereas § 216 is a de facto privileged qualification of § 212, yet in the form of a separate offence (see § 216(2)). Indeed, a number of commentators take this view. However, most academic writers would view § 212 as the basic offence in the empirical sense (the naked act of intentional killing), § 211 as an aggravated qualification of § 212, and § 213 and § 216 as above. The courts, especially the BGH, however, have traditionally seen § 211 and § 212 as totally separate offences. This classification has a serious impact, for example, in the area of accomplice liability under § 28.

This overview cannot—and need not—cover all the possible permutations and minor sub-classifications of offences, but it shows, at one small example, the tendency of German law to drift into logical exercises of trying to put everything neatly into separate drawers that are as small and homogenous as possible, and not to allow their contents to mix if it can at all be helped; at the same time this obsession with categorisation and classification necessarily founders when faced with the vagaries of real life and the banal fact that real persons do not live or act according to pre-set categories. The more one relies on categorisation and the logical interaction between categories for building the structure of law's house, the more important exact definitions of each concept down to the most minute level will become, and experience shows that it is very difficult to sustain that level of exactitude and logical rigour, especially when there is a myriad of academic opinion on almost any conceptual matter.[24]

Handlung and *Unterlassen*—Act and Omission

Positive Acts

Regardless of which type of offence we talk about, all of them have one common element without which there can be no liability: even in systems that rely on strict liability offences, there is agreement that triggering criminal liability requires at the very least a human act or, if omissions liability is a feature of the criminal law, an emanation of a lack of human interference that is seen as socially relevant for the establishment of criminal responsibility. We are not yet looking at the legal parameters of omissions liability or causation, but at the mere philosophical question of when we can say that a human being has acted or did not act when there was a possibility to act. Over the centuries, German philosophers and legal theorists have struggled with this conundrum and have come up with different definitions, which, after Hegel's statement[25] about the human will as the defining element for creating criminal liability, have more or less referred to different aspects of human will control over body movement or external factors. At the end of the day, all of these highly erudite elucidations of the several aspects of human behaviour cannot hide the fact that it is very difficult to explain a theoretical concept as basic as an 'act' because, on the one hand, it is almost impossible to keep normative elements based on societal models out of

[24] Although it is a more general observation, it may be apposite to make it at this time: German criminal law, as any law across the world, has to face the fact that logic is only one part of the application of the law, but that this needs to be tempered by common sense. The sometimes illogical reliance on common sense in English law as in *Majewski* takes up, from a German point of view, too much of the (practical) legal debate and begins too early in the deduction process, but at the end of the day one may well wonder whether the German-professed preference for strict logic is not equally to blame for falling into the other extreme and for being methodologically dishonest into the bargain, by claiming overall dogmatic and doctrinal purity, while at the same time hiding the influence of obvious common sense and public policy arguments by adapting the elements of its doctrinal definitions at the micro-level to these arguments and then pretending that the overall edifice is still all logic.
[25] Hegel, Grundlinien der Philosophie des Rechts, 1821, § 117.

the definition and, on the other hand, because the human language is restricted in its conceptual vocabulary: very often one will find that definitions either only use (vague) synonyms whose substance in itself is in need of explanation, or that they do, in essence, try to define a basic idea by its derivative higher-order concepts. The current state of affairs in Germany[26] appears to be that a grand unified definition of what is an act that could be applicable to all types of offences is not feasible and the definition will depend on the substance of each offence.[27] Fascinating as the history of philosophical thought[28] on the matter may be,[29] for our purposes we shall stick to a more pragmatic approach of definition by exclusion: common experience makes it easier to tell what is *not* seen as an act (or an attributable omission); what is not excluded by this process stands a good chance of being an act.

The first category that one would find it easy to agree with is that mere thoughts, feelings and attitudes which do not yet manifest themselves externally are not acts—but they might qualify as criminally relevant omissions if there is a duty to act (see below).[30] There appears to be some uncertainty as to whether mere thoughts without bodily movement can,[31] outside offences of omission, states of affairs and possession scenarios, qualify as acts.[32] From a strictly physical and neurological point of view, Jakobs[33] is right in pointing out that doing mental maths or planning a crime are of course human actions controlled by willpower and thus could on the face of it qualify as acts. Indeed, if the mental math was being done by an offender who, being present at the place where he or she wants it to explode, had his fingers around a 'dead man's switch'[34] trigger of an explosive device, and

---

[26] It would appear that the development in Spain has been influenced to a similar degree and with a similar result by the German debate; see, eg the discussion by Santiago Mir Puig in *Derecho Penal, Parte General* (7th edn, Barcelona, Editorial Reppertor, 2004) 188.

[27] Sch/Sch-Lenckner/Eisele, Vorbem. §§ 13 ff, Mn. 23–42, at 37.

[28] Sch/Sch-Lenckner/Eisele, Vorbem. §§ 13 ff, Mn. 23–42.

[29] See for an overview Roxin, AT I, § 8.

[30] Roxin, AT I, 266; Wessels/Beulke, AT, 36.

[31] The matter appears not to be addressed at any length in mainstream English legal writing. Glanville Williams in 1983 still defined an act as a 'willed bodily movement' (*Textbook of Criminal Law* (2nd edn) 47–148). See also David Ormerod in Smith and Hogan, *Criminal Law* (11th edn, Oxford University Press, 2005) 44 for similar approaches. One of the more incisive recent philosophical books on the question of what is an act, Jonathan Bennett's *The Act Itself* (Oxford, Clarendon Press, 1995), does not deal with this specific issue, either. The bodily movement or external manifestation requirement seems to pervade many different legal systems; for example, Dutch law appears to be based on the same idea of a physical component; see J de Hullu, *Materieel Strafrecht* (2nd edn, Deventer, 2003) 160. Jean Pradel in his *Droit Pénal Comparé* (2nd edn, Dalloz, 2002) 273, denies liability for thoughts '*indépendamment de tout acte matériel*'. He repeats this in his *Droit Pénal Général* (15th edn, Paris, Editions Cujas, 2004) 327. American law and especially the Model Penal Code, according to Wayne R LaFave, *Criminal Law* (4th edn, St Paul, Thomson/West Publishing, 2003) 302, subscribe to the requirement of a bodily movement. Islamic criminal law under the Shari'a also adheres to the external manifestation requirement; see Abdul Qadir 'Oudah, *Islamic Criminal Law*, Vol II (New Delhi, Kitab Bhavan, 1999, reprint 2005) 42–4.

[32] See the discussion in Sch/Sch-Lenckner/Eisele, Vorbem. §§ 13 *ff*, Mn. 23–42, especially at 37.

[33] Cited in Roxin, AT I, 266, fn 135.

[34] A trigger that operates when a restraining control mechanism is released rather than when a button is pushed; hand grenades work on that principle: once you pull the safety pin, the grenade will explode as soon as the handle is released and the safety time has elapsed. It takes its name from the fact that it will operate even if the person holding it is killed.

patient, may, according to (controversial) case law, for example,[67] require the doctor to inform persons about the HIV infection of their partners,[68] to protect hospital patients from dangers posed by other patients[69] and to protect minors from suicide.[70]

Duty Based on Specific Qualities of the Offender

Many people, whether in the work place or otherwise, are subject to certain duties arising from that very position. Chief executive officers will be under a duty to safeguard the financial interests of their enterprises and if they do not, they may be liable under § 266 for causing damage to the assets of the enterprises by omission. A large segment of these job-related duties occur in public service, especially with civil servants, whose office not only empowers them to perform certain functions, but also makes them liable if they omit to do so properly. An obvious example is the police officer who lets a thief get away on purpose because the thief is a friend of his or her own son; by omitting to arrest the thief, the officer is guilty of an offence under § 258.[71]

Duty Based on Creation of Dangerous Situations

As in English law under *Miller*[72] scenarios, German law[73] recognises a duty to act arising out of prior conduct which created a source of risk or danger, to take all necessary steps in order to prevent the risk from materialising. The risk-causing conduct may in turn have been an omission in violation of a duty to act.[74] The exact conditions regarding the nature and qualities of the dangerous conduct are unclear, but it would appear that the prevailing view does not tend to require any fault on the part of D. However, his or her conduct must have been dangerous as

[67] See for more examples Sch/Sch-Stree, § 13 Mn. 28.
[68] OLG Frankfurt, NJW 2000, 875; NStZ 2001, 149.
[69] BGH NJW 1976, 1145.
[70] OLG Stuttgart, NJW 1997, 3103.
[71] For an overview, see Sch/Sch-Stree, § 13 Mn. 31 with further references.
[72] [1983] 2 AC 161. See, for a similar German case with an almost bizarre course of events, BGH NJW 1989, 2480: D spends the night in the hay loft of V's barn. On the next morning he lights his cigarette lighter to have a look at his watch; this causes the hay around him, and consequently himself, to burn. He jumps down from the loft to get outside to put the fire out, only to be suddenly confronted by V who is in shock at the sight of burning D. She instinctively raises her pitchfork and the two engage in a struggle during which D grabs her throat and V faints. D leaves her in the barn and runs outside to extinguish the fire at a pond. He omits to tell the neighbours who have come to help about V; V's charred corpse is found later in the completely destroyed barn. The autopsy finds that she must have died before the smoke or fire engulfed her because there were no smoke or soot particles found in her upper airways. The trial court convicted D of negligent arson and acquitted him of attempted murder; the BGH quashed the acquittal and remanded the case for re-trial with an instruction that, depending on the circumstances of the case and the evidence, D could be guilty even of attempted aggravated murder under § 211.
[73] For an overview of categories and examples from the case law, see Sch/Sch-Stree, § 13 Mn. 32–42.
[74] RGSt 68, 104.

such in relation to the legal interest threatened as a result of his or her actions, and it must have been in breach of a duty itself, meaning that behaviour which is legal cannot normally give rise to omissions liability. Exceptions to this are the cases where the legal reasons for creating a certain source of danger cease to apply after a while: in that case, D is required to eliminate the danger source as soon as the reasons for its creation have ceased. An example is V, who was locked up by the police because he or she was found drunk in public and posed a danger to others; he or she must be released as soon as the drunkenness ends. A road block set up because of road flooding must be removed as soon as the flooding has subsided.[75]

Causation (Acts and Omissions)

A general element of all result offences is that of causation: D cannot be held liable for any event unless he or she did cause it and, we should add immediately, cause it in the legal sense. Just as under English law, German law has realised that the physical concept of causation would lead to an excessive scope of liability. The miner who dug up the ore from which a factory worker made metal which was then used in the production of the first nuclear bomb could thus be liable for the mass murder of the citizens of Hiroshima. This is clearly going too far, yet it is strictly speaking not a question of causation in the meaning of the relationship between cause and effect, but one of legal and thus moral ascription of responsibility. We can see the difference clearly when we imagine that the miner was one of a carefully selected few working in a special mine under government control, knew what the ore was going to be used for and approved of its intended use, and compare that to our reaction if he worked in a normal mine and knew nothing at all. In both cases, criminal liability may be lacking, and his knowledge is irrelevant for causality, yet we seem to attach great moral importance to it to the extent that we do not merely wish to negate the necessary *mens rea*, but exclude the person already from the chain of causation. This has led to the development of *legal concepts of causation* or conceptual restrictions on the *ascription of legal responsibility* for physically causal acts. English law has taken the former approach when it establishes categories such as the *novus actus interveniens* by a free, deliberate and informed act of a third party as breaking the chain of causation, whereas German legal thinking has in recent decades tended towards a clinical separation of the two issues which brings it closer to the second solution. Things are far from settled in all areas and there is considerable dogmatic uncertainty both in the literature and the case law. It is probably down to common sense in the individual case that the results rarely ever differ seriously in practice.

---

[75] Examples by Sch/Sch-Stree, § 13 Mn. 36. It would, of course, be an apposite observation to say that in the latter examples, the conduct giving rise to omissions liability is itself an omission, namely not to remove the previously legally created danger. However, the permission to create the danger source is by interpretation a conditional one dependent on the need for its continuation. In effect, this is less a case of liability because a danger was created, but one based on the law directly, where the law allowing the creation also demands its cessation when the conditions for its establishment no longer apply.

issues. Depending on the view and theory adopted, the examples may be treated under causation or as part of the ascription criteria outside causation.

Contributory Acts of the Victim

D cannot evade liability by arguing that V's own actions contributed to the result in its actual form. The same applies if V's physical or mental constitution is special or even abnormal (see the 'thin skull rule' in English law). Fortuity of consequence has no room in negating causation.[88]

Free, Deliberate and Informed Third-party Interventions

The ability of D to plead the above very much depends on whether or not the intervention, which may again be by the victim, breaks the causal chain started by D. The rule is that as long as the conduct of D is still operating as a cause of the intervener's acts, even if these are made intentionally and on a free, deliberate and informed basis, there will be no *novus actus* breaking the chain. Only if the act of the defendant has no more influence on the result will there be a lack of causality. Examples for the former category include:

a) death of a rescuer as a consequence of arson;[89]
b) refusal by the victim to have an operation after an accident;[90]
c) improper use of products by the victim;[91] and
d) provocation of the victim leading to lethal outcome, even if D was then acting in a state of self-defence.[92]

Examples for the second category include:

a) perjury in civil proceedings for the purpose of defrauding V through deceiving the court if the judge arrives at the incorrect decision in favour of D without any recourse to the false statement;[93] and
b) D1 tries to import drugs, which are then stolen and imported by D2.[94]

Obviously, there is no bright line that would allow for clear delineation in every case. The general rule is that the less D's acts continue to operate on the final result, the less likely they are to be considered as causal.

---

[88] Sch/Sch-Lenckner/Eisele, Vorbem. §§ 13 *ff*, Mn. 76.

[89] BGHSt 39, 324.

[90] OLG Celle NJW 2001, 2816.

[91] BGHSt 37, 112—Leather Spray Case. It must, however, be mentioned that the BGH did hold that an abuse or a use that did not comply with the normal conditions of use could affect the liability of the accused, even if it did not impact on causation.

[92] BGH NJW 2001, 1077.

[93] RGSt 69, 47.

[94] BGHSt 38, 32. See for a critique of that decision Sch/Sch-Lenckner/Eisele, Vorbem. §§ 13 *ff*, Mn. 78.

Alternative and Cumulative Causes

These scenarios occur, for example, when there are several offenders acting separately and not as joint principals, etc. Alternative causation covers those cases where two or more causes, each of which would have been sufficient to cause the result, impact at the same time: D1 and D2 each independently administer a lethal dose of poison to V, V dies of the simultaneous effect of both poisons. D1 and D2 are both guilty of murder. If, however, it cannot be established whether one of them did not take effect before the other, both D1 and D2 are each only guilty of attempted murder[95] (based on *in dubio pro reo*, because each cause could be seen as breaking the chain started by the other). Alternative causality may also apply if D initiated two causes, each of which in itself could have caused the result alone; this can be important with respect to the *mens rea* in which the causes were set. The BGH[96] had to decide the case of D, who had been drinking heavily together with V; late at night when D had retired to his room he heard noises downstairs. He took his pistol and, with conditional intent to kill, fired a short at the person he saw standing at the bottom of the stairs, who was V, whom D did not recognise. The injury caused by the shot was lethal, but could have been treated successfully had V been given immediate medical care. D returned to his room and a few minutes later heard more noises downstairs. He went back to the stairs and fired a random shot in the assumption that there might be several people downstairs. V was hit a second time; again the injury caused was lethal in itself. V died as a cause of the injuries received by both shots. The BGH considered the first shot as a sufficient cause of V's death and D was found guilty of murder already through firing the first shot, and of negligent killing through firing the second—although the BGH criticised the trial court for not examining the question thoroughly of whether D did not also have conditional intent for the second shot. Based on the doctrine applying to multiple charges, the negligent killing was, however, a subsidiary offence to the murder anyway and D was thus only convicted of murder.

If, in the above example of D1 and D2 using poison on V, the lethal result was only reached by the *combined* effect, we speak of *cumulative* causality. In this context, both are still causal. The question of whether V's death could be fully attributed to both D1 and D2 as in the case of alternative causality is much more difficult.[97] The tendency appears to be not to do so and, depending on the *mens rea* of D1 and D2, convict of attempted murder and/or causing grievous bodily harm or administering noxious substances.

The issues of alternative and/or cumulative causation are also highly relevant for environmental offences[98] and the criminal liability of members of decision-making committees, such as boards of directors, etc. Unless it can be proved that they acted intentionally as joint principals, which is hardly ever likely, the court

---

[95] Sch/Sch-Lenckner/Eisele, Vorbem. §§ 13 *ff*, Mn. 82; BGH NJW 1966, 1823.
[96] BGHSt 39, 195.
[97] See Sch/Sch-Lenckner/Eisele, Vorbem. §§ 13 *ff*, Mn. 83 for a discussion of the different views.
[98] Sch/Sch-Lenckner/Eisele, Vorbem. §§ 13 *ff*, Mn. 83.

will be faced with the dilemma that each one of those who voted for the activity that gave rise to the damaging result could argue that his or her vote did not make a difference if the sum of the other votes already passed the required majority, and was thus not causal. The case where D's vote was necessary to pass the threshold is incomparably easier to solve. However, even in the first scenario, the prevailing view is to hold all those who voted affirmatively as causal for the result.[99] The reasoning for this is complex and depends on which causation model one chooses to adopt. Because of the difficulty of establishing joint commission, academic writers have thought of the idea of a negligent co-perpetratorship (*fahrlässige Mittäterschaft*), which, as we shall see in the chapter on multiple actors and complicity, is strictly speaking a contradiction in terms.[100]

Lack of Creation of a Legally Relevant Danger

This category would appear to be clearly anchored in the realm of objective ascription. It covers such cases as the textbook example of D sending her uncle V, from whom she will inherit a fortune, on a plane trip in the hope that the plane will crash and V will die, which it and V actually do.[101] Generally speaking, as long as D acts lawfully, any consequences arising from that lawful behaviour cannot be attributed to her, regardless of any negative consequences she may wish upon others. However, the BGH[102] in a questionable judgment has held, in a case involving accident insurance fraud by arranged car accidents, that even if D is outwardly acting in compliance with the rules of the highway code, his criminal intention may make him causal and liable for fraud *and* endangering road traffic. D had caused a series of road accidents by exploiting the potential lack of attention by other road users; for example, he had set the left indicator light when nearing a junction, but had then braked and turned left into a garage yard before reaching the junction. In a number of cases, the following cars whose drivers had thought D would turn left at the junction bumped into his, which he had hoped for, and he then made fraudulent claims against the drivers' accident insurance. His outward behaviour as such was not, as the BGH accepted, in violation of the traffic rules, yet his motivation was 'hostile'. This may be an acceptable position as far as the fraud is concerned, but it presents enormous difficulties with respect to the offence of endangering road traffic.[103]

---

[99] BGHSt 37, 107. See also BGHSt 48, 95 regarding recalls of defective products and omissions liability.

[100] See the discussion in Sch/Sch-Lenckner/Eisele, Vorbem. §§ 13 *ff*, Mn. 83a for an overview of the opinions regarding the topic.

[101] Sch/Sch-Lenckner/Eisele, Vorbem. §§ 13 *ff*, Mn. 93.

[102] BGH NJW 1999, 3132.

[103] See the commentary in Sch/Sch-Lenckner/Eisele, Vorbem. §§ 13 *ff*, Mn. 93.

of care, or to be more precise, of diligence. As a general principle, any degree of negligence[120] can be the basis of liability in criminal law, yet the legislator has in recent times displayed a tendency to restrict it to cases of gross negligence (*Leichtfertigkeit*).[121] As mentioned above, the category of the result-qualified offences (*erfolgsqualifizierte Delikte*) plays a special part in the scenario of negligence liability, because contrary to the concept of constructive liability under English law, § 18 requires negligence with regard to the extended result. Negligence offences can be committed by omission if all other criteria for that form of liability are fulfilled.

The general structure of negligence offences is divided into an objective part and a subjective part, the latter being part of the third stage, guilt. The objective part is situated in the *objektiver Tatbestand*. A traditional view had held that for negligence offences, the only objective criterion was causation, everything else being a question of the personal abilities of the offender[122] and thus of guilt. This is no longer the prevailing view, because it became apparent that there had to be something already on the objective level that justified the theoretical inclusion of human frailty and error into the criminal law's remit, something that made a conceptual comparison with the intentional offences justifiable. Because everyone makes mistakes that may have severe consequences based on mere fortuity of circumstances, a criterion was needed that excluded imperfect behaviour where criminal sanctions were obviously out of place. We should also remind ourselves of the general fact that negligence liability requires a specific statutory prohibition; there is no general principle of liability for negligently caused harm in German, or indeed English, law. The criminalisation of negligence is thus virtually always a function of the societal value of the legal interest endangered, or of the degree of carelessness exhibited by the offender, or both. The sanction of the law represents society's verdict of what is and is not an acceptable and therefore permissible risk to the interests of its members.

The modern view, therefore, requires a breach of a duty of diligence already on the objective level.[123] Leaving aside the issue that German law does not erect a minimum threshold of gross negligence, the situation is similar to the principles under English law of gross negligence manslaughter, which requires the negligent violation of a duty of care and causation of the result by that negligent breach. It is commonly accepted that for positive acts in the context of dangerous activities, the situations giving rise to such a duty are 'limitless'.[124] For omission offences, such duties are, of course, less abundant, and under German nomenclature they would be primarily listed under the general heading of duty to act, as we saw above. The *actus reus* standard for deciding whether due diligence was violated is similar to that under civil law. It is, according to the prevailing view, an objective one, which means that any special skills or defects that D may have will not normally enter

---

[121] Sch/Sch-Cramer/Sternberg-Lieben, § 15, Mn. 105–8.
[122] Sch/Sch-Cramer/Sternberg-Lieben, § 15, Mn. 111–15 with a critique of that view.
[123] Sch/Sch-Cramer/Sternberg-Lieben, § 15, Mn. 116.
[124] See, eg Ormerod in Smith and Hogan, cited above n 1, 483–4.

into the evaluation. A minority view would wish to see these reflected in the *actus reus* already: why, for example, should a surgeon with skills and experience above the average, who does not do his or her best to employ them during a complicated operation, yet for which he or she may have been specifically requested, be able to argue that he or she should be measured by the standards of the average colleague? So far, this strand of opinion has not been able to dominate the field.[125] However, this does not mean that certain generalised categories of abilities and skills expected of certain classes and groups of persons will not play a role:[126] there may be general requirements over and above that asked of the average man and woman, such as for the members of a certain trade, profession or public service. However, these must be distinguished from the individual special abilities of persons working within one of those categories.

What is meant by a violation of due diligence can be summed up in the concepts of foreseeability and avoidability.[127] If D cannot foresee that his or her actions might cause harm, or even if he or she foresees it, cannot avoid causing that harm, then it would be unfair to hold him or her liable for the consequences of his or her actions.[128] However, there are some activities which contain both foreseeable and avoidable risks of potentially disastrous magnitude, which are nevertheless legal, such as, for example, the operation of a chemical factory[129] or the production of cars. In both cases, there are great risks involved that may, and statistically at some stage will, lead to harm to or even loss of life, possibly on a grand scale. Yet society accepts these activities as socially adequate risks, because based on a balancing of costs and benefits it is commonly seen as more beneficial to society to run these risks and try to contain them as much as feasible, than not to have their benefits and have no risks. The measure for deciding whether a certain result was foreseeable is the ex ante standard from the point of view of the offender at the time the harmful conduct occurred. This is no hard and fast rule and it may therefore be useful to look at some examples from practice, where the courts have held that a certain result was or was not foreseeable.

Foreseeability of the result by D, but not necessarily liability, has been accepted in the following circumstances:

a) use of a pistol left by theatre spectator D in his coat in the killing of V by another;[130]

b) death of drug addict V after D supplied heroin to him which V had then used;[131]

---

[125] See the discussion at Sch/Sch-Cramer/Sternberg-Lieben, § 15, Mn. 116–19. Note, however, that within the examination of guilt, personal abilities can play a role.

[126] Sch/Sch-Cramer/Sternberg-Lieben, § 15, Mn. 134, 141.

[127] Sch/Sch-Cramer/Sternberg-Lieben, § 15, Mn. 124–5.

[128] Note that, in this context, there is an unexplained conceptual gap between the English aversion against criminal liability for simple negligence on the one hand and the easy acceptance of criminal strict liability on the other.

[129] Examples by Sch/Sch-Cramer/Sternberg-Lieben, § 15, Mn. 127.

[130] RGSt 34, 91.

[131] BGH JR 1982, 341.

c) fatal accident of V after V uses D's car for a joyride, when D had not locked the car;[132]
d) death of V who was lying on a road when D did note that there was an object lying on the road, but ran over V nonetheless with his car without closer inspection;[133] and
e) wounding of V, a child, by D's aggressive dog, even if until that time the dog had shown aggressive behaviour only towards other dogs.[134]

The courts[135] rejected a finding of foreseeability in the following cases:

a) fatal consequence of the normal use of a harmless anaesthetic necessary because of harm caused by D to V;[136]
b) harm caused to child V through corporal punishment if V is a haemophiliac;[137]
c) death through shock and cardiac arrest of V when overtaken by D in normal road traffic;[138] and
d) death of V, who suffers from heart disease, as a consequence to excitement caused by minor traffic accident.[139]

A common thread that runs through these cases is that foreseeability is more likely to be accepted if and when the harm is caused by a factor which is under the control of D, rather than that of V or under no one's control. As such, one might say that the thin skull rule does avoid breaking the causal chain, yet its effects cease when the foreseeability of the causal chain is concerned.

[132] BGH VRS 20, 282.
[133] BGHSt 10, 3.
[134] OLG Stuttgart, Justiz 1984, 209.
[135] Compare also the recent case in the Canadian Supreme Court, *R v Beatty*, 2008 SCC 5 <http://scc.lexum.umontreal.ca/en/2008/2008scc5/2008scc5.html> accessed 26 June 2008. [From the summary of the judgment:] The accused was charged with dangerous operation of a motor vehicle causing death under s 249(4) of the Criminal Code. The accident that gave rise to these charges occurred when the accused's pick-up truck, for no apparent reason, suddenly crossed the solid centre line into the path of an oncoming vehicle, killing all three occupants. Witnesses driving behind the victims' car observed the accused's vehicle being driven in a proper manner prior to the accident. An expert inspection concluded that the accused's vehicle had not suffered from mechanical failure. Intoxicants were not a factor. The accused stated that he was not sure what happened but that he must have lost consciousness or fallen asleep and collided with the other vehicle. The question that divided the courts below was whether this momentary act of negligence was sufficient to constitute dangerous operation of a motor vehicle causing death within the meaning of s 249(4). The trial judge concluded that these few seconds of negligent driving could not, without more, support a finding of a marked departure from the standard of care of a reasonably prudent driver. The Court of Appeal set aside the acquittals and ordered a new trial, finding that the accused's conduct of crossing the centre line into the path of oncoming traffic could only be viewed as objectively dangerous and a 'marked departure' from the requisite standard of care. The determining question then became whether there was an explanation for the accused's conduct that would raise a reasonable doubt that a reasonable person would have been aware of the risks in the accused's conduct. The appeal of the defendant was allowed and the acquittals restored. Interestingly, the judges were divided over whether the *actus reus* was already excluded or whether the defendant lacked subjective negligence and therefore *mens rea*.
[136] RGSt 29, 219; OLG Hamm, VRS 18, 356.
[137] BGHSt 14, 52.
[138] OLG Stuttgart, VRS 18, 365.
[139] OLG Karlsruhe, NJW 1976, 1853.

4

The *Tatbestand*—Part Two

In this chapter, we will be examining the subjective side of the *Tatbestand*, ie forms of intent (*Vorsatz, Absicht*), the subjective criteria of liability for negligence (*Fahrlässigkeit*) for the purpose of distinguishing it from intent, as well as mistakes of fact concerning elements of the offence (*Tatbestandsirrtum*).[1] The last chapter dealt with what we called the *objektiver Tatbestand*; this one will explore the *subjektiver Tatbestand*. Special *mens rea* problems relating to multiple participants will be addressed in the chapter on joint principals and secondary participation below.

§ 15 is the basic norm which states: 'Unless the law expressly provides for criminal liability based on negligence, only intentional conduct shall entail criminal liability.'

The ground rule, much as in English law, is that the law requires intent as the form of *mens rea* before criminal liability can be established. Negligence is the exception and must be explicitly provided for by law.[2] There is, in fact, no provision prescribing negligence liability that does not have an intentional counterpart.[3] To that extent, the academic debate concerning whether negligence is a lesser form of *mens rea* included within intent or something different, an *aliud*, is of little practical importance.[4] Note, however, that unlike English law, German law does not restrict negligence liability to gross negligence. Simple negligence may suffice, the safety-valve for overreaching judicial punitiveness being the generally

---

[1] For reasons of space, special subjective elements such as specific intentions, motives, etc (*subjektive Unrechtsmerkmale*) will not be examined in this chapter. Some of the most relevant ones arise in the context of homicide offences and will be treated in a later chapter.

[2] Note that this was not the case before the reform of the General Part of the Criminal Code in 1975. Until that time, the judicial practice was that a court could establish negligence liability by judicial interpretation if the judge thought that the purpose of the law called and its structure allowed for it. See RGSt 48, 118; BGHSt 6, 132. This approach was expressly precluded by the new law under § 15.

[3] Sch/Sch-Cramer/Sternberg-Lieben, § 15 Mn. 109.

[4] See on the debate Sch/Sch-Cramer/Sternberg-Lieben, § 15 Mn. 3 with further references. A case cited by the afore-mentioned commentators where it arguably might be relevant is that of D who has tried to kill V by poisoning her, but then gives up the further commission of the offence in the negligently mistaken belief that the dose he has given her was not large enough to have lethal consequences, if V later dies from the ingested poison. Under the majority view, D should be able to withdraw successfully from the attempted murder under § 211, but it is questionable whether D could still be convicted of inflicting bodily injury causing death under § 227 because he acted negligently with regard to his belief. I am not sure whether the question of lesser included form of *mens rea* or *aliud* is really decisive in this respect. The real issue is whether the subsequent negligence displayed in D's error about the effects of the poison is a sufficiently immediate cause of V's death. There one may have different opinions.

lower sentencing scales for negligence offences. § 15 also precludes any liability without individual fault, such as strict liability of any sort. Reverse burdens of proof are seen as a problem of procedural, not substantive law. They do not exist in German law, as they are considered to be a violation of the presumption of innocence and are unconstitutional.

Before we continue with the description of intent, we need to understand that the typical tripartite structure applied to intentional offences is different for negligence offences, at least as far as the prevailing opinion is concerned. To that extent, it is not quite correct to speak of *mens rea* as understood for intentional offences. The subjective element of negligence is seen as part of the third tier, the offender's guilt. Thus, the *Tatbestand* for negligence offences, according to the majority view, consists only of an objective part, which was addressed in the last chapter.

Vorsatz—Intent

It is immediately apparent when looking at the Code's General Part that the law does not define the meaning of intent. It must therefore be deduced from the totality of the provisions relating to *mens rea* issues. The most important provision in this respect is § 16:

> (1) Whosoever at the time of the commission of the offence is unaware of a fact which is a statutory element of the offence shall be deemed to lack intention. Any liability for negligence remains unaffected.

> (2) Whosoever at the time of commission of the offence mistakenly assumes the existence of facts which would satisfy the elements of a more lenient provision, may only be punished for the intentional commission of the offence under the more lenient provision.

The required intent is always tied to the ambit of the individual offence and according to § 16 it means being aware of the statutory elements of the offence. However, the definition would be too short if it only related to the written statutory elements and neglected general substantive ingredients that apply to any offence, such as, for example, voluntary action or causation, or unwritten[5] ones specific to certain offences, such as the victim's disposition of his or her assets in fraud (§ 263). § 16 must be read to include those as well, in so far as they are under law relevant to the offender's intellectual decision-making process. As we will see, § 16 is applied by analogy to mistakes about facts underlying a recognised defence. The prevailing opinion also requires D to have knowledge of facts that serve as general or specific sentencing factors, for example, the different categories of § 243 on aggravated theft; these are not offence elements in the strict sense, but factors

---

[5] Unwritten elements are usually in *addition* to written ones based on the latter's interpretation and thus do not violate what was said about German law not knowing customary law-making to the detriment of the offender.

that turn theft under § 242 into its aggravated form. This makes sense because it would be unfair to use certain facts to increase the blame and thus the sentence unless D was aware of them. Otherwise, how can he be blamed for them? The general sentencing formula of § 46(1) is ample justification for that approach. However, intent is not required to cover categories such as *objektive Bedingungen der Strafbarkeit*, ie objective requirements for liability that do not form part of the offence elements, such as, for example, the question of whether there are diplomatic relations between Germany and another state within the meaning § 104a, or whether the asserted fact within § 186, the offence of defamation, is untrue or cannot be proved to be true—this is a risk that D takes and he must take the consequences, too. The same applies to procedural conditions, such as the fact of whether a necessary request to prosecute has been made.

As § 17 makes clear, (unavoidable) mistakes about the general element of unlawfulness, the second tier of the tripartite structure, affect only the third tier, the offender's guilt, not his or her intent under the first tier:

> If at the time of the commission of the offence the offender lacks the awareness that he is acting unlawfully, he shall be deemed to have acted without guilt if the mistake was unavoidable. If the mistake was avoidable, the sentence may be mitigated pursuant to § 49(1).

Until the advent of §§ 16 and 17, the courts and most prominently the BGH had adhered to the so-called *Vorsatzschuldtheorie*, which included knowledge of the general unlawfulness into the intent. This led to the consequence that if an honest but avoidable mistake had been made, the offender could only be punished for the negligent crime, whereas the new law cut off this retreat by stating that the defendant will remain liable for the intentional offence, but may receive a reduced penalty. The (complex) academic debate about this matter is still not finished, but for all practical purposes the consensus appears to be that the new law has rejected the previous approach.[6] The BVerfG has held that the new law is constitutional.[7]

Some of the statutory elements of offences by their very nature may merely require the actual knowledge of the offender; for example, in the context of theft (§ 242), D's awareness that the car he or she is trying to steal is the property of another, V. Others will require an exertion of willpower to achieve the completion of the offence: to remain within our example, D must also want to take the car away from V. Thus, intent in most cases requires a combination of cognitive and voluntary or volitional elements, or to put it another way, knowledge of the elements of the offence and the will to bring about its completion. This is a paraphrased translation of the traditional German short formula memorised by every law student in their first year: '*Vorsatz bedeutet das Wissen und Wollen der Tat*'. For offences of omission, this applies *mutatis mutandis* with the additional requirement that D must know about the *facts* giving rise to the duty of care and to the

---

[6] See Sch/Sch-Cramer/Sternberg-Lieben, § 15, Mn. 104.
[7] BVerfGE 41, 121.

duty to act, unless it is a genuine omission offence such as § 323c—omitting to effect an easy rescue—about the mode of action that can avert the danger and that acting as required would avert the result from occurring with a probability bordering on certainty.[8] It is necessary to remember that, like in English law, the offender is not required to understand the elements of an offence in their correct legal meaning, but it is sufficient if he or she can make the correct evaluations about their substance in layman's terms (so-called *Parallelwertung in der Laiensphäre*).

It is obvious that this formula is a mere shorthand reference to the basic principles and applies to the vast majority of intent-based offences only in what we might call fair-weather conditions if will and knowledge are 100 per cent congruent. In many cases, however, the very question will be what exactly the defendant knew and which degree of knowledge or will is sufficient for each offence. This is a problem which plagues every legal system and has, in England and Wales for example, been forcefully highlighted for the law of murder by the string of cases leading up to *Woollin*[9] and *Matthews and Alleyne*,[10] which confirmed the fallback principle that even if D did not actually desire the death of V, the virtual certainty of that result occurring from D's actions and D's realisation of this certainty and its degree will suffice. Whether one views this as a substantive principle or a rule of evidence or an unhelpful confusion of both[11] is of secondary importance; the real issue in my view is that it is a public policy extension of the common-sense meaning of intent in order to catch the cases where D's advertent taking of an obvious and overwhelming risk of a certain result is considered to be just as deplorable as if it had been his or her primary purpose to bring about the result regardless of his or her views about the certainty of the risk.

It does not sound quite right to say that because a result is virtually certain and D knows that, he or she intended, in the meaning of *wanted*, the result to occur. This is easily demonstrated at the example of irrelevant mistakes about identity: D wants to kill V, who has for years been blackmailing her husband H, extorting large sums of money from their marital assets. One night she decides to lie in wait when V and H are to meet again for another instalment. Under the failing light of a street lantern, she can only make out their silhouettes, but for some reason is sure one of them is V. She shoots that person, who turns out to be H. English (and German) law nevertheless holds her liable for the intentional murder of H, but it would strain the common sense meaning of the word 'intend' to say that she *wanted* to kill her husband; in fact that was the last thing she desired. We can only say that under law she intended to kill H because again for public policy reasons the law denies her to argue the ordinary meaning of intent. One might even go so

---

[8] BGH MDR/D 1971, 381; NJW 1994, 1357. The appreciation of being under a duty to act is not part of the intent for the *Tatbestand*, but is dealt with under § 17 as a mistake of law; see BGHSt 16, 155; 19, 295.

[9] [1998] 4 All ER 103 (HL).

[10] [2003] 2 Cr App R 30 (CA).

[11] See Ormerod, Smith and Hogan, 95.

far as to say that the current view is a further outcropping within the substantive law theory relating to intent of the general principle that motive is irrelevant to intent: D is to be prevented from arguing 'I did not want to kill her because of φ' when she knew that there was virtually no chance that a lethal result could be avoided and still went ahead. In other words, lack of purpose can be compensated for by an excess of knowledge.

German law has, of course, faced the same problems. Given its above-mentioned propensity to address matters of principle on the substantive rather than the evidential or procedural level, distinct categories of intent have been created.

Categories of Intent and Delineation from Advertent Negligence

Depending on the degree of knowledge and will employed, German law traditionally recognises the following degrees of intent, in descending order:

a) direct intent in the first degree: *Absicht, wissentlich, wider besseres Wissen, 'um zu'*;
b) direct intent in the second degree: *Direkter Vorsatz or dolus directus*; and
c) conditional intent: *Bedingter Vorsatz or dolus eventualis*.

The first degree category is usually explicitly mentioned in the wording of the provision in question by using one of the phrases set out in German above, and excludes conditional intent, and in most cases also mere direct intent in the second degree. Great care must be taken not to confuse the issues to which the intent has to relate. For example, the offence of theft under § 242 requires the intention to appropriate the object of the theft unlawfully: Here it is necessary that D acts with direct intent in the first degree regarding the appropriation,[12] but it is entirely sufficient if he or she has only conditional intent with respect to the question of whether the appropriation is unlawful.[13] Similar problems exist in English law in relation to the problem of whether recklessness can be sufficient for the *mens rea* of a given offence, or whether full direct intent is required. Note that German law has no category of *mens rea* that fully equals the concept of recklessness as understood in English law. Recklessness does not require a volitional element of approval of the result of D's actions to the same extent as *dolus eventualis* does; it therefore straddles the fence between the German concepts of conditional intent and advertent negligence, as will be evident from the explanations below.

Intent in the first degree and second degree are similar in substance; however, the former requires D to have the completion of the offence (element) as his purpose,

[12] Which is not to be confused with the English concept of appropriation in theft; see the explanations below in the chapter on property offences.
[13] See Sch/Sch-Eser, § 242, Mn. 61–5.

albeit not necessarily his main or only purpose. He will be deemed to have that intent also with regard to any fact that is a necessary or indispensable interim or ulterior consequence of his primary purpose: for example, if D shoots at V through a window, he will also have direct intent to damage the window. It will not be enough if he merely realises or is aware of a certain consequence or its high likelihood. However, *Absicht* does not require D to be certain that the result will occur: if D shoots at V for the purpose of killing him, when V is standing 300 metres away and D knows that he is a poor shot, but hopes he will hit V nonetheless because he hates him utterly and wants to rid the world of his presence, D will have intent in the first degree to kill V.[14] The same applies to the members of a gang of thieves if they want to steal the Pink Panther from a museum in the knowledge that their chances of getting caught in the security installations are at over 90 per cent and that therefore they may very well not be able to appropriate the diamond. Direct intent in the second degree, or *direkter Vorsatz*, does not require the same purposive degree as *Absicht*; yet certain knowledge of the facts and elements of the offence and the clear will to bring them about as just explained for *Absicht* will suffice,[15] also with regard to necessary interim and ulterior consequences.

Much more of a problem is the concept of *dolus eventualis*, or conditional intent, and its demarcation from advertent negligence. There are several major schools of thought addressing the question of how to define conditional intent. What is common to all of them is that D must have been aware of the fact that his actions *may* lead to an offence being committed.[16] This awareness of possible harmful consequences may be lacking, for example, if D was handling a gun and was sure that he had removed all bullets from it,[17] of if he had thrown counterfeit money into a waste bin and thought that it would be destroyed and not circulated.[18] (Liability for negligence may still exist in such cases.) The cognitive element may already be lacking for reasons that impair the offender's ability to realise the degree of danger. Although alcoholic intoxication is usually a matter for §§ 20 and 21 in the third tier and does not, with exceptions in egregious cases, exclude the defendant's capacity to form an intent, or more precisely a *will*, at all, it may have a *factual* impact on the defendant's *actual cognitive ability* to realise the danger or its degree; the same applies if D finds himself in a situation of extreme excitement, uncontrollable rage or similar states of mind.[19]

The more controversial issue is the volitional element: does the law require one and, if so, how do we define it? If a certain behaviour is still intentional, the sentence will be more severe, secondary participation by others in the act will be possible, etc. If it is merely negligent, there may not even be liability, let alone the

[14] BGHSt 18, 248; 21, 283. Note, however, that murder does not normally require intent in the first degree.

[15] For all of this, see Sch/Sch-Cramer/Sternberg-Lieben, § 15 Mn. 64–70.

[16] See, eg BGH MDR/H 1981, 630.

[17] BGH NStZ 1987, 362.

[18] BGH JR 1988, 119, but see BGHSt 44, 62, which overruled the former decision to some extent on offence-specific grounds.

[19] BGH NStZ 1994, 482; 2001, 86; 2002, 214.

possibility of participation by others in D's offence. The different theories pro-pounded by academic commentators and the courts, at the end of the day, hardly ever lead to different results. They range from theories that decline to entertain, to differing degrees, any volitional element, for example from the mere awareness of a possibility of the result occurring, to its probability, the requirement that D must envisage an unreasonable risk, or a manifestation of avoidance efforts, to those that require a volitional element, again to differing degrees, such as the approval theories which make the mental consent of the offender to the result, should it occur, the decisive parameter, to those that let an attitude of reckless indifference suffice, in other words if D says 'I could not care less'.[20] The courts, following the tradition of the *Reichsgericht* and the jurisprudence of the BGH in effect adhere to a somewhat watered-down approval theory, yet the approval does not need to be explicit and the offender need not *morally* approve[21] of the result—it is sufficient if he or she accepts it nevertheless in order to reach his or her ulterior goal.[22] In the more recent case law, a strong emphasis has been put by the courts on distin-guishing between the substance of the cognitive and volitional elements and inferring their existence from the evidence about the external conduct of the defendant.[23] The BGH has taken the line that if D is acting in an objectively highly dangerous situation and still goes ahead with his or her plans without being able to claim realistically that nothing bad will happen, the volitional element may be more easily inferred than in less clear-cut situations, where the danger is not read-ily recognisable.[24]

An illustrative example is a case decided by the BGH:[25] D, from a distance of four to five metres, threw a hatchet with full force through a glass door at a police-man, P, who was standing behind it. The BGH held that the trial court was right to infer the volitional element for killing P because of the short distance, the use of full force and the fact that the door's glass was merely a negligible obstacle for a hatchet thrown in that manner. Another frequent scenario are those cases where D is about to be stopped at a police road checkpoint and, because he is either sub-ject to an arrest warrant or has something else to hide, drives straight at the police-man standing in the road; the latter can barely save himself by jumping into the roadside ditch. Moral indignation at such behaviour would make it easy to infer that D would have driven over P had he not managed to get out of the way, if nec-essary accepting a lethal result. However, the courts have gone the other way and argued that offenders in these situations rather bank on the reaction of the police-men: they accept endangering them, but do not actually contemplate that they will be killed. Coupled with the generally accepted high psychological threshold for intentional homicide offences, the BGH has consistently tended to reject trial

[20] See for all this and further references Sch/Sch-Cramer/Sternberg-Lieben, § 15 Mn. 72–89.
[21] BGH NJW 1989, 781.
[22] See the references to the jurisprudence at Sch/Sch-Cramer/Sternberg-Lieben, § 15 Mn. 85–9
[23] See, eg BGH St 46, 35.
[24] BGHSt 36, 1.
[25] BGH JZ 1981, 35.

courts' findings that D acted with conditional intent with respect to P's death.[26] As with the cognitive element mentioned above, the courts have also negated the volitional element or, more to the point, the inference of a volitional element merely from external circumstances[27] if the offender was, for example, either drunk[28] or generally immature.[29] Sometimes the circumstances of the defendant's profession may be sufficient reason to doubt that he has formed even a conditional intent. The BGH[30] has thus held that an attorney as an organ of the administration of justice, or in common law terms an 'officer of the court', will not without further evidence be considered to have the volitional element for submitting falsified documents to the court.

An area of law, much as in the United Kingdom after *Dica*[31] and *Konzani*,[32] where the question of intent has become a problem concerns the cases where D infects V with HIV. Apart from the issue of consent, which will be looked at later,[33] the courts had to struggle with the question of whether the fact that once the HIV virus is contracted, the chances of developing AIDS with a lethal outcome are near 100 per cent, should mean that anyone who knows he or she is HIV positive has a conditional intent to cause bodily harm—which the infection undoubtedly is—to or maybe even kill the person whom he or she infects. The BGH has been reluctant to accept a generalisation of such inference[34] from D's mere knowledge of his or her *own infection*. However, D's knowledge of the dangerousness of unprotected sexual *activity* in the individual case may well be a sufficient basis for such a conclusion, especially if sexual contact occurs repeatedly. While tending to accept conditional intent for the mere bodily harm on such grounds, the BGH has rejected a similar inference for the conditional intent to kill V, because D may have hoped that V will not develop AIDS or only after a cure has been found. This is self-contradictory, as has rightly been pointed out by commentators,[35] to the argument regarding bodily harm. Recent research has shown that once an HIV infection has occurred, everyone develops AIDS and everyone, all other circumstances being equal, dies of AIDS. Based on the level of common knowledge about this in the general population, D can be taken to be aware of the lethal danger, too, ergo if he or she has conditional intent to infect, he or she has conditional intent to kill. The BGH has, however, been criticised by the same commentators for its approach in general, because the relatively low probability of infection in the first place could give rise to a justifiable argument by D that he or she trusted that nothing would happen, which would mean mere advertent negligence. In this context,

[26] BGH StV 1992, 420; VRS 50, 94; NStZ 1983, 407.
[27] BGH StV 1991, 262; 1993, 641; 2003, 214.
[28] BGH NStZ-RR 2004, 205.
[29] BGH StV 1994, 303.
[30] BGHSt 38, 345.
[31] [2004] 3 WLR 213.
[32] [2005] EWCA Crim 706.
[33] See the chapter on justificatory defences below.
[34] BGHSt 36, 1.
[35] Sch/Sch-Cramer/Sternberg-Lieben, § 15, Mn. 87a.

much will depend on one's own stance regarding the public policy issues involved in such a highly controversial field as that of the treatment of HIV infection by unprotected sexual activity.

Advertent negligence (*bewußte Fahrlässigkeit*) in the subjective sense will accordingly be present if only the cognitive component is fulfilled, but if there is no volitional element. D appreciates the danger he or she causes to V, but he or she hopes that the damage will not materialise, and based on the evidence of external factors, there is no safe basis to infer that he or she (must have) had an attitude of acquiescence in the face of the likelihood of the result occurring.

With the exception of offences falling under the category of direct intent in the first degree, the rule is that any intentional offence may be committed with direct intent in the second degree or conditional intent, unless the nature of the offence element to which the intention refers precludes conditional intent.[36] An example of the latter is § 316, driving whilst under the influence of drink or drugs. The activity of driving or steering a car cannot really be imagined without the direct will to do so, whereas the driver may have mere conditional intent as to his or her drunken or drugged state and its influence on his or her ability to drive safely. Another example is the offence of poaching under § 292, where D may be indifferent as to whether the game is somebody else's property or subject to another's hunting rights, yet he or she can hardly hunt the game indifferently.[37]

Coincidence of Intent and *Actus Reus* Elements; Deviations from the Imagined Chain of Causation

English and Welsh law in cases such as *Le Brun*[38] and others had to deal with how to solve the question of what the offender must have known about the offence elements and their underlying facts, and at which point in time. The general rule is that there has to be full coincidence of *mens rea* and *actus reus* at the time the offender acts. However, this rule has known exceptions based on public policy considerations and matters of interpretation. Similar matters apply in German law.

The rule is that D must have the necessary intent for the offence at the time she acts. What she knows or wants before or after her actions is in principle irrelevant.[39] If D ties up and gags V in order to take him to another place where he intends to torture V, force him to sign a document and then kill him, but V dies while being gagged, then D will not have the necessary intent for murder; she can only be held liable for negligent homicide.[40] Similarly, D cannot be found guilty of

---

[36] Sch/Sch-Cramer/Sternberg-Lieben, § 15, Mn. 88–9.
[37] Examples coined by Sch/Sch-Cramer/Sternberg-Lieben, § 15, Mn. 88–9.
[38] [1992] QB 61.
[39] BGH JZ 1983, 864.
[40] BGH NJW 2002, 1057.

handling stolen goods under § 259 if she bought a necklace in good faith and only later finds out that it had been stolen. Previous knowledge will not suffice if the offender no longer has that knowledge, because she has forgotten; for example, D will not be liable for sexually abusing minors under § 176 if he was no longer aware of the age of the girl at the time of the sexual activity, even if he had known her age at an earlier time.[41] Obviously, much will in practice depend on whether or not D's protestations are credible to the judges. Again, as mentioned above, the knowledge may be lacking because of intoxication which can impair a person's ability to perceive certain facts relevant for the offence.[42] Yet the cognitive requirement does not mean that D must be *actively* reflecting on all the elements at any time during the commission of the offence; some things he will just generally know.

The most important area where coincidence can be lacking is that of the chain of causation. We remember that causation is a general unwritten offence element for all result offences, and as such D's intent must cover it as well. What then, for example, if D stabs V in the chest, intending to kill her, and then believing her to be dead throws her into a pond to hide the body, where she is killed by drowning? Deviations from the causal chain were already examined in the last chapter when we dealt with the *objektive Zurechnung*, but they also become relevant with regard to the offender's intent.

The general rule is that any deviation that is still within the parameters of what can be ordinarily foreseen in the normal course of events is irrelevant to the question of coincidence.[43] This test combines an objective criterion with the original plan of the offender: based on what D intended to do, and bearing in mind all the attendant circumstances and consequences, was it still ordinarily foreseeable that things turned out the way they did? This is, naturally, no clinically precise test. It relies on the general life experience of the average person and the courts' jurisprudence has not always been consistent. The BGH has held, for example, that for the purposes of the offence of importing unlawful drugs, a relevant deviation exists when the drugs intended for import and carried by a drug courier are stolen and then imported by the thief.[44] This is a typical case of *novus actus interveniens* by a free, deliberate and informed third-party act as one would understand it in English law. However, the BGH in another case held D liable for murder even though the death of the victim was speeded up by the intervention of a third person.[45] The RG had held that it was a relevant deviation and intent was consequently lacking if a hit on the head led to the loss of an eye, if only a hit on the head was planned,[46] and the BGH saw a relevant change in circumstances if V did not suffer bodily harm from the beating that D had intended for her, but from stomach aches caused by the fear of being beaten.[47] These cases are somewhat difficult to reconcile.

[41] See, eg BGH NStZ 2004, 202.
[42] BGH NStZ 1983, 365.
[43] BGHSt 7, 392; 23, 135; 38, 34.
[44] BGHSt 38, 32.
[45] BGH NStZ 2001, 29.
[46] RGSt 73, 257.
[47] BGH MDR/D 1975, 22.

Another scenario where the issue of coincidence can become virulent is that of an offender who is acting in a state of legal insanity. If D began her actions in a state of full capacity, but only became insane during the commission of the offence, she may certainly be liable for attempt provided her actions before she became insane had already crossed the threshold of more than merely preparatory acts.[48] She may, however, in the view of the courts also be liable for the full offence, if the result occurs in the state of insanity, if the chain of causation started by her when she was still *compos mentis* continues without any serious deviations in her new state,[49] or according to a growing literature opinion, if the danger in the form as it was caused in the sound state of mind materialises in the result even after D becomes insane.[50] The BGH has held, on the one hand, that there is no serious deviation if D planned to kill V with one knife stab and after stabbing her once, is overcome by blood lust and knifes her many times.[51] On the other hand, if D intended to Kill V with a knife, but in the state of insanity then lays her in front of her car and runs her over with the car, she can only be liable for attempt.[52] Unless D has put herself in the state of insanity voluntarily, for example by intoxication, and in a culpable manner (*actio libera in causa*) any changes in intent after she becomes insane must be treated according to the actual state at the time the intent was formed: if she originally only intended to hurt V, but in the state of insanity then went on to kill her, she can only be found guilty of the completed offence of bodily harm; liability for negligent killing only arises in the case of an *actio libera in causa.*

The cases mentioned at the beginning of this section (D stabs V and thinking she is dead, throws her body into a pond where she drowns) are sometimes addressed under the heading of *dolus generalis,* or general intent, although the BGH has criticised the use of that term.[53] The general prevailing opinion views these as irrelevant deviations from the planned course of events that are still covered by general life experience, especially as long as the *result* was intended in the first, for example, the killing of V.[54] The converse case, where D intends to kill V by a certain act but already causes her death by preparing for the actual killing, is treated similarly, for example, if D knocks V over the head to stun her first and then kill her, yet already kills her by the blow.[55] There is a limit to this, however, as the BGH has held that the deviation will be relevant and serious if the result is brought about in the preparatory stage before the attempt phase has even been entered.[56] D must have passed into the latter stage before her actions can be

---

[48] BGHSt 23, 356. If D becomes insane before the attempt stage is reached, it is irrelevant whether the offence then unfolds as planned.

[49] BGHSt 7, 329; 23, 133; 23, 356; NStZ 1998, 31.

[50] See the references in Sch/Sch-Cramer/Sternberg-Lieben, § 15 Mn. 56.

[51] BGH 7, 325; 23, 133.

[52] BGH GA 1956, 26.

[53] BGH 14, 193.

[54] RGSt 67, 258; BGHSt 7, 329; 14, 193.

[55] BGH GA 1955, 123; NJW 2002, 1057; NStZ 2002, 475.

[56] BGH NJW 2002, 1057.

utilised for establishing a merely irrelevant deviation. The case in question decided by the BGH in 2001 concerned a husband who wanted to kill his wife; his plan was to tie her up and drug her first in order to put her in the trunk of his car, transport her to a secret location and kill her there. In order to prove the guilt of D, the trial court (and the BGH) had to rely on the *in dubio* principle, because the exact sequence of events could no longer be established. This meant that the factual alternative that was most favourable to D was that V had already died as a consequence of the tying up or drugging. Based on this, the BGH, contrary to the trial court, held that D had not yet passed into the attempt phase for murder and that consequently the deviation was relevant. The BGH quashed the trial court's judgment and remanded the case for a re-hearing with the instructions that if the new trial could not shed more light on the events, D could only be liable for negligent homicide, unlawful imprisonment causing death or bodily harm causing death (§§ 222, 227 and 239(4)).

The scenarios mentioned above must be distinguished from a specific problem related to the so-called *zweiaktige Delikte*, namely, composite offences that require two (or more) separate stages to be fulfilled before liability for the composite offence can accrue. There are so-called genuine composite offences where the first stage serves the completion of the second, and offences that merely have several stages without a purposive link. The rule is that for the former, D must have the intent to fulfil the second stage when he embarks on the first. Examples are rape and robbery: For rape, D must use force in order to have intercourse with V; for robbery, D must use force in order to take away V's property. If D uses violence against V in both cases and only then decides either to have intercourse or take away the property, he will not normally be liable for rape or robbery. The other category very often comprises situations where the second stage is embarked upon on the occasion of the first stage having been completed. An example, to use the robbery scenario again, is theft and use of force to retain stolen goods under § 252. For this, it would be enough if D formed the intent to use violence against V after he had already taken away her property, in order to keep it against her attempts to get it back.[57]

Mistakes of Fact and Missing the Target

As we saw above, § 16 states that if D acts without knowledge of all the elements of the offence, he acts without intent and can only be punished for a negligent offence, if the law provides for one. This seems straightforward in theory. Yet there remain some areas of uncertainty. Mistakes as to mere factual elements of offences present the least problematic cases. They rarely happen in practice in their pure form. How do we treat D in the context of theft under § 242 if he is aware that the

---

[57] Sch/Sch-Cramer/Sternberg-Lieben, § 15 Mn. 25.

property belongs to V, but mistakenly believes that he has a right to appropriate it? What do we do if it is not one of the elements of the offence that D is mistaken about, but the identity of the victim—he means to shoot a person whom he thinks to be A, but who in reality is B? Will he be liable for murder if he throws a knife at V1 with the intent of killing her, but instead hits her husband, V2, who is standing next to her? Does it matter in the context of § 16 whether the mistake could have been avoided, whether it is honest or reasonable?

Let us look at the final question first and give a very simple answer: it does not matter.[58] Even if D is to blame for his error, for example because he did not bother to make prior enquiries, etc, it will still exclude his intent and lead to mere liability for negligence if there is a negligent (lesser included) offence, or for another 'catch-all' provision if there is one. An exception, which we will look at in the context of self-defence,[59] is § 33, which excludes even negligence liability if the excessive self-defence was based on fear, terror or confusion.

Transposed to the situation under English law, for example under the Sexual Offences Act 2003, this would mean that if D honestly but unreasonably believed that V consented to intercourse, he would not be guilty of rape, unlike under the new English sexual offences law, which requires a reasonable belief. In a way, the German approach is thus more akin to the case law under *Morgan*,[60] *B*,[61] *K*[62] and *G*.[63] German law, leaving aside the differences in the offence structure for rape, would in principle also subscribe to Lord Hailsham's view in *Morgan* when he said:

> Once one has accepted ... that the prohibited act in rape is non-consensual sexual inter-
> course, and that the guilty state of mind is an intention to commit it, it seems to me to
> follow as a matter of inexorable logic that there is no room either for a defence of honest
> belief or mistake, or of a defence of honest and reasonable belief or mistake. Either the
> prosecution proves that the accused had the requisite intention, or it does not. In the for-
> mer case it succeeds, and in the latter it fails.[64]

German law does not view a mistake of fact under § 16(1) as a defence, either, but as the mere absence of an offence element, namely, intent. This also has the consequence that D need not have a wrong idea of what is going on; it is enough if she does not know, in other words, it is lack of knowledge, not an actual error, which is at the heart of the rule.[65] This excludes scenarios where D allows for the possibility that a certain element may be fulfilled, because then she will be moving into the area of conditional intent if she still goes ahead. Logically, this also means that if D is mistaken only about an element of an aggravated version of a basic

---

[58] Sch/Sch-Cramer/Sternberg Lieben, § 16, Mn. 12.
[59] See the chapter on excusatory defences below.
[60] [1976] AC 182.
[61] [2000] 1 All ER 833.
[62] [2002] 1 AC 462.
[63] [2003] UKHL 50.
[64] [1976] AC 182 at 214.
[65] Sch/Sch-Cramer/Sternberg-Lieben, § 16, Mn. 4.

offence, she will still remain liable for the basic offence if she is aware of all of its elements. For example, if D1 and D2 spontaneously decide to steal a briefcase with £10,000 in it from V, and D2, unbeknown to D1, carries a firearm for the purpose of breaking V's resistance if need be, D2 will be liable for the aggravated form of theft under § 244, whereas D1 will only be guilty of basic theft under § 242. Incidentally, from a German point of view it would be rather questionable to establish different levels of mistake for different offence categories—reasonable for sexual offences, but honest even if unreasonable for all others, as is the law in England at present. This different treatment would appear to lack sufficient justification and might face a challenge under constitutional law based on article 3(1) GG.

As indicated above, a mistake about the identity of the object attacked is irrelevant, as long as the objects are of the same nature. Thus if D aims at V who is standing 20 metres away from him thinking it is A, whereas it is A's twin brother, B, he will be guilty of B's murder if he kills B. However, if D is a hunter and during a hunt at night in the forest shoots at a shape he takes for a wild boar, but which in fact is his fellow hunter V, he will only be guilty of negligent homicide, because the objects are of an unequal nature. The question of how to treat errors about different alternatives in one criminal provision has not yet been finally solved: what if D thinks he is destroying a police car if in fact it is an army vehicle? Can he still be liable under § 305, or merely under § 303? The initial feeling is to say that there is no difference because both alternatives are equal within § 305 and why should D profit from this kind of error, yet a strict application of § 16(1) would lead to the conclusion that D cannot be held liable for a completed offence under § 305 at all.[66]

Offences do not only contain descriptive elements (a human being in § 212, an object in § 242, etc), but very often so-called normative elements that require the offender to be aware of certain legal implications (for example, the unlawfulness of the appropriation in § 242). Does the law require D to have the full legal knowledge to make this evaluation? The answer, as indicated earlier in this chapter, is no. Otherwise, as Frank has aptly stated, 'only lawyers could commit crimes'.[67] All D needs to be aware of is the substance of the legal concept as a layman would ordinarily understand it. As with any issue, the borderline between what is and is not a relevant error is sometimes difficult to draw. What is certain is that legal fineries that are not part of everyday legal folklore, as it were, cannot be attributed to the offender: if D takes £25 from V's wallet because V owes him that sum, he may think that he has a right to help himself and that thus the appropriation is not unlawful. This example is a borderline case, as normally the ordinary person will still frown on this sort of behaviour. However, if D has, after signing a written contract, bought a car from V and then without V's knowledge takes the car from V's yard after transferring the price to V's bank account, thinking that title to the car has passed to him on conclusion of the contract and payment of the price, he will

---

[66] See for an overview of the discussion and the different solutions proposed Sch/Sch-Cramer/Sternberg-Lieben, § 16, Mn. 11.
[67] Cited in Sch/Sch-Cramer/Sternberg-Lieben, § 15 Mn. 43–3a.

be mistaken about the (legal) fact that the car is still V's property because of the generally little-known 'principle of abstraction' in German civil law, which distinguishes between the contractual obligation to pass title to the buyer and the act of transferring title itself. If V, even after payment by D, does not hand over the car to D, all D can do is either rescind the contract and get his money back or sue for specific performance by V to hand over the car. He is not yet the owner of the car.[68] Yet, what do we do if D has made such a mistake that is relevant to his intent? Is it not in reality a mistake of law, rather than a mistake of fact? Should it then not be treated according to § 17 and questions about its avoidability asked? The rule is, however, that § 16(1) applies *stricto sensu* even to normative elements; D's fault in the occurrence of the mistake is irrelevant and liability will be excluded unless there is a subsidiary negligent offence. Looking at the situation under English law, matters are not that different as it is accepted that mistakes about, for example, preliminary questions of civil law are also treated like mistakes of fact and subject to the general honest belief standard.[69]

Of course, it would be too simple if that was the end of the matter: There are cases where one could imagine that D's mistake about and element of the offence description leads to a general error of law on the level of § 17. For example, D knows that the car she is taking away is owned jointly by her and V, yet she thinks that 'property belonging to another' within the meaning of § 242 means only exclusive sole property. She would thus be aware of the legal facts of the case, but could be said to labour under a misinterpretation of the ambit of the whole provision. Some appear to think that this kind of error should be treated under § 17.[70] In one case under the old law of § 237 on kidnapping, the BGH had held that D's opinion that the concept of kidnapping required that V was taken away from her usual residence over a longer distance was not merely a mistake about an offence element, but about the scope of the entire provision, which was to be treated under § 17.[71] The whole topic is still highly controversial.[72]

Cases of mistake imply a discrepancy between misinformed imagination and reality. What about those situations where the best laid plans simply go astray? We are talking about cases that English law covers under the heading of transferred malice: D is aiming at V1, and because D is a miserable shot, he hits V2 who is standing next to V1. Or instead of V, he hits V's precious Ming vase. English law basically transposes the reasoning of the mistaken identity scenario to this one: as long as the victims or objects are equal in nature, the intent remains unaffected, the malice is transferred to the new victim or object; if they are unequal, the malice is not transferred. The argument is simple and rather convincing: if the law of

---

[68] See more examples at Sch/Sch-Cramer/Sternberg-Lieben, § 15 Mn. 43–3a.

[69] See the discussion and references in Ormerod, Smith and Hogan, 122 and 294.

[70] See Sch/Sch-Cramer/Sternberg-Lieben, § 15, Mn. 44 with references.

[71] BGH NJW 1967, 1765.

[72] One can, of course, also ask the question of how to treat D who misinterprets a provision as establishing liability when in fact it does not. Depending on the circumstances, this may lead to an imaginary offence (*Wahndelikt*) without liability or an impossible attempt (*untauglicher Versuch*), which is in principle an offence. See further the chapter on attempts below.

murder, as it does, only requires D to have the intent to kill 'a human being', what does it matter if it is not the one that he planned to kill, but another? Regrettably, too simple for many a Teutonic soul: German law uses the concept of *aberratio ictus* to solve this problem, a formula which can be translated loosely as an 'attack gone astray'. In a leap of reasoning which is difficult to reconcile with the argument around errors of identity, the prevailing academic opinion and the courts now say that in these cases the offender's intent has become 'specific' and is attached to the concrete person that D is taking aim at. This has the consequence that if D misses V1 and hits V2, he can only be found guilty of attempted murder of V1 and, depending on the circumstances, of negligent homicide of V2.[73] Yet, if D takes aim at V1 thinking him to be V2 and hits him, he is liable for murder. It is difficult to see why in that case the intent should not have become specifically attached to the identity that D imagined. The stringent application of this view can also lead to absurd consequences: D intends to kill his arch-enemy V; he lies in wait near V's house. When M arrives, whom D thinks is V, D shoots at him but misses. In the meantime, V has come out of the house and is hit by the erring bullet and killed. The representatives of the view described above maintain that because of the specific attachment of the intent to the *physical* person of M, there is an *aberratio* regarding M, leading to D being guilty of the attempted murder of M (because his identity is irrelevant) and merely a negligent killing of V, even though killing V was D's intent all along, and had it not been for the *aberratio* and the prevailing view advocating the specific intent attachment to M, one might have viewed the whole course of events as an irrelevant deviation from the imagined causal chain under the general principles described above.[74]

The reasoning behind the prevalent view would appear to be that D did want to hit the *physical* person (whose identity would be irrelevant) in front of him and missed. That sounds like something has gone *physically* wrong, like a relevant deviation from the imagined causal chain, which in turn should exclude intent for the actual consequence. The reason is thus a divergent public policy choice in both cases that is not logically reconcilable. It is in my view to some extent based on subconscious attitudes to motive that are allowed to reach into the doctrine of intent: our ethical value code rejects the idea that D should be held liable for murdering his beloved wife when it was the woman who was blackmailing her that he wanted to kill, but whom he missed. Yet the same would apply if in the dark D mistook his wife for the blackmailer—but then he would be a murderer.

---

[73] BGHSt 34, 55; 37, 219. See further references to case law and academic commentary, including views that coincide with the English approach, in Sch/Sch-Cramer/Sternberg-Lieben, § 15, Mn. 57.
[74] Sch/Sch-Cramer/Sternberg-Lieben, § 15 Mn. 57.

Mistake and General Defences

Finally, as far as mistakes of fact are concerned, we need to address errors that occur in the context of general defences, such as, for example, where D thinks she is being attacked by V and acting in self-defence hits her over the head with a stick, when in fact V was not attacking her at all. In this area we encounter similar problems as in the *Tatbestand*. Dogmatically, errors about general defences are strictly not part of the first tier, but because they relate to the second tier of general unlawfulness, they should normally be addressed in the third tier, which under the traditional structure would mean that they form part of the category of mistake of law under § 17. Yet, much as in English law,[75] German law has recognised that because general justificatory defences take away the opprobrium of unlawful action and not only the guilt of the defendant, it would appear unsatisfactory to employ the strict regime of unavoidable error to mistakes about *facts* which, if they existed, would provide the grounds for a recognised justificatory defence (*Erlaubnistatbestandsirrtum*). After all, the *Tatbestand* itself is merely a formalised segment of the required general unlawfulness that the offender's conduct must show.[76]

This has led to models which see the first and second tier as a so-called '*Gesamtunrechtstatbestand*', meaning a composite offence description existing of a positive component, namely, the *actus reus* and *mens rea* elements, and a negative component, namely, the absence of justificatory defences (so-called '*negative Tatbestandsmerkmale*'),[77] with a subjective element built in the second tier as well. As we will see later, this ties in with the idea that D must not only *objectively be* in a situation where he may employ self-defence, etc, but he must also *want to act* in its exercise. While these composite theories have not become the prevailing view in their pure form, their underlying concern has to be recognised. It is therefore equally difficult to accept the solution offered by the so-called *strenge Schuldtheorie*, or 'strict guilt theory', which puts the issues squarely under § 17. The majority view in the literature (as well as in the courts) has for a long time subscribed to the application of § 16, either directly if they favour the composite offence description approach, or by analogy to the benefit of the offender if they reject the composite idea. The courts and especially the BGH have adopted the latter position.[78] A mistake about facts giving rise to a recognised defence therefore excludes intent with the consequence of § 16(1) that D may be liable for a negligent offence. The error about the legal scope of an existing general justificatory

---

[75] Compare Ormerod, Smith and Hogan, 122 and 294.

[76] See the overview of the arguments in Sch/Sch-Cramer/Sternberg-Lieben, § 16 Mn. 14–20.

[77] This leads to problems as to where to examine the mistake about facts underlying recognised justificatory defences in the tripartite model hierarchy. A convincing solution is that advanced by Beulke, when he requires the split of the second tier into objective and subjective elements, the error about such facts being dealt with under the second heading. See Wessels/Beulke, AT, 352.

[78] BGHSt 3, 106; 31, 286; 32, 248. See for further references Sch/Sch-Cramer/Sternberg-Lieben, § 16 Mn. 14–20.

defence remains, in principle, a mistake of law (*Erlaubnisirrtum*) under § 17.[79] However, there can be areas of overlap, especially where facts are concerned that are akin to the above-mentioned normative *actus reus* elements, as, for example, in the case of the so-called *Putativnotwehr* (putative self-defence) if D is mistaken about the strength of the attacker and consequently about the degree of force necessary to repel him. In that case, D will be treated according to § 16 although he has also been in error about a question of law, namely the meaning and scope of 'reasonable force'.[80]

D may, however, be mistaken doubly in certain cases. Imagine the following 'battered woman' scenario which had been decided by the BGH:[81] D had been humiliated and maltreated by her husband V over a long period of time and wanted to get a divorce. When V learned of her intention, he said, 'I'm going to waste everyone now!' and began looking for his pistol. D had previously taken his gun out of the drawer where he kept it. While the altercation was going on, their daughter started crying in her room upstairs. V then said words which led D to believe that he was going to kill the child, and V went to another room looking for something, which D thought was an axe. She positioned herself in front of the door and drew the loaded gun, taking off the safety. When V entered the room, V fired four shots at him from a distance of two to three metres without looking at him; in fact, she had closed her eyes. V was hit by all four shots and killed by two of them. He had not been carrying an axe.

The trial court argued that D was mistaken about the fact that she was under attack by V and was thus acting in self-defence. She was acquitted[82] of murder, but convicted of negligent homicide by application of § 16. The private prosecutor (*Nebenkläger*) appealed the verdict and the BGH quashed the trial judgment, remanding the case for re-trial. The BGH argued that even if one accepted that D was under a misapprehension regarding the attack, which would normally afford her the defence of § 16, she had to be treated exactly the same as if she had really been acting in self-defence. In that context, the (potentially and uncontrolled, because she did not take proper aim) lethal use of a firearm was normally a means of last resort and the trial court had not established clearly whether that stage had been reached (clearly it had not) and whether D could have avoided an error about her being entitled to use the gun to avert the danger of V's killing their child, because this mistake would fall squarely under § 17.

It should be added that these principles only apply to mistakes in connection with justificatory defences. For excusatory defences, the rule now appears to be, based on § 35(2), that any error will only be taken into account if it was avoidable, even if it was about facts and not about the legal scope of an excusatory defence.[83]

---

[79] Wessels/Beulke, AT, 170.

[80] Wessels/Beulke, AT, 171.

[81] BGH NStZ 1987, 322.

[82] Untechnically speaking, because German procedural law does not allow for a separate acquittal as long as the defendant is convicted of some offence based on the same facts.

[83] See Sch/Sch-Lenckner/Perron, § 35, Mn. 39–45.

5

Justificatory Defences— *Rechtfertigungsgründe*

In the last chapters we examined the question of which elements make up the offence description or *Tatbestand* as the first tier of the tripartite hierarchy. The next rung up on the structural ladder is the tier of general unlawfulness. We remember from the chapter on basic concepts and the tripartite structure that some defences, such as, for example, consent, can already play a role in negating the *Tatbestand* of certain offences if the offence description itself requires absence of such a defence; consent as an element in the first-tier *Tatbestand* is translated by the technical term *Einverständnis*,[1] as opposed to the second-tier justificatory defence of consent, which is called *Einwilligung*. An example mentioned above is that of theft under § 242, which is based on the concept of 'taking away' (not 'appropriation' as in English law), and 'taking away' by definition includes the absence of the owner's consent. If, therefore, D takes €500 from V's wallet and V allows this because he owes D that sum of money, D is not considered to be 'taking away' the €500. The fact that V owes the money to D is irrelevant if and when V does not want D to rummage through his wallet, for whatever reason. General unlawfulness similarly requires absence of justificatory defences, because as stated earlier, once the *Tatbestand* has been fulfilled by D's actions, the general unlawfulness will be presumed, unless D has a defence that negates it. Remember that under procedural aspects it is *not* for the defendant to provide proof, evidentiary or otherwise, for any defence, but it is for the court to establish its own conviction of whether or not any defence raised by D is a valid one. German law does not know reverse burdens of proof.[2]

This chapter is going to provide an overview of the main justificatory defences and the major problem areas in each one of them. We will first address some overarching issues relevant to the concept in general, and then move on to the individual defences. Because they are to some extent fallback defences, self-defence (§ 32) and necessity (§ 34) will be treated at the end to put them in the proper context of the other, more specific defences.

---

[1] See on the *Einverständnis* the summary overview at Sch/Sch-Lenckner, Vorbem §§ 32 *ff*, Mn. 31–2.
[2] See for the leading case in the United Kingdom, *DPP ex p Kebilene* [2000] 2 AC 326 (HL).

General Issues

Conceptual Basis and Cumulation of Defences

Justificatory defences operate on the second tier of the tripartite structure. They do not, therefore, impact on the *actus reus*, as they may do in English law, or the *Tatbestand*. Rather, they regulate when a certain behaviour that would normally fulfil the *Tatbestand* and entail criminal liability is exceptionally permitted based on the moral value system of society. Their exact theoretical foundation has been controversial for some time, but under the current state of affairs it seems right to say that there is some basic conceptual consensus that depending on their nature, justificatory defences either give the offender what *Lenckner* calls a 'right to interfere' (*Eingriffsrecht*) or a 'licence to act' (*Handlungsbefugnis*) by way of a mode of conduct that would in all other circumstances be described as criminal.[3]

In this context, a *right* to interfere on behalf of legal interest A, which materially and morally overrides legal interest B, ie the sacrificed position, will usually exist if there is an *actual* danger to a legal interest, but *not normally* where, based on an ex-ante view of the *underlying facts*, such a danger may be pending on a reasonable prognosis based on the known circumstances. In other words, if V does not actually attack D, D's honest and even reasonable belief in such an attack will not materially *justify* her hitting V over the head to ward off the presumed attack, although depending on which theory one follows on this category of mistake, it may exclude D's intent or guilt.[4] An exception to this exists with respect to those elements of a materially justificatory defence that are prognostic in nature themselves (for example, the concepts of danger, appropriate and necessary means of defence, etc). A right to interfere, most importantly, normally excludes any recourse to a justificatory defence by the victim: there is no self-defence by V against an act committed by D in self-defence against V; there is, however, if D is mistaken about the situation and 'defends' herself against a harmless V.[5]

A *licence* to act is said to cover scenarios where such a material moral override based on actual facts as mentioned above does not exist and where on that basis any interference by D would normally remain unlawful, but where, for example, prognostic decisions to act must be taken at a certain stage and it would appear

---

[3] See on the development of these ideas and the following discussion, Sch/Sch-Lenckner, Vorbem §§ 32 *ff*, Mn. 9–12.

[4] Similar principles apply if D's actions are based on facts that only partially support a defence or if they exceed the ambit of a defence. In both cases, the acts remain unlawful, although clearly there may be a differing degree of blameworthiness involved in these scenarios. Any exemption from or mitigation of liability can, however, only arise on the level of guilt or in sentencing. See OLG Stuttgart NJW 1981, 995 and generally Sch/Sch-Lenckner, Vorbem §§ 32 *ff*, Mn. 22.

[5] This shows another difficulty with regard to the theory that would exclude intent in the *Tatbestand* directly: if D has no intent, then the *Tatbestand* is not fulfilled and he is not acting unlawfully at all in the first place. One has to interpret the meaning of 'attack' in § 32 in a broad manner (see below) to allow V to exercise self-defence, with potentially lethal force (!), against mistaken D.

unfair to punish the decision-maker for the ensuing conduct, yet the decision remains subject to autonomous influence and counteraction by V as, for example, in the case of presumed consent of the victim. To use an old standard example: D, a doctor, finds unconscious V alone at a roadside accident and needs to perform an immediate tracheotomy to prevent V from dying from asphyxiation; all she has with her is a rusty flick-knife. D may assume that V would, were she conscious, consent to the risk involved in this. Any actions by D based on this presumed consent must stop once V is awake and capable of voicing her views. Alternatively, if D intends to publish negative facts in a newspaper about V which may as such exceptionally be permitted under the principles of § 193,[6] V may under certain circumstances still try to prevent D from doing this by destroying D's notes and files as an act of 'pre-emptive self-defence', which, as we will see below, would, however, most likely be classified as a case of necessity according to § 34, not § 32, under German law. Because of the existence of pertinent provisions for most of these cases and of principles that have been more or less well defined by the courts over time, direct recourse to this conceptual distinction is rarely, if at all, necessary to decide a particular question.

Much of this is still controversial in conceptual detail, but the issues involved will become clearer once we address the individual defences. These defences cannot only be found in the criminal law, but also in civil law or other areas of public law or even international law. The principle of the so-called *Einheit der Rechtsordnung* ('unity of the legal order') militates for the more or less uncontested assumption that what is permitted under civil law is permitted under criminal law and vice versa; what is a defence under the one is a defence under the other.[7] If more than one defence could apply per se to a certain situation, ie if there is a cumulation of defences, the rule is that they do not normally apply cumulatively but that the most appropriate one has to be found by referring to the substance and purpose of each. If there is a clear relationship of *lex specialis* and *lex generalis*, the principle that the more specific law abrogates the more general one will apply.[8]

Subjective Elements

Similar to English law,[9] there has been a debate about whether justificatory defences require a subjective element, ie the will or at least an awareness to

---

[6] § 193 Fair comment; defence

Critical opinions about scientific, artistic or commercial achievements, utterances made in order to exercise or protect rights or to safeguard legitimate interests, as well as remonstrations and reprimands by superiors to their subordinates, official reports or judgments by a civil servant, and similar cases shall only entail liability to the extent that the existence of an insult results from the form of the utterance of the circumstances under which it was made.

[7] Sch/Sch-Lenckner, Vorbem §§ 32 *ff*, Mn. 27.
[8] Sch/Sch-Lenckner, Vorbem §§ 32 *ff*, Mn. 28.
[9] See, eg *Williams (Gladstone)* [1987] 3 All ER 411.

exercise the defence in question before the defence can operate as such on the level of justification. The courts have clearly stated so only for a few of them, but importantly with respect to the most significant ones under §§ 32 and 34.[10] The majority view in the literature does, however, subscribe to a subjective element in one form or another,[11] and mostly the mere awareness, as opposed to the actual desire to act in exercise of the defence, is seen as sufficient, even if D may also be acting out of other (acceptable) motives. The question of whether D has applied due diligence in ascertaining whether the relevant circumstances exist is, of course, irrelevant as long as he reaches the correct result; if his imagination and reality do not coincide, the defence fails anyway and the lack of due diligence will have a bearing on a potential liability for negligence because of mistake or negate the defence entirely leading to liability for the intentional offence.[12] In the context of negligence offences, there is a controversy about whether the subjective elements apply to them as well. While a large part of academic commentary disputes that there is any place for them in negligence, the courts[13] and other commentators appear to see no reason why not to apply the same arguments of principle.[14] This clearly matches the basic setup of criminal offences as consisting of blameworthy conduct on the one hand and socially disapproved result on the other: if D objectively finds herself in a situation of self-defence vis-a-vis V, but is not aware of it and harms V because she has a long-standing grudge against her and was waiting for an opportunity to beat V up anyway, it would seem wrong to accord her the defence as society disapproves of her attitude. The ensuing question of how to treat D's behaviour and how to characterise it legally is difficult, because despite the fact that the element of blameworthy conduct is present, the undesired result as such—there is objectively a defence against an actual attack—is not. The situation is therefore structurally similar to that of an attempted offence where the result is also missing. Indeed, some commentators would therefore treat D as if she had merely attempted the offence, whereas the courts are not clear on the matter.[15] In the case of murder under § 212, that can mean the difference between a minimum sentence of five or two years (§§ 23(2), 49(1)), even given the fact that the law does not strictly require a reduction in sentence for attempts.

---

[10] Sch/Sch-Lenckner, Vorbem §§ 32 *ff*, Mn. 13 and the references to the case law at the individual defences below.

[11] See the references at Sch/Sch-Lenckner, Vorbem §§ 32 *ff*, Mn. 13.

[12] See Sch/Sch-Lenckner, Vorbem §§ 32 *ff*, Mn. 17–20 on the structural differences in this context with regard to the categories of *Eingriffsrecht* and *Handlungsbefugnis.*

[13] BGH NJW 1985, 490; OLG Hamm NJW 1962, 1169.

[14] See the overview of the different approaches at Sch/Sch-Lenckner, Vorbem §§ 32 *ff*, Mn. 97–9.

[15] The BGH has opted for full liability in the context of necessity, BGHSt 2, 114, whereas the *Kammergericht*, KG GA 1975, 213, has subscribed to the attempt approach, which was also adopted by the BGH in BGHSt 38, 155 in the context of abortion under the old law of § 218. See for references regarding the academic debate, Sch/Sch-Lenckner, Vorbem §§ 32 *ff*, Mn. 15.

Provocation of Defence

What if the situation gives rise to a defence, but D is somehow to blame because his own actions brought the situation about, for example, if D provoked V by taunting him about some physical deformity? To what extent, if at all, will this impact on D's ability to rely on the defence? Similar problems have recently been addressed in the courts of England, for example, for the use of self-defence.[16] We will revisit this matter later in the examination, mainly with §§ 32 and 34, but generally it should be clear that not every blameworthy causation of an emergency situation which under normal circumstances would give rise to a defence can be taken as justifying the total exclusion of that defence in the individual case. An instructive example given by *Lenckner*[17] is that of D who goads V's dog, maybe even with the aim of making the dog attack him so he can wound or kill the animal out of sheer ill-will towards its master, to a point where the animal does attack D and D is in serious danger of suffering grievous bodily harm or even death from the dog's fangs. It cannot be right to tell D that he must not defend himself against the dog because it is his own fault that he is being attacked. Clearly, human life and bodily integrity still rank above that of the dog and the interests of its owner even then, so that whilst V may use self-defence against D when D is egging the dog on, V cannot be allowed to stop D once he is defending himself against the dog's attack under necessity. Whether D may still be held liable for criminal damage under § 303 by applying the principle of an '*actio illicita in causa*', ie by shifting the focus of the criminal blame to the course of events before the dog attacks, when D is still at fault, is another matter.[18]

Rule-of-law Aspects

As we already saw in the chapter on basic concepts, there are several classic rules of law ideas embedded in the Criminal Code, such as the principles of *nullum crimen* and blameworthiness, the ban on retroactive penalisation, etc. The ban on extension of liability by way of analogy is one of the facets of these principles. Originally, the analogy ban and the rule against retroactive penalisation were meant to cover the creation of new offences. No ban exists against inventing new or extending existing rules that solely benefit the offender. However, rule-of-law concerns can also be raised by changing the interpretation of previously existing defences, especially in the context of transitional justice situations, as was the case in Germany after unification. By restricting the ambit of a defence *ex post*, or by giving it a new interpretation, one can de facto increase the field of penalised conduct indirectly, and there appears to be agreement that this is forbidden by natural

---

[16] See *Rashford* [2005] EWCA Crim 3377; and *Duffy v Chief Constable of Cleveland* [2007] EWHC 3169 (Admin) 2007 WL 4190665.
[17] Sch/Sch-Lenckner, Vorbem §§ 32 *ff*, Mn. 23.
[18] Favoured by Sch/Sch-Lenckner, Vorbem §§ 32 *ff*, Mn. 23.

justice as embodied in constitutional and international law.[19] In the times of the transition from the GDR to a unified Germany, this became a vitally important factor for members of the GDR's armed forces who served at the former inner-German border (*Mauerschützen*) and who were under orders to shoot at GDR citizens trying to flee the communist regime across that border. Under the application of the formally valid GDR law, especially as *practised* at the time, they could claim to be justified in their actions. The post-unification jurisprudence, however, substituted that practice by its own human-rights-guided interpretation, relying partially on *Radbruch's* formula, and held that the proper interpretation even at the time would have shown the soldiers that they were committing or participating in extremely serious state crimes; they were thus not deserving of having their trust in the validity of the GDR's law on the issue honoured.[20]

Individual Defences

We will start with the more specific justificatory defences to put the general catch-all principles of self-defence and necessity in §§ 32 and 34 in proper perspective.[21] This chapter can only scratch the surface of the respective defences and highlight some of the more general issues.

Consent

Consent on the second tier (*Einwilligung*) as a defence is based on the idea that if the victim approves of D's actions, the indicative function of the *Tatbestand* for the actions' general unlawfulness is abolished by the person whose interests the offence *Tatbestand* is meant to protect in the first place. It is thus a waiver of protection by the law.[22] In principle, the same applies to the *Einverständnis*, yet some aspects of what we will address in the following are not necessarily congruent with the related aspects in the context of the *Einwilligung*. This applies particularly to the question of capacity to consent: whereas in the context of *Einwilligung* this may be an issue (legal ability or mere factual capacity required), for the *Einverständnis* a merely factual basic capacity to form a will is in the view of the majority of commentators sufficient if the offence element addresses merely the natural mental faculties of basic decision-making, with the consequence that an insane or otherwise mentally ill person may be abducted 'against his or her will'

---

[19] See for a discussion BVerfGE 95, 96, which left the issue of whether this is a general principle for all defences open.

[20] See BVerfGE 95, 96; BGHSt 39, 15; 40, 232; 41, 105; 42, 70.

[21] The sequence of description follows loosely that of Sch/Sch-Lenckner, Vorbem §§ 32 *ff* for ease of reference.

[22] BGHSt 17, 360.

or, vice versa, may be able to consent to being 'abducted'.[23] The same is true for the already mentioned element of 'taking away' in theft. If, however, more complex and far-reaching decisions must be taken, for example, when V is to consent to medical treatment if one follows the view that already excludes the *Tatbestand* of bodily harm under § 223 in the case of valid consent, then a higher-order capacity to reach a conclusion of informed consent is required. Similar considerations apply to a possible vitiation of consent based on mistake and deception.[24]

Capacity to consent in the context of *Einwilligung* requires first and foremost that V is a person holding 'title' to and the power to dispose over the legal interest that is affected, for example, her property or bodily integrity. Consent with regard to attacks on common or public interests is, as a rule, of no effect.[25] The holder of a certain legal interest may not effectively consent even if the interest is an individual one, if public policy does not allow him to dispose freely over it; the best example is the protection of one's own life and bodily integrity. As can be deduced from a systematic analysis of § 216[26] and § 228,[27] a person is not free to allow another to hurt her if public policy militates against the *act*, and not free at all as far as her life is concerned: any consent by V, even—and only if—it is earnest and express, to be killed can only be pleaded by D in mitigation of sentence, not to exclude liability. This principle, according to some academic commentators,[28] does not apply to the same degree to V's consent to D's merely knowingly *endangering* her life with *negligently* caused consequences, an approach somewhat reminiscent of *Dica*.[29] The courts also present a divided picture: some appear to have made this result contingent on the fact of whether or not death did actually occur or how serious the consequences are for V; if V died or suffered serious harm, the consent to the endangerment was held to be void.[30] Others argue based on public

---

[23] § 181(1) no 2; see on the parallel situation under the old law BGHSt 23, 1.

[24] See the overview at Sch/Sch-Lenckner, Vorbem §§ 32 *ff*, Mn. 32

[25] Sch/Sch-Lenckner, Vorbem §§ 32 *ff*, Mn. 35–6. If the offence is of a mixed nature containing both individual and public interests, consent may be effective if the two are protected cumulatively, but not if they are protected alternatively.

[26] '§ 216 Killing at the request of the victim; mercy killing

　(1) If a person is induced to kill by the express and earnest request of the victim the penalty shall be imprisonment from six months to five years.
　(2) The attempt shall be punishable.'

[27] '§ 228 Consent

Whosoever causes bodily harm with the consent of the victim shall be deemed to act lawfully unless the act violates public policy, the consent notwithstanding.'

[28] See the references at Sch/Sch-Lenckner, Vorbem §§ 32 *ff*, Mn. 103–5.

[29] [2004] 3 WLR 213.

[30] BGHSt 4, 93 (according to which an exception may be made by negating a breach of duty), BGH VRS 17, 277 and OLG Hamm MDR 1971, 67; both against RGSt 57, 172. This ex post approach is problematic for an offender (and victim) who must, after all, make a decision ex ante. It basically tells both parties involved that they are not just taking a risk as to the actual legal interest, but also with respect to the potential effect of the consent: if something goes wrong, despite any precautions they may have taken, the consent will be void and one of them will be criminally liable. From the point of view of deterring risky behaviour for the overall good of society and the purpose of protecting people from their own stupidity, ie a paternalistic attitude, this appears logical, yet seen through the filter of

policy reasons similar to § 228[31] or whether the consensual endangerment of another in all the circumstances of the case equals a self-endangerment.[32] The debate is still ongoing, yet it seems fair to say that if the consent to intentional bodily harm under § 228 is void, this has the same consequence for a negligent causation of death by causing that bodily harm,[33] whereas the fact that a certain course of conduct may be life-threatening does not in and of itself make the consent to the bodily harm void under § 228.[34] Care must also be taken not to extend the public policy restriction in § 228 as a general principle to other individual legal interests, as was the case under some of the older academic literature.[35] A careful distinction must also be made between the fact of whether the *consent* violates public policy or whether the *act consented to* does so; only the latter is relevant. An example given[36] by *Lenckner* is that of D taking blood from V with V's consent, which V had only given after asking an extortionate price from D: asking for a large sum of money as consideration for giving blood as such may be violating public policy, yet the act under § 223 of causing bodily harm does not therefore become unlawful, because giving blood as such is not infringing public morals and the consent to the physical invasion by D stands. Generally speaking, one may say that circumstances surrounding the obtaining and giving of the consent are typically irrelevant,[37] with the exception of deception and threat or force, as we will see below.

Capacity to consent also requires that V has the necessary intellectual maturity to understand what she is consenting to, and that she can make an informed decision and understand the consequences of her actions. The prevailing opinion in the jurisprudence these days does not tie this capacity to the civil law categories of contractual capacity or certain age brackets; what is required is the natural ability and intellectual insight into the circumstances.[38] However, some commentators argue that there should be no discrepancy between the criminal and civil law rules on when a consent can be valid, which may after all impact on such issues as to whether a contract based on fraudulently obtained consent is binding or void(able), or whether or not a bodily injury is a tort.[39] Therefore, the civil law rules should be applied *mutatis mutandis*. It would indeed be an unfortunate result if the consequences under criminal and civil law were to differ in such cases. There is much to commend that view on the basis of the unity of law, yet the courts have so far not sanctioned it. However, it is open to question whether the sensible applica-

---

the right to personal self-determination, it may cause hardship. The courts who take this line clearly share the public policy concerns of the English courts, as, eg in *Armstrong-Braun*, [1999] Crim LR 416 and the related cases.

[31] OLG Düsseldorf NStZ-RR 1997, 327; OLG Karlsruhe NJW 1967, 2321.
[32] OLG Zweibrücken JR 1994, 518.
[33] BGH NJW 2004, 1054.
[34] Compare BGH NJW 2004, 1054 and BGH JZ 2005, 102.
[35] Sch/Sch-Lenckner, Vorbem §§ 32 *ff*, Mn. 37.
[36] Sch/Sch-Lenckner, Vorbem §§ 32 *ff*, Mn. 38.
[37] *Ibid.*
[38] RGSt 71, 349; BGHSt 4, 90; 5, 362; 8, 357; 12, 382; BGH NStZ 2004, 205; BGHZ 29, 33.
[39] Sch/Sch-Lenckner, Vorbem §§ 32 *ff*, Mn. 39–40.

or if the balancing of the pros and cons of a course of action are materially affected, as, for example, in the case of V deciding whether an operation is necessary.[59] Mistakes relating to V's motive, unless they pertain to material qualities as just mentioned, are irrelevant;[60] the treatment of errors which, although related to the substance of the legal interest, are based on incorrect personal views of the victim is controversial: while the courts[61] in principle also wish to extend the protection to the victim in these cases, some commentators would deny the relevance of the mistake.[62] The effects of fraudulently obtained consent are also disputed. While again some courts[63] and parts of the literature take a strict view and will always hold the consent to be void if it has been caused by a deception, because after all it was the offender's intentional doing that brought the consent about, others wish to differentiate here, too, according to which circumstances the deception covered. If they relate to facts that are not material to the legal interest's protection, the tendency is to declare the error irrelevant, as, for example, in the case of V donating blood because D told him V's neighbour had also given blood[64] and V merely wanted to 'keep up with the Joneses'—whereas the cases become more difficult if V was told that the donated blood was meant to be used by a charitable organisation when in reality it was intended for commercial purposes.[65] Some courts will include in this category borderline cases such as the undisclosed medical placebo treatment of V if it results in a positive effect for the victim's health.[66] According to this view, deceptions will be likely to be considered as relevant if their

---

[59] Sch/Sch-Lenckner, Vorbem §§ 32 *ff*, Mn. 46.

[60] RGSt 41, 396. Compare the recent English case of *R v Devonald* [2008] All ER (D) 241 (February): the complainant, a 16-year-old boy, had been in a relationship with the defendant's daughter. Following the breakdown of the relationship, the defendant posed as a 20-year-old woman called 'Cassie' on the internet and struck up a friendship with the complainant. On two occasions, the defendant encouraged the complainant to masturbate in front of a 'webcam', which he did. The defendant was subsequently arrested and charged with offences of causing a person to engage in sexual activity without consent, contrary to s 4 of the Sexual Offences Act 2003. The defendant accepted that that he had posed as Cassie in order to humiliate the complainant. The issue which arose was consent under the conclusive presumptions in s 76 of the Act. The judge ruled that it was open to the jury to decide that the complainant had been deceived as to the purpose of the act of masturbation. Following the judge's ruling, the defendant pleaded guilty to two counts of causing a person to engage in sexual activity without consent. The defendant applied for leave to appeal against his conviction to the full court and submitted that the judge had wrongly ruled that the conclusive presumption in s 76(2)(a) of the Act applied. The application was refused, the Court of Appeal stating that the judge had correctly ruled that it was open to the jury to find that the complainant had been deceived as to the purpose of the act. The complainant had been deceived into believing that he was masturbating in front of the webcam for the sexual gratification of a 20-year-old woman, and that was why he had agreed to do it. '*The defendant had over-theorised the issues.*' The nature of the act had undoubtedly been sexual, but the purpose of the act had encompassed more than sexual gratification. [Emphasis added.] The question remains, however, whether a person who engages in such an activity and relinquishes all control over what the viewer does with the webcam data has been deceived at all, or whether he was not taking a clear and obvious risk that the viewer might use them to humiliate or maybe even blackmail him.

[61] BGH NJW 1978, 1206.

[62] Sch/Sch-Lenckner, Vorbem §§ 32 *ff*, Mn. 46.

[63] OLG Stuttgart NJW 1982, 2267.

[64] Sch/Sch-Lenckner, Vorbem §§ 32 *ff*, Mn. 47.

[65] Sch/Sch-Lenckner, Vorbem §§ 32 *ff*, Mn. 47.

[66] OLG Hamm NStZ 1988, 546.

effect is equal to a compulsory situation that leaves the victim no real choice, such as, for example, the mother who is untruthfully told that she must urgently give blood for an emergency treatment of her child, because the impression this will inevitably leave on the mother is that otherwise she will be condemning her child to death.[67] Finally, any consent will be void if it has been obtained by force or threats if these reach a certain threshold that excludes the freedom of choice by V. They need not reach the level of duress under § 35, but neither will any threat be sufficient. The standard is subjective, not that of a reasonable man or woman in V's circumstances: the BGH has coined the rule that the decision will depend on 'whether it can be expected of *this* threatened person in *his* circumstances to withstand the threat in cool-headed fortitude',[68] which means that, for example, elderly people who tend to be more timid than younger ones will not have to withstand a threat to the same degree as a 25 year old in the prime of her health and physical powers.

What happens if D is unaware of V's mistake and could not have found out even though he had employed all reasonable diligence? Obviously this question can hardly arise in the categories of deception, threats or force. Especially for those who see any consent or its absence as an unwritten part of the *Tatbestand* and do not split consent into *Einverständnis* and *Einwilligung*, the consequence is that D's actions lack subjective unlawfulness (*Handlungsunrecht*), do not fulfil the *Tatbestand* and thus are not unlawful—a view which entails the logical corollary that V cannot defend herself against D through self-defence according to § 32 because the attack by D is not unlawful, but possibly only on the basis of necessity under § 34.[69] If one follows the theory that applies § 16 to such errors by analogy, the consequences are in effect similar.[70]

Presumed Consent

Often it will be impossible for D to ascertain in time whether V or a representative approves of a certain course of conduct. Examples are the above-mentioned medical emergency cases where V is unconscious and in dire need of immediate medical intervention. The common view in literature and jurisprudence is that in such cases D's actions may nevertheless be justified by presumed consent if an evaluation of all circumstances, conducted with due diligence at the time of the act by D, leads to the conclusion that, if asked, V would consent.[71] The justificatory defence of presumed consent applies both to *Einwilligung* and *Einverständnis*. If ex post the assumption proves to be incorrect, that will not vitiate the defence as long as D

---

[67] Example used by Lenckner in Sch/Sch-Lenckner, Vorbem §§ 32 *ff*, Mn. 47.
[68] BGHSt 31, 201; BGH NStZ 1992, 378.
[69] So Sch/Sch-Lenckner, Vorbem §§ 32 *ff*, Mn. 50.
[70] See for further discussion the references cited by Sch/Sch-Lenckner, Vorbem §§ 32 *ff*, Mn. 50–52.
[71] BVerfG NJW 2002, 2615; BGHSt 35, 246; 45, 221 and Sch/Sch-Lenckner, Vorbem §§ 32 *ff*, Mn. 54.

acted with due diligence.[72] Presumed consent is no sub-category of necessity as some say,[73] but a justification *sui generis* because it does not operate on the basis of an objective balancing of interests, but on the hypothetical will of the victim alone.[74] This becomes clear when we look at the situation where D assumes a certain attitude by V, but then finds out that V has a totally different view of things, which in addition is entirely unreasonable and possibly even dangerous. Because presumed consent as a justificatory defence is only triggered if the real will of the victim is not clear, it ceases to operate as soon as V has voiced or can voice that will and as with consent in principle, the question of whether V's will is sensible or utter nonsense is typically of no consequence.[75] Any problems remaining in this context must then be solved by recourse to the general principles of necessity under § 34.[76] Mistakes by D despite his exerting due diligence will not void the defence, as with consent proper. If a doctor realises or considers it possible that V opposes a certain treatment, but still goes ahead with it because she thinks it is a medically warranted and reasonable course of action, she will be treated under § 17 as labouring under a mistake of law.[77]

Official Authorisation

In the modern world, many activities, especially in trade and commerce, rely to a large extent on official permits and concessions. Persons or legal entities intending to operate a dangerous enterprise, such as, for example, a chemical factory or nuclear power plant, need to go through a rigorous examination by government authorities. It is thus not unreasonable to conclude that such persons or entities will want to rely on these authorisations to justify, in the wider meaning, their activities and provide cover if something goes wrong, provided they have abided by all the requirements of the particular trade or business and the demands attached to the permission. Doctrinally, German law distinguishes between authorisations that already exclude the *Tatbestand*, on the one hand, which is mostly the case where a permission is merely required to ensure that D abides by the proper standards, but where the activity that D intends to engage in is as such not materially forbidden and may in fact be even part of the provision of necessary goods

---

[72] See BGHSt 35, 246, a case concerning the question of sterilisation as a possible additional measure in the course of another operation.
[73] See references at Sch/Sch-Lenckner, Vorbem §§ 32 *ff*, Mn. 54.
[74] BGHSt 35, 246; 45, 221.
[75] Naturally, if V's views are unknown and there are no clues as to how he might decide, D may and indeed should act on what would be seen as a sensible solution by the reasonable by-stander based on objective standards. Additional problems may arise if V could have been asked earlier but was not out of lack of diligence, or could be asked later. In both cases, the effect of presumed consent may depend on whether V would either still have presumably decided as D now assumes had he been asked earlier, or whether he would want to have D act now rather than wait for the opportunity allowing D to ascertain V's will. This is of eminent importance in the medical arena. See on this most instructively BGHSt 35, 246 and 45, 221.
[76] Sch/Sch-Lenckner, Vorbem §§ 32 *ff*, Mn. 56.
[77] BGHSt 45, 225.

or service unit, such as, for example, the Armed Forces.[89] D may act *propio motu* on her own power, or may be instructed or ordered by her superiors to do so. It is important to keep the unlawfulness under general public law and criminal law apart in this context: D as an individual may be justified in acting as she did vis-à-vis a criminal prosecution, but the state as such may in certain circumstances still be liable for damages if the action was objectively unlawful.

The mere fact that D is acting in her official capacity does not provide her with any justificatory defence; her actions must comply with the requirements of public law and normally be within the scope of the law authorising the scope and powers arising from her position. Apart from any other particular conditions imposed by specific provisions, all public administrative and governmental acts must comply with the overriding constitutional doctrine of proportionality as developed by the BVerfG: they must be apt and capable of bringing about the desired result (*geeignet*), they must be the least intrusive means possible (*erforderlich*) and, finally, they must be proportionate in the strict and narrow sense, ie can the victim be expected to submit to the intrusion into his personal sphere even if the first two criteria are fulfilled, which may not be the case, for example, if the actions by the state violate the core substance of a right (*zumutbar, verhältnismäßig im engeren Sinne*).[90] As mentioned above, if the action by D objectively complies with the required criteria, it is irrelevant whether he exercised due diligence in arriving at his conclusion;[91] if it does not so comply, that factor will have a significant bearing on his criminal liability. According to the prevailing but controversial opinion in jurisprudence and literature which applies a specific 'criminal law concept of lawfulness' in this context, the actions of D will be justified, not merely excused, if he employed due diligence when exercising his ex ante judgment on the situation before him.[92] This result can be supported if one views the justification in this case not as a privilege of the state to make mistakes (*Irrtumsprivileg des Staates*) or as a right to interfere, but as a licence to act,[93] which is often coupled with those scenarios where ex ante views must decide whether or not an action can be taken. If one does not wish to follow this view, then an error about the *facts* will lead to the analogous application of § 16 and consequently to a lack of *Tatbestand*. The consequence in both cases again is the loss of self-defence against the action of the official and the mere possibility of recourse to necessity in situations when D's actions may cause severe and irreparable damage.[94] If D is

---

[89] We shall leave aside in this context the question of whether international (humanitarian) law or the law of armed conflict is capable of providing independent justificatory defences. The German courts have had the opportunity to decide the cases of counter-measures by the Gestapo against resistance fighters (no defence—BGHSt 23, 103) and the application of the retaliation principle of '*tu quoque*' (no defence—BGHSt 15, 214).
[90] BVerfGE 19, 348; BGHSt 4, 377; 26, 99; 35, 379.
[91] BGHSt 35, 387; BayObLG JR 1981, 28.
[92] See BGHSt 24, 125 and the further references at Sch/Sch-Lenckner, Vorbem §§ 32 *ff*, Mn. 86.
[93] Sch/Sch-Lenckner, Vorbem §§ 32 *ff*, Mn. 86.
[94] *Ibid.*

mistaken about the *scope* of his powers based on a proper perception of the facts, he will be treated under § 17 as acting under mistake of law.[95]

D will in principle also be justified when acting under superior instructions as long as the instructions are lawful; their unlawfulness makes the action by D unlawful. This principle is subject to some exceptions, especially if and when the instructions are binding for the subordinate.[96] The case is rather clear if the action taken is as such not covered by any legal authorisation: any error here can only be relevant for deciding whether D or his superior laboured under a mistake of law.[97] If, however, the law provided in principle for such a measure, but D and/or his superior were honestly and despite due diligence mistaken about the *facts*, they may be justified; this applies especially to the subordinate, because under German civil service law the subordinate has no general duty to examine whether a superior instruction is lawful; he may and sometimes must obey it unless its unlawfulness is positively known to him or so glaringly obvious that any diligent civil servant would have been expected to notice it.[98] However, if the subordinate is aware that his superior exercised due diligence, but knows that the facts on which the superior based his decision have changed, he must not carry out the instructions; if he does, his actions will be unlawful and may be resisted by self-defence under § 32, regardless of whether or not he could have remonstrated with his superior.[99]

This general debate is subject to further qualifications regarding the controversial concept of the 'unlawful but binding order'.[100] The general debate originally centred around whether this should provide a justificatory defence or merely an excuse, with the supporters of a justificatory defence apparently having carried the day.[101] Specific legislation in the areas of police officers, prison guards, soldiers and the service provided by conscientious objectors (*Zivildienst*) now states that an order must not be followed if its execution would entail the commission of a criminal offence, yet if the subordinate obeys it, nevertheless she will not be liable unless the fact that the act will be criminal *is known to the subordinate or is obvious.*[102]

---

[95] BGH NStZ 1981, 22; BGH JR 1990, 170 (= BGHSt 35, 379, yet the section in question was not printed in the BGHSt reference).

[96] Sch/Sch-Lenckner, Vorbem §§ 32 *ff*, Mn. 87.

[97] Sch/Sch-Lenckner, Vorbem §§ 32 *ff*, Mn. 88.

[98] Consistent jurisprudence of the courts, see BGHSt 4, 162; BGHSt 39, 32.

[99] BGHSt 19, 22 and 231.

[100] See for the category of the merely 'dangerous order', ie when the execution would entail the danger of the commission of negligence offences, Sch/Sch-Lenckner, Vorbem §§ 32 *ff*, Mn. 90: The general principles apply, with a liability of the subordinate in practice being reserved for those cases where the risk is grave and there is a high degree of probability of its materialising. *Lenckner* gives the example of a superior ordering the driver of a military vehicle on the way home from an exercise at night to exceed the speed limit when driving through a sleeping village on the one hand, and on the other ordering him to drive in combat mode without lights during the exercise on a busy road at night. In the first case, the order could provide a justificatory defence for the driver for negligent homicide, in the second it could not, according to *Lenckner*.

[101] See the references at Sch/Sch-Lenckner, Vorbem §§ 32 *ff*, Mn. 89.

[102] See, eg §§ 7(2) UZwG; 97(2) StVollzG; 11(2) SoldatenG; 5(1) WStG and 30 (2) and (3) ZDG.

However, the general civil service law[103] requires the subordinate to follow an unlawful order if it is affirmed by the next-higher superior of her own superior or if the latter requires the subordinate to execute the order forthwith because of a state of emergency, unless the order entails commission of a criminal offence and *D can realise that.* This results in the order being binding and providing a justificatory defence already if D as an individual does or cannot realise the criminal quality, either for factual or legal reasons, with the consequences of § 16 or 17 about mistake of fact or law.[104] In cases of a dispute between superior and subordinate about the lawfulness of an order, the presumption is that the superior's view shall prevail because she will normally be in a better position to overlook the facts and consequences of the instructions and because the hierarchy of the civil service is in favour of that solution for reasons of administrative efficiency, with the subordinate's duty of obedience ending only when the superior's views are clearly unacceptable under any circumstances.[105] As mentioned earlier, these limits were in principle exceeded by the GDR border guards if they acted with (conditional) intent to kill[106] and in the context of the Nazi regime's policy of genocide and persecution.[107]

A final note must be made in this context of two provisions in the Special Part of the Criminal Code, §§ 113 and 114[108] on resisting enforcement officers, which contain specific regulations on how to treat the resister's views of the lawfulness of an officer's actions as the flipside of the coin:

§ 113 Resisting enforcement officers

(1) Whosoever, by force or threat of force, offers resistance to or attacks a public official or soldier of the Armed Forces charged with the enforcement of laws, ordinances, judgments, judicial decisions or orders acting in the execution of such official duty shall be liable to imprisonment of not more than two years or a fine.

(2) In especially serious cases the penalty shall be imprisonment from six months to five years. An especially serious case typically occurs if

1. the principal or another accomplice carries a weapon for the purpose of using it during the commission of the offence; or
2. the offender through violence places the person assaulted in danger of death or serious injury.

(3) The offence shall not be punishable under this provision if the official act is unlawful. This shall also apply if the offender mistakenly assumes that the official act is lawful.

(4) If the offender during the commission of the offence mistakenly assumes that the official act is unlawful and if he could have avoided the mistake the court may mitigate the sentence in its discretion (§ 49(2)) or order a discharge under this provision

---

[103] See, eg § 56(3) 2nd sentence and (3) BBG.
[104] Sch/Sch-Lenckner, Vorbem §§ 32 *ff*, Mn. 89.
[105] KG NJW 1972, 781; OLG Karlsruhe NJW 1974, 2142.
[106] BGHSt 39, 15; 39, 183; 40, 232; 41, 105; 42, 70; 45, 270.
[107] BGHSt 2, 234; 3, 271 and 357; 5, 238; 15, 214; 22, 223.
[108] For commentary on these provisions, see Sch/Sch-Eser, §§ 113 and 114.

if the offender's guilt is of a minor nature. If the offender could not have avoided the mistake and under the circumstances known to him he could not have been expected to use legal remedies to defend himself against the presumed unlawful official act, the offence shall not be punishable under this provision; if the use of remedies could have been expected the court may mitigate the sentence in its discretion (§ 49(2)) or order a discharge under this provision.

§ 114 Resistance to persons equal to enforcement officers

(1) Acts of enforcement by persons vested with the powers and duties of police officers or who are investigators of the public prosecution service without being public officials, shall be equivalent to the official act of a public official within the meaning of § 113.
(2) § 113 shall apply mutatis mutandis to persons who are called upon to assist in the execution of the official act.

Collision of Duties

Although at first glance this category of justificatory defence appears to be a special case of the general principle of necessity,[109] German doctrine tends to treat it as a separate defence *sui generis*, especially in the field of offences by omission;[110] doctrinally, this is questionable and produces tensions with the concept of necessity as will be explained below when we look at necessity. D has two or more conflicting duties to act, but can only obey one with the necessary and unavoidable consequence that he will be violating the other.

a) The duties may be of an equal nature: D's daughter and son, one and two years old, fall into a wide river with a strong current; both of them are still within reaching distance of the shore, but D, who cannot swim and has to hold on to a tree because of the slippery rocks on the shore, is only able to grab one of them at a time, which means that in the time it takes to rescue one, the current will have carried the other away to the middle of the stream and beyond rescue.
b) The duties may be of an unequal nature, for example, if D, who runs a professional dog care service, had taken V's dog out for a walk and brought his little daughter along, and both fall into the river. Under the contract with V, D is obliged to try and save the dog and, as a father, he has to try and save his child.
c) Duties to act may conflict with duties not to do a certain act; legal duties might conflict with moral obligations: the defence attorney who knows his client is a serious child abuser and works in a kindergarten must not tell anyone about his knowledge because of the attorney-client relationship, but he may feel

---

[109] See, eg the somewhat ambiguous stance in Spanish law in Santiago Mir Puig, *Derecho Penal, Parte General* (7th edn, Editorial Reppertor, 2004) 447–9.
[110] Sch/Sch-Lenckner, Vorbem §§ 32 *ff*, Mn. 72.

morally bound to inform his client's employer in order to ensure that the children are taken out of harm's way.[111]

Although in theory D may also be subject to several conflicting duties *not* to do certain acts that leave him no choice but to follow one at the expense of the other, which could in principle trigger the collision defence,[112] it will not be a frequent scenario. In practice, therefore, collision of duties as a justificatory defence applies in the case of conflicting duties to act. Any other of the conflicts mentioned above would appear to be solved by application of necessity standards under § 34.[113] The collision of duties defence is based on the principle that the law cannot ask the impossible: if D has no choice but to violate one duty by being a law-abiding citizen with respect to the other, it seems unfair to expose her to criminal sanctions. This—the lack of choice and the inevitability of violating one or more duties—is also the rationale that is said to conceptually distinguish the defence from necessity. Indeed, in a legal system that has a basic murder definition such as England and Wales, where causing death with intent to kill or cause grievous bodily harm is sufficient, and which ties this basic offence to a mandatory life sentence, non-recognition of such a defence would lead to unbearable results that should not be 'solved' by reference to prosecutorial discretion. German law has thus accepted that the collision defence applies to conflicting duties even of an equal nature and even if the consequence of D's informed[114] choice is loss of human life. In our first example above, D would thus be justified for the murder of the child he can no longer reach,[115] a consequence that would be impossible under necessity rules. Interestingly enough, German doctrine appears to view utilitaristic arguments, such as the scarcity of resources, as unacceptable criteria for the exercise of the discretion of which duty to follow, especially in the context of hospital and other medical waiting lists.[116]

---

[111] See for the scenario of a doctor who feels he must inform the inhabitants of a block of flats about a serious contagious disease of one of his patients who lives there: RGSt 38, 62; and see further BGH NJW 1968, 2288; OLG Köln VRS 59, 438.

[112] D is driving his car on the *Autobahn* at 90 mph when V1-3, three boys on a truth-or-dare mission, jump on the road in front of him; close behind him, as he knows, is a car driven at the same speed by V4, in which V4's three children V5-7 sit as well. He cannot evade V1-3 because the fast lane is blocked by overtaking cars and there is no hard shoulder. Here D can only choose between driving on and hitting V1-3 or braking hard and risking the almost certain impact of V4's car, which at that speed would also mean almost certain death for V4-7. See also with respect to this kind of scenario the cases OLG Hamm VM 70, 86; OLG Karlsruhe JZ 1984, 240.

[113] Sch/Sch-Lenckner, Vorbem §§ 32 *ff*, Mn. 72.

[114] The general subjective requirement that D must act in awareness of the facts applies. See Sch/Sch-Lenckner, Vorbem §§ 32 *ff*, Mn. 76.

[115] Compare BGHSt 48, 311. Yet, it also allows D to make value judgments regarding which object or person is worth saving over the other which may have a shaky foundation: D may decide to save a seriously wounded person rather than another who is only relatively lightly hurt—even though the person saved may be so seriously hurt that he will die anyway and the other will develop a serious complication from the lack of attendance by D while D cares for the first one; from a cynical point of view of balancing societal costs and benefits it might thus have been better if D had saved the second victim.

[116] Sch/Sch-Lenckner, Vorbem §§ 32 *ff*, Mn. 74.

use self-defence,[146] whereas modern commentary[147] appears to view this as going too far as long as V has not actually shown any signs of his intention to use the gun immediately.

If the attack is not imminent[148] in the manner described above, D will not be able to rely on § 32, but will in principle have to have recourse to necessity under § 34, although the courts have apparently recognised a special justificatory defence of so-called 'quasi-self-defence' or 'pre-emptive self-defence'.[149] This concept was developed against the background of secret recordings made by D of calls from V wherein V was insulting or blackmailing[150] D etc and D made the recordings in order to expose V to the police and prevent any future infringement of his rights by V.[151] However, on a strict analysis of the issues involved, the academic commentators that consider this scenario to fall squarely under necessity would appear to have the better arguments on their side.[152] Note that the approach under s 3 CLA 1967 and the case law of *Kelly*[153] and *A-G's Reference (No 2 of 1983)*[154] seem to suggest a somewhat more lenient attitude with respect to the use of self-defence in pre-emptive fashion. An attack will remain ongoing until the aggressive conduct and infringement of the legal interest have been *factually* completed either by abandoning the attempt, by its failure or by causing the definite violation of the protected interest with the consequence that there is no more further harm that could be averted by self-defence.[155] The completion of the legal elements of an offence is not necessarily determinative: if V steals D's bag and runs away, the attack will be ongoing until V has secured full and safe possession of the bag, which is why pursuing D may still act in self-defence[156] and use force to regain

---

[146] RGSt 53, 132; 61, 216; 67, 337.

[147] Sch/Sch-Lenckner/Perron, § 32, Mn. 14.

[148] See for the question of whether the use of automated protective installations that are meant to repel potential intruders can be subsumed under § 32, Sch/Sch-Lenckner/Perron, § 32, Mn. 18a and 37. The problem here is not the issue of the attack not being imminent, because these installations are meant to be activated only in the event of an actual attack. The problem is whether their use is reasonable force; this has been held not normally to be the case if the installations were not recognisable to V, and consequently could not act as a deterrent. If V went on to overcome these obstacles, the *Tatbestand* of any offence based on D's actions may already be excluded by the free and informed self-endangerment of V (compare the *Kennedy*-type scenarios); if one did not already wish to adopt that stance, then the fact that he perseveres serves as an indicator of the dangerousness of V's attack, which is a factor to be taken into account when deciding whether the use of force is reasonable. In sum, the majority view seems to be that hidden installations are highly problematic, especially if their use can have lethal consequences for the attacker. See BGHSt 43, 177 (poison trap) and OLG Braunschweig MDR 1947, 205 (electric installation).

[149] Sch/Sch-Lenckner/Perron, § 32, Mn. 17.

[150] See for the similarly controversial question whether and to what extent D can use self-defence against *actual* blackmail by V when the threatened consequences for non-compliance are not immediately imminent, and whether the continuing pressure on D's freedom of choice is an attack the references at Sch/Sch-Lenckner/Perron, § 32, Mn. 18; the majority view seems to be in favour of allowing quasi-self-defence in some form or another in this context.

[151] See BGHZ 27, 289; BGH NJW 1982, 277.

[152] Sch/Sch-Lenckner/Perron, § 32, Mn. 17.

[153] [1989] NI 341.

[154] [1984] QB 456.

[155] BGHSt 27, 339.

[156] RGSt 55, 84.

possession.[157] If V has unlawfully taken photographs of D, the attack on D's right to privacy continues from pressing the camera's trigger until the production of the photos themselves.[158]

The attack[159] must be unlawful. However, this does not mean that it has to be a criminal offence, and it especially means that the attacker need not act with full guilt.[160] Any aggression that is at odds with the mandates of the legal order as a whole will in principle qualify.[161] A good example in this context is the protection of the embryo or *nasciturus* against abortion under § 218. The BVerfG[162] still views an abortion as being in principle an unlawful act against the embryo, which is protected by § 218. This would in theory trigger the right of anyone to defend the embryo, despite the fact that an abortion that is carried out in accordance with the law is not an offence. Yet the court without any doubt excluded the right to self-defence in the case of abortion[163] as an obvious consequence. At the end of the day, one will not be able to solve this conundrum by doctrinal reasoning, but one will have to accept that this is a case of public policy restricting the application of the criminal law for the solution of societal conflicts. As mentioned earlier, self-defence will not lie against behaviour by V which is in itself lawful,[164] especially if based on a justificatory defence, or if V commits a mistake of fact under § 16 which negates the *Tatbestand* or is treated in an analogous manner. In such cases, where the denial of self-defence may lead to unbearable results, D may be able to rely on necessity under § 34.[165]

The defence[166] must be directed against the attacker; collateral damage caused by the actions of D to a third party T when defending herself against V is in prin-

---

[157] It is, of course, a truism that D may at any time take his property back if he meets V later on, yet it is hard to make the average person understand why he should then not be allowed to use force anymore if V refuses to return the item, especially if V is carrying it with him. It is unclear whether that would be a case of necessity, either, because generally D would be required to use the legal process to get his property back as even the generous civil law protection of possession rather than title under the BGB would no longer allow him to enforce his rights without recourse to the courts; see §§ 859 and 861 BGB.

[158] OLG Düsseldorf NJW 1994, 1972.

[159] Note that in cases of a consensual fist-fight between several persons, nobody is considered to be 'attacking' the other and thus if one of them is losing he will not be entitled to use a weapon (knife, etc) to defend himself; the situation only changes if one of the participants exceeds the level of violence, as it were, that the parties had agreed to use. See, eg BGH NJW 1990, 2263.

[160] BGHSt 3, 217 and the further references at Sch/Sch-Lenckner/Perron, § 32, Mn. 24.

[161] Sch/Sch-Lenckner/Perron, § 32, Mn. 19–20.

[162] BVerfGE 88, 203 at 251.

[163] BVerfGE 88, 203 at 279.

[164] If D is coming to the aid of a third person T who chooses not to defend herself against V, he will in principle not be able to rely on § 32 as long as T is aware of and fully capable of consenting to the attack and as long as the attack does not endanger legal interests not under the control of T; see BGHSt 5, 248.

[165] Sch/Sch-Lenckner/Perron, § 32, Mn. 21.

[166] D must be acting with the intention of defending himself, as was mentioned above with respect to all justificatory defences; this includes cases where D is acting in knowledge of the defence situation, but also has other motives unless he merely abuses the objective situation, as, eg in the case of intentionally provoked self-defence; see Sch/Sch-Lenckner/Perron, § 32, Mn. 63.

ciple not covered by § 32.[167] A case in point, similar to *Pagett*,[168] was decided by the BGH[169] in 1993: D had been beaten up and humiliated by V during a fight in a bar, and had about 16,000 DEM stolen from him by V. D returned with a sawn-off shotgun and threatened V with it, asking him to return his money. V refused, grabbed T and used him as a human shield whilst firing twice himself at D.[170] D in return fired two shots at the group consisting of V and T; V was wounded superficially and T died. D argued that the unintended killing of T was covered by self-defence. The BGH rejected that D was acting in self-defence vis-a-vis V in the first place and thus could not rely on it with respect to T anyway, and even if he had acted in self-defence, § 32 did not cover collateral harm to third parties who were not part of the attack. An exception is made by the courts for collateral damage to *objects* belonging to third parties[171] and for the violation of *public order offences* in the course of self-defence, such as, for example, disturbing the course of a church service when replying to insulting remarks by the priest from the pulpit.[172] This issue can be brought to a head in 9/11 scenarios, when the only defence against terrorists using a plane with hundreds of innocent passengers as a weapon to cause immense havoc and the death of many more people on the ground, is to shoot it down.[173] One can doctrinally view this as a case of necessity or of acceptable collateral damage under self-defence—the ethical issues are the same. Glanville Williams had the following to say for the English practice:

> One can imagine a case where the use of mild force against an innocent third party would be adjudged reasonable and lawful. But injuring or endangering third parties would be unlikely to be held reasonable unless to avoid even greater danger to life, when the question in effect becomes one of necessity.[174]

We will examine 9/11 scenarios more closely under the heading of necessity below. However, if an otherwise proper exercise of the right to self-defence has unintended consequences for any legal interest of the attacker which, had they been intended, would not have qualified for § 32, then these consequences may be justified as 'quasi-collateral' damage.[175] This may even include the death of the attacker.[176] The stress in this context lies on the fact that German law asks whether the act of defence chosen is necessary, not on whether the result that occurs is.[177]

---

[167] RGSt 58, 29; BGHSt 5, 248.
[168] [1983] Crim LR 394.
[169] BGHSt 39, 380.
[170] In fact, one of V's shots hit another person who was also killed.
[171] RGSt 58, 29.
[172] RGSt 21, 168. See also BGH StV 1991, 63; 1996, 660; NStZ 1986, 357 (where the court argued that it was a case of necessity); 1999, 347.
[173] The German Government had tried to provide for such an option of last resort in the *Luftsicherheitsgesetz* (Air Traffic Security Act), which was, however, struck down by the BVerfG in 2006; see my article 'In Extremis—Hijacked airplanes, "collateral damage" and the limits of criminal law' (2006) Criminal Law Review 579–92 and the discussion below at necessity.
[174] *Textbook of Criminal Law* (2nd edn, 1983) 497.
[175] BGHSt 27, 313; 336; BGH MDR 1977, 281; 1979, 985; BGH NStZ 1986, 357; BGH StV 1999, 143.
[176] Sch/Sch-Lenckner/Perron, § 32, Mn. 39.
[177] Sch/Sch-Lenckner/Perron, § 32, Mn. 38.

The defence against the attack must be the least intrusive and serious measure that promises the immediate cessation of the attack on an ex-ante basis;[178] that means must also be employed in the least intrusive manner possible. There is no longer a general duty to retreat,[179] yet D will generally have to employ merely defensive means (*Schutzwehr*) before moving towards a counter-attack (*Trutzwehr*),[180] but he must never risk the endangerment of his own legal position in order to spare the attacker.[181] The measure for this evaluation is the actual 'combat situation' (*konkrete Kampflage*[182]), which means that the characteristics of the persons involved, their age, strength, whether they are armed, etc can and must be considered.[183] These principles also apply to the use of firearms in defence which may be permissible in certain circumstances even if the attacker is unarmed; however, because of the extreme dangerousness of firearms and the serious consequences for the attacker's health or life, their use must, wherever possible, be threatened first, be it by the use of a warning shot or otherwise, unless such prior warning would render the defensive action futile.[184]

In principle, the question of proportionality of value between the attacked interest and the interest endangered or sacrificed in the course of the defence is neither here nor there.[185] If no less intrusive course of action is available, D may sacrifice a higher interest of V to her own defence. There are exceptions to this principle, however, which are based on the idea of abuse of rights or general considerations of a gross discrepancy between the goods involved, the blameworthiness of the attacker or special relationships between the actors.[186] Thus the defence may be restricted:

a) in cases of *de minimis* attacks, such as shining a light into someone's face[187] or touching another person in the course of an argument without the intention of physical aggression;[188]

---

[178] BGH NJW 1969, 802; BGH StV 1999, 143.

[179] Sch/Sch-Lenckner/Perron, § 32, Mn. 40, although in the older case law, much like under the common law of self-defence in England, there was a tendency to require D to retreat if that could be done without dishonour or violating his dignity or other interests. However, even under the present law, D may be required to desist from defending himself if help from third parties, especially public authorities such as the police, is readily available and as effective as his own defence: equally effective police assistance must always be accepted, see BGHSt 39, 137. Private help must only be accepted if it is offered and leads to the possibility of the use of a less intrusive means of defence: D is weaker than V and would have to use a knife to defend himself, but T who is a Taekwondo trainer offers to help and will be able to stop V's attack with a few punches; compare RGSt 66, 244.

[180] BGHSt 24, 356; 26, 147.

[181] BGHSt 25, 229; BGH NJW 1980, 2263; NJW 1991, 503.

[182] Sch/Sch-Lenckner/Perron, § 32, Mn. 36.

[183] RGSt 55, 83; BGHSt 26, 256; 27, 336; BGH NStZ 1998, 508.

[184] Consistent jurisprudence of the courts: RGSt 55, 83; 58, 27; BGHSt 24, 356; 25, 229; 26, 143; 27, 336 and the many further references in Sch/Sch-Lenckner/Perron, § 32, Mn. 37.

[185] RGSt 69. 310; 72, 58; BGH GA 1968, 183; 1969, 24; BGH VRS 30, 281; BGH StV 1982, 219; 1996, 146.

[186] See for an overview, Sch/Sch-Lenckner/Perron, § 32, Mn. 46–7.

[187] Sch/Sch-Lenckner/Perron, § 32, Mn. 49.

[188] BGH MDR 1956, 372.

b) if there is a gross and unacceptable discrepancy as in the cases (some of which emanated from the hard times after the Second World War[189]) of protecting a peach tree by means of a lethal electric installation,[190] a shot with fatal consequences at a thief fleeing with a bottle of syrup worth 10 pence,[191] defending a lien on a chicken by hitting its owner over the head with an axe,[192] threatening to set dogs on cross-country walkers and to use firearms against them because they use D's private path;[193]

c) if the attacker is acting without guilt, as for example in the cases of children, insane persons or those labouring under an unavoidable mistake of law, where D may be required to resort only to defensive action, or at least more so than against an average person, the reason here being that the law as such is not being disobeyed by V to the same extent as in the ordinary case;[194]

d) if there is a special relationship between D and V, such as, for example, husband and wife or family members, which may at the very least require D to avoid lethal means of defence,[195] which does, however, not apply to broken-down relationships and situations of long-standing abuse such as in battered-women scenarios;[196] and

e) if D has provoked[197] the attack, which—apart from raising concerns about whether D is actually acting with the intent to defend herself if the attack was intentionally provoked[198]—may restrict D's alternatives to purely defensive action and may additionally give rise to a duty to retreat, and in the case of an intentional provocation, depending on the circumstances of the case, lead to an absolute exclusion of the right to self-defence.[199]

The use of torture, be it by representatives of the state or by private persons, can never be an appropriate means of self-defence; a state governed by the rule of law should not embrace this idea which may have uncontrollable consequences for the psyche of the general public and its civil servants—in addition, the practicalities are too repulsive even to contemplate them: will torture have to be ordered by a judge, will a doctor have to supervise the application of the treatment, will the police officers have to undergo special courses to find the most effective means of

---

[189] Note, however, that financial and social hardship in those times has for public policy reasons been consistently held not to be sufficient grounds for a defence of necessity: see Sch/Sch-Lenckner/Perron, § 34, Mn. 41d and compare the English case of the squatters in *Southwark LBC v Williams* [1971] 1 Ch 734 (CA).

[190] OLG Braunschweig MDR 1947, 205.

[191] OLG Stuttgart DRZ 1949, 42.

[192] BayObLG NJW 1954, 1377.

[193] BayObLG NJW 1965, 163.

[194] BGHSt 3, 217; BGH GA 1965, 148; BGH MDR 1974, 722; BSG NJW 1999, 2302.

[195] BGH NJW 1969, 802; 1975, 62; 1984, 986; 2001, 3202.

[196] BGH NJW 1984, 986; BGH NStZ 1994, 581.

[197] This does not include those cases where the provocation was already an attack in itself and V's reaction is in exercise of § 32: see BGH NStZ 2003, 599.

[198] BGH NJW 2001, 1075.

[199] BGH NJW 2001, 1075; 2003, 1958 and the references at Sch/Sch-Lenckner/Perron, § 32, Mn. 54–7.

torture for certain groups of people or ethnicities?[200] For the parents of an abducted child, this refusal to even engage in preliminary[201] reflection of admitting torture in restricted cases is a hard and unbearable attitude, but in the words of US Supreme Court Justice Antonin Scalia in the context[202] of allowing the evidence of abused children[203] without fully honouring the defendant's right to confront the witnesses under the Sixth Amendment's confrontation clause: 'It is a truism that constitutional protections have costs'.[204]

Necessity

Unlike in England and Wales,[205] necessity had been recognised in German law as a defence even for serious crimes involving the taking of pre-natal human life at the very latest after the decision[206] of the *Reichsgericht* in the 1927 abortion case, where the court held that the principle, although at the time not enshrined in criminal legislation, had to be recognised as a 'supra-legal' defence. The rule of necessity is now included in the Criminal Code under § 34:

§ 34 Necessity

A person who, faced with an imminent danger to life, limb, freedom, honour, property or another legal interest which cannot otherwise be averted, commits an act to avert the danger from himself or another, does not act unlawfully, if, upon weighing the conflicting interests, in particular the affected legal interests and the degree of the danger facing them, the protected interest substantially outweighs the one interfered with. This shall apply only if and to the extent that the act committed is an adequate means to avert the danger.

However, § 34 is not the only provision that impacts upon the criminal law of necessity: based on the principle of the unity of the legal order, there are, for exam-

---

[200] Rightly in this vein Sch/Sch-Lenckner/Perron, § 32, Mn. 62a–b. See also the case of the Frankfurt Chief of Police Daschner, who in 2002 had ordered the police officers investigating a child abduction to threaten the suspect Gäfgen with the infliction of pain, should he not tell them where the child was hidden. Gäfgen then admitted that the child had already been dead for some time. Daschner was subsequently indicted and convicted for giving this order; see on the issue LG Frankfurt NJW 2005, 692.

[201] Which was not always the case in the German debate after the Daschner case, see Sch/Sch-Lenckner/Perron, § 32, Mn. 62a and the preceding footnote.

[202] Although I do not agree with his conclusions in that particular case: see my article 'Zum Einsatz von Videotechnologie bei der Vernehmung kindlicher Zeugen' (1995) 107 *Zeitschrift für die gesamte Strafrechtswissenschaft* 87.

[203] See the US Supreme Court landmark cases of *Coy v Iowa*, 101 LEd 2d 857 (1988) and *Maryland v Craig*, 110 S Ct 3157 (1990).

[204] *Coy v Iowa*, 101 Led 2d 857 (1988) at 866.

[205] I have argued elsewhere that the continuing English debate about necessity and the taking of human life overlooks the fact that it had been partially accepted long ago in legislation relating to abortion and child destruction before the case of *Re A* highlighted the matter again in recent years. See my article 'Of Shipwrecked Sailors, Unborn Children, Conjoined Twins and Hijacked Airplanes—Taking Human Life and the Defence of Necessity' (2006) 70 *Journal of Criminal Law* 147.

[206] RGSt 61, 252; 62, 137.

ple, two provisions from the Civil Code (*Bürgerliches Gesetzbuch*—BGB) that need to be borne in mind as well, namely §§ 228 and 904 BGB:[207]

§ 228 Necessity

A person who damages or destroys an object belonging to another in order to avert from himself or from another a danger arising from the object does not act unlawfully if the damage or destruction is necessary to avert the danger and the damage is not out of proportion to the danger. If the person acting in this manner caused the danger, he is obliged to pay damages.

§ 904 Necessity

The owner of an object is not entitled to refuse another to interfere with the object if the interference is necessary to avert an imminent danger and if the impending damage is disproportionately high if compared to the damage caused to the owner by the interference. The owner may claim damages for the damage caused to him.

The provisions cover two different scenarios: § 228 is concerned with dangers arising from an object and a simple proportionality rule, whereas § 904, the so-called 'aggressive necessity exception' (*aggressiver Notstand*), deals with damage caused to objects that have no relation to the danger, and will often be related to uninvolved third parties, which is why there is a qualified proportionality rule. The fact that these previously codified necessity rules from the civil law were not applicable to personal injury partly prompted the decision of the *Reichsgericht* mentioned above.[208] § 34, according to some, contains a proper right to interfere[209] (*Eingriffsrecht*) and is based on the 'lesser of two evils' test. As we saw above, it does not apply to the scenario of collision of duties, which follows its own rules and is actually both narrower and wider than the necessity rule. The relationship of § 34 to the above-mentioned and other specific justificatory defences is that of a subsidiary norm and normative corrective at the same time: as long as there is a specific defence, its triggering criteria will usually trump the general clause of § 34, as, for example, the criteria for allowing interference with non-involved property set out in § 904 BGB derogate the general weighing exercise under § 34, yet the material rules developed specifically for the criminal law under § 34 will correct the application of § 904 BGB in certain cases.[210] An important case where no recurrence to § 34 is thought to be feasible is § 218a(2) and (3) on the reasons when an abortion is legal, because that rule was set up as an exclusive defence; however, it only goes as far as its elements—if the abortion is not performed by a medical doctor, § 218a does not apply and one may have to refer to § 34 after all.[211]

[207] Translation of § 904 by the author; § 228 is taken from the website of the Federal Ministry of Justice (<http://www.bmj-bund.de> accessed 30 June 2008) in slightly revised form.
[208] Sch/Sch-Lenckner/Perron, § 34, Mn. 2.
[209] Sch/Sch-Lenckner/Perron, § 34, Mn. 1.
[210] Sch/Sch-Lenckner/Perron, § 34, Mn. 6 give the following examples: D who has been sentenced to life imprisonment breaks down the door of his cell; or D, who does not have sufficient means, steals a sum of money in order to pay for his medical treatment.
[211] Sch/Sch-Lenckner/Perron, § 34, Mn. 6 with further references.

The question of whether § 34 is applicable to state action must in principle be answered as it was for § 32: in theory, § 34 can apply, but in practice it will in a large number of cases be excluded by specific provisions.[212] Note that in recent years, the BVerfG twice had the opportunity to clarify the special relationship between state action, general principles of justificatory defences (such as necessity) and the fundamental rights under the *Grundgesetz*, and there most particularly articles 1 on human dignity and 2 on the freedom of the person. On 15 February 2006,[213] the BVerfG partially struck down the Air Traffic Security Act 2005, which contained the following crucial provision in its § 14(3), which was declared unconstitutional and void:

> (3) The direct use of weapons is only allowed if under the circumstances it must be assumed that the airplane will be used against the lives of human beings and that such use is the only means of averting that present danger.

The court referred to its long-standing case law regarding the concept of human dignity, which enjoys the highest degree of protection within the canon of fundamental rights under the Basic Law. One of the main tenets of this is that the principle of human dignity is violated if and when a person is treated as a mere object for the fulfilment of somebody else's purposes, in other words when they can no longer decide for themselves. This principle does not attach any significance to the question of how long a life will last. The court expressly recognises that the passengers have already achieved this 'object status' based on the actions of the terrorists, yet it goes on to say that the state would also treat them as objects if it negated their interests by making them the necessary sacrifice for the purpose of saving the lives of the people on the ground. The court said at paragraph 124:

> By instrumentalising their killing *as a means to save others* [emphasis added], they are turned into mere objects and stripped of their rights . . .

But what of the people on the ground who cannot flee and will only be saved by the passengers' sacrifice? Are they not turned into objects, too, in order to give the passengers a short extension of their doomed lives? The BVerfG, however, refused to engage in *any* balancing exercise at all on this issue as it made clear in paragraphs 137 to 138 of the judgment, where it held that the fact that the killing is meant as a means to save the lives of others does not enter into the equation. This means that German constitutional law now requires the state to stand by and watch passively as a fully-fuelled civilian plane with one kidnapped pilot who

---

[212] Especially the use of undercover agents or so-called *agents provocateurs* in the context of investigating and prosecuting organised crime, and particularly their committing offences for the purpose of gaining credibility and blending in with the criminal group to be observed is highly controversial. The prevailing opinion still appears to accept that § 34 could in principle be a basis for such actions if and when there is no legal way around it, until such time as there are proper provisions established by the legislature. After all, the state of the rule of law is, by condoning such behaviour of its representatives, crossing the border into illegality itself and betraying its very principles. See the discussion at Sch/Sch-Lenckner/Perron, § 34, Mn. 41c.

[213] Online at <http://www.bverfg.de/entscheidungen/rs20060215_1bvr035705.html> accessed 30 June 2008. There is a link to an English press release on that page.

steers it, and one terrorist who forces him at gunpoint to do so, crashes into a foot-ball stadium where 25,000 spectators are watching a game, or into a nuclear plant that is destroyed and contaminates an area of hundreds of square miles and tens or hundreds of thousands of citizens. Moreover, this kind of reasoning also applies when it is not a civilian but a military plane, for example, a bomber carrying nuclear warheads that are going to be dropped on a large city, just as long as the terrorists make sure they have at least one innocent passenger on board.

On 27 February 2008,[214] the BVerfG, in a decision on the covert surveillance law of one of the German Member States, put a provisional stop to the federal government's wide-ranging plans to conduct secret online searches of private computers for the purposes of the war on terror and serious crime investigations. Operational necessity had been one of the key arguments advanced by its propo-nents. Here are the central findings as set out by the court itself:[215]

1. The general right of the freedom of the person (Art 2(1) and Art 1(1) 1 GG) encom-passes the fundamental right to the confidentiality and integrity of information techno-logy systems.

2. The secret infiltration of an information technology system through which its use can be monitored and the contents of its storage media be downloaded is constitutionally unacceptable unless there are factual reasons for a concrete danger for an overwhelm-ingly important legal interest. Such important interests are the life, limb and freedom of persons or such other common interests the threat to which touches upon the founda-tions or the existence of the state or the foundations of the existence of humanity. The measure may be justified even if it cannot be said with sufficient certainty that such a danger will occur in the near future, as long as certain facts point to a danger caused by individual persons in the individual case to such an overwhelmingly important interest.

3. The secret infiltration of an information technology system must in principle be based on a judicial order. The law authorising such an intrusion must make provision for the protection of the core area of privacy.

4. If an authorisation merely concerns a governmental measure aimed at monitoring and evaluating the contents and circumstances of currently ongoing communications in the computer network, the measure must be compliant with Art 10(1) GG [= secret of postal and telecommunications—MB].

5. If the state acquires knowledge of the contents of internet communications in the technical manner envisaged, an intrusion into the right under Art 10(1) GG will only occur if the public authority has not been authorised to do so by participants to the com-munication process. If the state acquires knowledge of publicly accessible communica-tion contents on the internet or if it participates in publicly accessible communication processes, it does not in principle infringe fundamental rights.

These cases show that on a proper reading of fundamental rights as enshrined in a constitution with primacy over the law-making prerogatives of Parliament and the Executive, it does make a difference whether an individual or the state engages in certain acts.

[214] <http://www.bverfg.de/entscheidungen/rs20080227_1bvr037007.html> accessed 30 June 2008.
[215] Translation by the author.

Just as under § 32, in principle, any legal interest can be defended[216] on the basis of necessity; similar reservations as to public and common interests apply[217]— there seems to be agreement that killing cannot be justified[218] with the possible exception of tyrannicide.[219] The evaluation of whether there is a danger for the legal interest D wishes to defend must be made on an ex-ante basis, according to the prevailing view. Yet, Lenckner and Perron are right to point out that just like in self-defence, in principle necessity as a right to interfere will only be triggered if there is actually a danger, which means that one may have to make a distinction, as stated previously, between realising the fact that there are on the one hand indicative circumstances that need to be *diagnosed*, and which on the other hand form the proper basis for the *prognostic* evaluation of whether there is a danger and which degree of danger there is; ie the ex-ante view as establishing the justificatory effect of necessity should be restricted to the prognostic part, while any mistakes about the diagnostic part would be treated as such, mistakes of fact.[220] The required degree of probability has been difficult to pin down; the efforts at arriving at a judicial definiton have ranged across the whole spectrum from a mere increased probability to a degree of probability bordering on certainty. These days, it seems right to say that the likelihood must be high, ie over the general risk to be expected in everyday life,[221] which is not a very helpful formula either, and much will depend on the circumstances of the individual case[222] and the pragmatic rule of 'I know it when I see it'.

There is no need for a human attack to be involved in the context of § 34[223]— the danger may arise from natural causes; in effect, a direct danger created to D

[216] D must be aware of the facts of the situation justifying recourse to necessity—see BGHSt 2, 114, which speaks of the 'will to rescue', which must be interpreted more widely as encompassing mere knowledge. However, the BGH has, it is worth noting, refused to grant recourse to necessity to D who professionally helped *bona fide* fugitives to flee from oppression in their countries, when D's only motive was the material gain from these operations (BGH MDR 1979, 1039).

[217] Sch/Sch-Lenckner/Perron, § 34, Mn. 11.

[218] RGSt 63, 215; 64, 101—these concern the so-called 'Fememord', ie vehmic murder or assassination attempt cases, committed in the beginning of the Weimar Republic against public figures such as Erzberger, Rathenau, Scheidemann and Gareis. The committee of the Reichstag which dealt with the phenomenon of the vehmic murders applied it to any politically motivated killings of persons who were accused of betraying the secrets of a certain political or ideological organisation. See on this topic, Irmela Nagel, *Fememorde und Femeprozesse in der Weimarer Republik* (Cologne/Vienna, 1991); and Bernhard Sauer, *Schwarze Reichswehr und Fememorde. Eine Milieustudie zum Rechtsradikalismus in der Weimarer Republik* (Berlin, Metropol, 2004).

[219] So the view of Sch/Sch-Lenckner/Perron, § 34, Mn. 11. See for a look at tyrannicide on the international law level as a way of avoiding collateral civilian damage my chapter 'Killing Many to Save a Few?' in Kaikobad/Bohlander, *Essays in Honour of Colin Warbrick* (Martinus Nijhoff, forthcoming 2009).

[220] Sch/Sch-Lenckner/Perron, § 34, Mn. 13 with references to the debate.

[221] Sch/Sch-Lenckner/Perron, § 34, Mn. 15.

[222] See, eg RGSt 61, 255; 68, 433; BGHSt 8, 31; 11, 164; 13, 70; 18, 272; 19, 373; 22, 345; BVerfGE 66,59; 77, 170.

[223] Indeed, a typical human-agency-related case would be duress by threats to commit criminal offences, which is generally classified as an excusatory defence under § 35 or as a separate supra-legal defence if the criteria of § 35 are not met; see Sch/Sch-Lenckner/Perron, § 34, Mn. 41b, also with reference to dissenting views. The reasoning behind this distinction is, apparently, that D, even if unwillingly, chooses to act against the law. I fail to understand the moral and structural difference to

through human agency finds its place mainly in the ambit of pre-emptive self-defence unless one takes the view of the opinion that subscribes to a separate sub-category of self-defence in this context as was mentioned above under the heading of self-defence.[224] There are, of course, also dangers created by humans[225] that need not be a direct attack on D, such as V operating a chemical factory in D's neighbourhood. Other than in § 32, the danger will be 'imminent' within the meaning of § 34 either if it is an ad hoc situation that is about to move from impending to real within a short time, as, for example, a person bleeding to death after an accident, or if it is a permanent danger that can be realised at any time without prior warning, such as a delapidated building falling down. In addition to these categories, the courts have also accepted a danger to be imminent if the damage may only arise in the future, but immediate action is required to prevent the future result.[226]

The action taken by D to avert the danger must be a necessary means; similarly to self-defence this requires that the defence is capable of ending the danger and is the least intrusive means to end it; to this extent the formula sometimes used by the courts that it must be the only way[227] to avert the danger can be misleading if there are several ways of achieving that goal.[228] In fact, if there is only one manner of reacting to the danger, the examination about the least intrusive means is pointless. In general, the rule for several possible avenues is as follows: if the least intrusive means is the one with the highest likelihood of succes, it is the only acceptable one; among several equally or nearly equally serious methods, the one with the highest likelihood is the only necessary one; and, finally, among several equally or nearly equally likely means, the least intrusive one is the only necessary one;[229] if there are several with equal chances of success and similar levels of intrusiveness, D can freely choose from among them. As § 34 does not in principle require an attack through human agency from which D is as a matter of public policy not required to retreat in cases of self-defence, D must normally try to retreat from the

---

necessity as a justification as long as the proportionality requirements set out below are met and the affected legal interest is lower in value than the threatened one: if D can commit an offence to save T's life and be justified under necessity, why should he not be able to save his own life and be justified in committing the same offence? The conceptual argument advanced against a justificatory defence is that because necessity gives D a right to interfere, V could not act in self-defence against D who is acting under duress. Yet, is it entirely unimaginable, for example, to request V to suffer the interference by D with his property if and when he knows that D is acting under threat to life and limb as he would have to if D was acting to save another's life under § 904 BGB? Any cases of V's ignorance could be caught by the pragmatic application of § 16.

[224] Sch/Sch-Lenckner/Perron, § 34, Mn. 16.

[225] As with self-defence, the fact that D caused or even provoked the danger herself does not in principle rob her of the possibility of relying on necessity; see the case law of RGSt 61, 255; BGH VRS 36, 24 and further references at Sch/Sch-Lenckner/Perron, § 34, Mn. 42.

[226] See for detail the case law in RGSt 36, 339; 60, 318; 66, 225; BGHSt 5, 373; 39, 137; 48, 258 and the references at Sch/Sch-Lenckner/Perron, § 34, Mn. 17.

[227] Eg RGSt 61, 254; BGHSt 3, 9.

[228] Sch/Sch-Lenckner/Perron, § 34, Mn. 18.

[229] BGHSt 3, 7; BGH NJW 1951, 769; BGH GA 1956, 382; BayObLG JR 1956, 307; OLG Celle VRS 26, 27; OLG Düsseldorf VRS 63, 384; OLG Hamm VRS 36, 37.

danger before he can choose to cause any damage or harm under the principle of necessity.[230]

§ 34, and this is a major difference to § 32, always includes an element of proportionality, not just in extreme cases: necessity is by definition a defence based on a balance of evils. The balancing exercise must not be based on a general view of the interests involved, as, for example, damage to property versus damage to health or life, but it must be based on the sum of the circumstances of the individual case,[231] also on the degree of damage caused or threatened to both sides on the scales of necessity[232] and the chances of saving each of the two.[233] According to a traditional view, there is one exception to this: lives can never be traded against each other,[234] as was mentioned above with regard to the 9/11 scenarios; to this extent German law shares the approach expressed in *Dudley and Stephens*.[235] The approach, according to the majority view, even applies to the well-known speluncan explorers, mountaineers and Zeebrugge ferry disaster situations as well as to 9/11 scenarios; for them it seems, according to some, only a supra-legal *excusatory* defence could exist.[236] As I have tried to argue elsewhere,[237] I find this difficult to accept, even more so given the ready general agreement to the collision of duties justification for murder explained above: collision of duties is ethically speaking not materially different from necessity, with the only difference that whatever D does in a collision scenario, she will violate the law. Whether that restriction of choice is a sufficiently delineating argument is doubtful. Yet, according to collision rules, killing is permissible under a *justificatory* defence. In the cases mentioned just now, the moral choice may be just as restricted for D and choosing the theoretical possibility of doing nothing would evoke the strongest moral condemnation from the majority of well-meaning and law-abiding people in some cases. To move the question one level to one of lack of guilt rather than lack of unlawfulness would mean that state action to prevent

[230] This may be subject to qualifications if § 34 is applied to scenarios of pre-emptive self-defence.

[231] Sch/Sch-Lenckner/Perron, § 34, Mn. 22.

[232] See for several categories of compound criteria (road traffic violations (eg drunken driving in order to save seriously wounded patient, etc), aggressive versus defensive necessity, human agency and necessity in general, being subject to a common and joint danger (*Gefahrengemeinschaft* = Zeebrugge cases), nature of the competing individual interests of the participants, special duties of some persons to undergo and accept risks, eg firemen, policemen and soldiers, etc, legislative intention in prohibiting the conduct of D (see, eg the recent UK cases on drug use for palliative purposes: *Quayle and others* [2005] EWCA Crim 1415), special provision for certain procedures to resolve conflicts between interests, and others): Sch/Sch-Lenckner/Perron, § 34, Mn. 22–41a, with numerous references to case law and literature. The fact that the situation of necessity arising in the first place was not D's fault is not in principle determinative of whether the scales are weighed for or against him, nor is the fact that D may have been under a duty to protect the threatened interest; see Sch/Sch-Lenckner/Perron, § 34, Mn. 42 with references to the case law.

[233] Sch/Sch-Lenckner/Perron, § 34, Mn. 25–9.

[234] See the above-mentioned decision of the BVerfG on the Air Traffic Security Act, and BGHSt 35, 350.

[235] [1881–5] 1 All E R Rep. 61 (QBD); (1884) 14 QBD 273.

[236] See the references to the debate at Sch/Sch-Lenckner/Perron, § 34, Mn. 24.

[237] 'In Extremis—Hijacked Airplanes, "Collateral Damage" and the Limits of Criminal Law' (2006) *Criminal Law Review* 579–92.

catastrophic consequences for the price of far fewer lives, as ethically unpalatable as that may appear, would be seen as something disapproved of by the law. The special status granted to human life is logically of little help, as all of the potential victims enjoy that special status and are thus, as far as balancing their interests goes, on an equal footing. In my view, the state's responsibility then is to diminish the sum of damage to the group with that special status, and as we must not under traditional views make differences among human beings according to their ethnicity, age, health, etc, the remaining criterion for the decision is the number of lives gained and lost. The traditional view becomes absurd and grotesque in the above-cited example of the nuclear bomber.

According to the prevailing view and tradition, the balancing exercise required by § 34 does not, as the wording might suggest, demand that 'the protected interest *substantially* outweighs the one interfered with' in the meaning of a high degree of substantial difference and importance, but merely that on an evaluation of all the circumstances of the case it *clearly* is of higher importance, leaving no doubt in the mind of the average reasonable person. The reference to adequacy in the last sentence of § 34, if it has any independent meaning at all, is a control clause that puts the whole concept under the scrutiny of a final instance of moral and ethical oversight, as it were.[238] The measure against which the balancing exercise is to be performed consists of the entirety of the positive legal order and generally accepted legal principles, as well as the communal ethical and moral frame of reference of society; consequently, all efforts at pinning it down to a ready-made formula will be doomed to failure.[239] Some guidance may be obtained by an overview of the case law. Apart from the examples mentioned above in this chapter, the courts have accepted or entertained in theory the idea of a case of necessity under § 34 in the following instances:[240]

a) criminal trespass (§ 123) by police informers into the house of a suspect for the purpose of uncovering facts about drug offences;[241]
b) leaving the scene of an accident (§ 142) in order to avoid physical abuse;[242]
c) disturbing the peace of the dead (§ 168) by performing an organ transplant if the consent of the relatives could not be obtained,[243] or by taking a blood sample from a deceased accident victim for the purposes of excluding drunkenness in the context of potential insurance claims;[244]
d) violation of the privacy of the spoken word (§ 201) by making secret phone recordings for the purpose of using them in civil or family proceedings, etc[245]

---

[238] Sch/Sch-Lenckner/Perron, § 34, Mn. 45–7.
[239] Further examples at Sch/Sch-Lenckner/Perron, § 34, Mn. 53.
[240] Further examples at Sch/Sch-Lenckner/Perron, § 34, Mn. 53.
[241] OLG München NJW 1972, 2275.
[242] BGH VRS 25, 196; 30, 281; 36, 25.
[243] LG Bonn JZ 1971, 56.
[244] OLG Frankfurt JZ 1975, 379. This issue is now expressly regulated in the law of insurance.
[245] BGH NStZ 1982, 254; OLG Frankfurt NJW 1967, 1047; KG NJW 1967, 115.

or to prove the bias of a judge in a criminal case for the purpose of recusing him;[246] and

e) taking away someone's car key to prevent him from driving whilst drunk (§ 240).[247]

A claim of necessity was rejected in the instances set out below:[248]

a) criminal trespass (§ 123) through occupation of a house by squatters (*Hausbesetzung*) in order to highlight and criticise issues related to the housing policy of the government,[249] or occupying military bases as a means of protest against stationing missile units there;[250]

b) participating in a criminal organisation (§ 129) as a member of a South Tirolean movement for self-determination;[251]

c) leaving the scene of an accident (§ 142) in order to attend a non-urgent medical[252] or business appointment;[253]

d) perjury before a former GDR court (§ 154) in order to avert danger to one's own life when simultaneously exposing another person to danger;[254]

e) secretly taping a phone conversation (§ 201) in order to use it as evidence through a audio-phonetic and linguistic analysis;[255]

f) beating prisoners of war (§ 223a) in order to combat theft;[256] and

g) environmental offences (§§ 324 *ff*) in order to save the jobs and the operation of a factory.[257]

---

[246] OLG Frankfurt NJW 1979, 1172.
[247] OLG Frankfurt NStZ-RR 1996, 136.
[248] Further examples at Sch/Sch-Lenckner/Perron, § 34, Mn. 54 Note that in some cases other reasons than the mere balancing exercise helped determine the issue.
[249] OLG Düsseldorf NJW 1982, 2678.
[250] OLG Stuttgart OLGSt § 123 no 2.
[251] BGH NJW 1966, 310.
[252] OLG Koblenz VRS 57, 13.
[253] OLG Stuttgart MDR 1956, 245.
[254] BGH GA 1955, 178.
[255] BGHSt 34, 39.
[256] BGH NJW 1951, 769.
[257] BGH MDR 1975, 723.

6

Guilt and Excusatory Defences

General Overview

On the third tier of the tripartite hierarchy, guilt, we find elements of liability that complement the first two tiers, such as subjective negligence or capacity (for example, § 3 JGG, see above in the chapter on basic concepts) and a number of defences whose function it is to eliminate that guilt. They are generally based on the idea that the law cannot ask of anyone more than they can be legitimately expected to do, either intellectually or emotionally.[1] What people do may be objectively unlawful vis-a-vis the victim or the legal interest involved for lack of a justificatory defence and, for example, create a claim in tort in certain circumstances, yet the criminal law recognises the fact that they could not help but act in an unlawful manner. As under § 29, everyone is liable according to his or her own guilt, some accomplices may still be fully liable even if one of them is not.[2] Thus, if D is in unavoidable error about the law, he should be excused from liability; the same applies if he is put under unbearable psychic pressure, if he has lost control of himself because of fear or confusion, if he is mentally incapable of understanding what he is doing or that what he is doing is wrong or to act on that insight, if he has it. In this chapter, we will look[3] at subjective negligence as the one missing element of negligence liability, followed by the defences of:

---

[1] See Sch/Sch-Lenckner, Vorbem § 32 *ff*, Mn. 108–11.

[2] This fact also militates against the demand heard time and time again in the United Kingdom of unifying all defences, whether excusatory or justificatory, because under the present system participation in a justified and therefore lawful act is not punishable and even if the participant has no subjective knowledge of the defence or an intent to act in its exercise he will likely be only liable for attempt, as we saw in chapter five in connection with § 16. Unifying defences would entail rules that take into account the differences in individual degrees of blameworthiness and involvement in an act.

[3] For reasons of space, we will leave out the question to what extent freedom of religion and conscience under art 4 GG can act as an excusatory defence; we already saw in the chapter on justificatory defences that it has an impact on the interpretation and scope of other defences such as consent, and while the issue is controversial, there is no denying that the constitutional freedoms generally influence the interpretation of any law beneath the level of the Basic Law. The freedom of religion will be more difficult to use as a defence when we look at offences by positive acts, yet for omission offences the door may be open a bit wider and there again often in a medical and palliative context, such as, eg the request of a seriously ill woman not to be brought to an intensive care unit in the case of BGHSt 32, 380. For a discussion and further references, see Sch/Sch-Lenckner, Vorbem § 32 *ff*, Mn. 118–20.

a) mistake of law (§ 17);
b) excessive self-defence (§ 33);
c) duress (§ 35) and supra-legal duress (*übergesetzlicher entschuldigender Notstand*);
d) insanity (§ 20); and
e) diminished responsibility (§ 21).

Regarding the last two defences, it is important to remember from the outset that the concepts of insanity (*Schuldunfähigkeit*) and diminished responsibility (*verminderte Schuldfähigkeit*) under German law do not have the same meaning as in English law, and for that reason their use in this context is one of terminological approximation only for want of a better word. Insanity in England has a very restricted meaning, and diminished responsibility is currently recognised as a *substantive* partial defence only in cases of murder; in Germany, insanity includes issues such as intoxication and scenarios that might fall under provocation and battered-women syndrome which would be viewed as separate and quite distinct defences in England. Diminished responsibility is not a partial defence to a certain crime that would alter the substantive designation of that crime, as it does, for example, in England with murder and manslaughter, but a mere sentencing provision that applies across the board to all offences and is based on the categories encompassed by insanity. § 21 is thus, one could say, the little sister of § 20, and both, according to a common interpretation, partially represent nothing but examples of unavoidable and therefore relevant mistakes of law under § 17, or avoidable ones where the law still wanted to highlight the offender's special position compared to the criminal who is fully *compos mentis* but merely intellectually mistaken about the law. Duress, for example, includes both English concepts of duress by threats and duress of circumstances. Excessive self-defence partially crosses over into the area of insanity and may also cover situations involving extreme provocation. Most importantly, the fact that somebody acted with full intent does not prejudice the question of whether she also acted with full, partial or no guilt, and voluntary causation of a state of insanity or diminished responsibility does not predicate the applicability of these defences; German law[4] does not know, for example, the distinction of basic and specific intent and the availability of intoxication as a defence based on that difference. However, it recognises the policy need for penalising some of those situations which led to the concept of *actio libera in causa* where prior guilt, intentional or negligent, may be the cause for criminal liability for actions committed under insanity. The latter concept has come under intense constitutional scrutiny in recent years because it extended criminal liability and circumvented the strict application of § 20, and at this time its remaining scope of application is unclear. Conversely, the characterisation of D's behaviour as falling under § 20 or 21 is only permissible if it had not already

---

[4] Interestingly enough, the law of the former GDR had rules that almost exactly mirrored the *Majewski* principle in §§ 15 and 16 of its Criminal Code, and the case law of the GDR Supreme Court also developed the distinction between basic and specific intent. See LK-Jähnke, *StGB* (11th edn, 1993) § 21, Mn. 96–7.

reached a degree that made his actions involuntary in the sense that legally he was not acting at all. This throws into sharp relief again the critical distinction between the ability to act as a basic natural attribute of human agency, intent as a form of *mens rea* attached to the elements of the *Tatbestand*, and guilt as an emanation of D's general capacity to abide by the law and to control herself. That said, this general (in)capacity of D will only be relevant if it had an effect on her actions that underlie the offence in question; there is no such thing as general insanity. One may be insane within the meaning of § 20 for the purpose of one offence, but not necessarily for another: a kleptomaniac may possibly be insane or suffer from diminished responsibility in relation to theft, but not for murder.

Individual Issues

Subjective Negligence

As was already indicated in the chapter on the subjective side of the *Tatbestand*, negligence in a subjective sense is not part of the general *mens rea*, but of the third tier, guilt. Subjective negligence is a positive prerequisite for establishing guilt in negligence offences. As we saw in the chapter on the *objektiver Tatbestand*, the standard for objective negligence is largely a reasonable or ordinary man standard, with some allowance or indeed increased expectation based on specific spheres of life or activities, such as trades or professions, etc. In the context of guilt, D's special abilities or defects will play a more prominent role, because the question that needs to be answered by the court is now whether *D* could have lived up to the objective standard, whether *he* could have foreseen the negative result and avoided it. The principle of individual blameworthiness (*Schuldprinzip*) requires that D's personal abilities are taken into account.[5]

A similar discussion took place in recent English jurisprudence regarding the problem of whether objective *Caldwell*[6] recklessness was a sufficient *mens rea* criterion in criminal damage or whether it was necessary to revert to the subjective *Cunningham*[7] standard, a question which was resolved by *R v G*[8] in favour of the latter, although there is still some uncertainty as to possible residual applications of *Caldwell* in other offences if that was to suit public policy requirements. Although this book is not concerned with commenting on the development of English law, I find it methodologically and morally difficult to accept that there should be different standards of interpretation of recklessness just because the protagonists and makers of public policy may wish to be stricter vis-a-vis certain

---

[5] Sch/Sch-Cramer/Sternberg-Lieben, § 15, Mn. 194–5.
[6] [1982] AC 341.
[7] [1957] 2 QB 396.
[8] [2003] UKHL 50; [2003] 3 WLR 1060; [2003] 4 All ER 765.

categories of offences based on their perceived greater danger to the public interest; very often the real reason may be mere prosecutorial expediency. The central moral statement from *R v G*, reminiscent of *Elliott*,[9] demands, in my view, general application:

> It is neither moral nor just to convict a defendant (least of all a child) on the strength of what someone else would have apprehended if the defendant himself had no such apprehension. Nor, the defendant having been convicted, is the problem cured by imposition of a nominal penalty.[10]

We find an interface with the above-mentioned concepts of insanity and diminished responsibility in that for reasons of §§ 20 and 21, D may not have been able to recognise the potential consequences of his actions[11] and abide by his duties of diligence. Generally, D may not be able to exercise his diligence to the appropriate level because of intellectual or physical defects, lack of experience or capacity to react, sudden and unexpected tiredness or feeling sick, being frightened and surprised, etc.[12] As far as the subjective foreseeability is concerned, the courts subscribe to the principle that it is D's ability to foresee certain events, ie a subjective standard, yet in practice the inference is often drawn that what is generally foreseeable to the average man is also foreseeable for the individual defendant.[13] The object of foresight, according to the courts,[14] must be the final result, not necessarily the actual causal chain and all the individual elements of the offence as such, but only the major ones, unless there is a major and highly unusual deviation from what could be expected to happen based on general experience.[15]

A final element of subjective negligence is that of the *Zumutbarkeit normgemäßen Verhaltens*, ie whether in the given circumstances D can legitimately be expected to abide by the letter of the law, in effect the general principle underlying the concept of duress in § 35. While the relevance of this concept is more or less uncontroversial for negligence offences as opposed to offences of intent and is actually not restricted to the ambit set out for duress proper under § 35 (see below), there is a debate about whether it is actually an element of guilt or whether one should not already subsume it under the objective negligence criteria in the *Tatbestand* or other parts inside or outside the tripartite hierarchy.[16] What is meant by these cases is exemplified very well by the decision of the *Reichsgericht* of 23 March 1897[17] in the so-called '*Leinenfängerfall*' (reins-catcher case): D was

---

[9] [1983] 1 WLR 939.

[10] *Ibid*, at [33].

[11] Sch/Sch-Cramer/Sternberg-Lieben, § 15, Mn. 191–2.

[12] Many of these situations will happen in the context of road traffic offences. See, eg the case law in BGH VRS 7, 181; 10, 123; 19, 108; 23, 369; 34, 434; 44, 431; BGH DAR 1956, 106; 1958, 194 and RGSt 58, 30.

[13] See, eg RGSt 29, 218; 56, 350; BGHSt 3, 62; 4, 185; 12, 78; and with a slightly more individualised attitude, BGHSt 40, 348.

[14] See the views of the literature at Sch/Sch-Cramer/Sternberg-Lieben, § 15, Mn. 199–203.

[15] RGSt 29, 221; 34, 94; 73, 372; BGHSt 12, 77; BGH VRS 16, 33; 17, 37; 22, 367; 24, 212.

[16] Sch/Sch-Cramer/Sternberg-Lieben, § 15, Mn. 204.

[17] RGSt 30, 25.

driving a horse-cart for his employer, E; one of the horses he worked with was, as both he and E knew, a so-called reins-catcher, ie it had the habit of swishing its tail across the reins held by the driver of the cart and pressing the reins to its body, thus making a controlled use of the reins by D extremely difficult if not impossible. One day while D was working with the cart, the horse caught the reins again. D tried desperately to regain control and to get the reins free again, yet his efforts made all the horses go wild. D lost control of the cart which then ran over a passer-by, V, who suffered a broken leg. D was charged with negligently causing bodily harm and while the *Reichsgericht* accepted that he could have generally foreseen that result, it held that he could not be expected to disobey the instructions of his employer to use that horse in his work and risk losing his livelihood by refusing to work with that particular horse at all, which would have been the only practicable way of avoiding those kinds of risks. D was consequently acquitted.

Mistake of Law

Just as in English law, the ground rule in German law is that one simply has to know the law; errors about it will not exonerate the defendant, unless the error was unavoidable. That is the consequence of the position taken by the BGH in its land-mark case of BGHSt 2, 194, which we referred to in the chapter on basic concepts above where the court said that an offender has to have the awareness that what he is doing is wrong and forbidden before he can be punished,[18] yet this assumption is the rule and the absence of knowledge the exception. While English law, which takes a very strict approach to errors of law, put the unavoidability threshold extremely high by the Privy Council decision in *Lim Chin Aik*,[19] a case referring to a scenario where the defendant could under no circumstances have had prior knowledge of an unpublished ministerial decree refusing immigration to him individually, and could not have arranged his conduct accordingly, German law takes a more relaxed attitude. § 17 provides:

> If at the time of the commission of the offence the offender lacks the awareness that he is acting unlawfully, he shall be deemed to have acted without guilt if the mistake was unavoidable. If the mistake was avoidable, the sentence may be mitigated pursuant to § 49(1).

As we saw in chapter four on the subjective part of the *Tatbestand*, there is a certain tension with the concept of mistake of fact when it applies to normative elements of the offence or to wrongfully assumed facts that would, if true, support a recognised defence on the level of unlawfulness. Here the prevailing opinion is to apply § 16 directly or by analogy, which has the consequence that D is deemed to

---

[18] That was not always the case under the previous interpretation, see RGSt 61, 258; 63, 218, where the *Reichsgericht* argued that the *Tatbestand*-related intent of D was in principle sufficient to establish his guilt.

[19] [1963] AC 160.

act without intent and may consequently only be found guilty of a negligence offence if his actions fulfil the elements of such an offence. The difference to § 17 is that a mistake of law, if unavoidable, leads to a full acquittal and if it is avoidable, D remains guilty of the intentional offence, but will get his sentence reduced under § 49(1).[20]

D, in addition to any other requirements of an intention related to the *Tatbestand* or subjective negligence, needs to be aware that he is also acting unlawfully in relation to the relevant legal interest involved in the offence.[21] As stated earlier, this will normally be the case if he has the *mens rea* for the elements of the offence on the first tier. He need not understand the full legal qualifications, but it will suffice if he has a layman's insight into the normative evaluation of the underlying facts (*Parallelwertung in der Laiensphäre*).[22] Similar to the situation regarding the intent in the *Tatbestand*, the awareness may be conditional[23] in the sense used in the context of *dolus eventualis*.[24] A person who acts out of certain firmly held beliefs (*Überzeugungstäter*) will as a rule have awareness of the unlawfulness of his actions, in fact very often he will want to oppose the state's very regulations by his actions, as, for example, in the case of terrorists or total draft resisters.[25] Recent German history provides an example of when courts have held out of historical-political considerations that the order to shoot at GDR citizens trying to flee across the border into West Germany was patently unlawful, based on egregious human rights violations, and that therefore GDR border guards were assumed to know, for the purposes of military law,[26] that they were acting unlawfully, even under GDR law.[27]

The central question of § 17 is that of avoidability. It is not a mere psychological criterion, but requires of D that he exerts all his individual intellectual abilities and if need be consults with reliable specialists, such as lawyers,[28] as to whether or not his intended action is lawful. Although not as strict as *Lim Chin Aik*, the threshold

[20] The courts have been confronted over time with widely differing scenarios where a delineation was required, yet the casuistic jurisprudence makes it difficult to define a bright line of distinction; see the examples listed at Sch/Sch-Cramer/Sternberg-Lieben, § 17, Mn. 12–12c.

[21] There is no *general* awareness of unlawfulness and in cases where D commits several offences by the same act, the awareness may exist for some and be lacking for others. Compare BGHSt 10, 35 and the further references at Sch/Sch-Cramer/Sternberg-Lieben, § 17, Mn. 8.

[22] BGHSt 10, 41.

[23] BGHSt 4, 4.

[24] For negligence offences, similar considerations apply if D is negligently unaware of the law; see the references at Sch/Sch-Cramer/Sternberg-Lieben, § 17, Mn. 9.

[25] So, eg the members of the Jehovah's Witnesses who refuse to do both military service and the replacement community service for conscientious objectors; the BVerfG has held that their punishment for *total* draft resistance is constitutional, see BVerfGE 19, 135; 78, 395; BVerfG NJW 2000, 3269.

[26] Military law carries a special rule regarding errors of law in relation to superior orders, where based on the exigencies of military efficiency D will be excused unless he knew the order was unlawful or if its illegality was 'obvious' (*offensichtlich*). Note, however, that in the context of superior orders (see the chapter on justificatory defences), a subordinate's mistakes may in some cases already lead to a justification of D's behaviour. See Sch/Sch-Cramer/Sternberg-Lieben, § 17, Mn. 22a.

[27] See BGHSt 39, 33.

[28] Sch/Sch-Cramer/Sternberg-Lieben, § 17, Mn. 18 with references.

is high,[29] especially if the relevant behaviour belongs to the traditional core area of criminally sanctioned conduct, less so if it crosses into the area of specific regulatory criminal offences. This may also apply to foreigners if certain circumstances should have given them cause to reflect on the lawfulness of his actions, such as, for example, the foreigner who supplies people with drugs in order to allow them to commit suicide, if there is a notorious 'suicide tourism' into his home country as evidence that the same behaviour encounters (legal) obstacles in Germany.[30] If new legislation enters into force, the standard for avoidability is somewhat relaxed unless the law's purpose is absolutely clear from its mere wording; in all other cases D will be safe from prosecution if his interpretation remains within the range of acceptable options; yet he will still have to obtain information from experts about the background to the new legislation.[31] D will also be able to rely on a long-standing jurisprudence in the case law which considered his conduct lawful at the time of his action, even if the courts reinterpret the law and reject the previous approach,[32] for the simple reason that the new decision attests the previous judges that they themselves were caught in a mistake of law; this will even apply if D did not know the previous case law, because if he had asked for clarification he would have received a 'wrong' answer[33] and there must be causality between the fact of non-consultation and the error.[34] If the case law is contradictory, D may in principle rely on the views of the higher court.[35]

Excessive Self-defence

Self-defence will normally only be available to D if he uses reasonable force and is under attack at the time of his 'defensive' action. What if he exceeds the degree of force necessary to repel the attack, or is mistaken about the fact that there is an attack and/or the degree of violence directed at him? These cases of excessive defence are also known as 'intensive excess' (first scenario), 'extensive excess' (second scenario) and may come in the mixed form of the 'putative excess' (third scenario). As we saw above when we looked at § 16 and § 17, these are in principle cases either of mistake of fact regarding the factual basis for a recognised defence[36] or of a mistake of law with regard to whether D exceeded the necessary force. § 33, however, has a partially modified answer for these problems:

[29] BGHSt 4, 5; 4, 237; 21, 20.
[30] BGHSt 46, 287.
[31] RG JW 1938, 947; BGH NStZ 1996, 237; OLG Braunschweig NJW 1951, 811.
[32] BGHSt 37, 55.
[33] Sch/Sch-Cramer/Sternberg-Lieben, § 17, Mn. 20.
[34] BGHSt 37, 67; BGH NJW 1996, 1606.
[35] OLG Bremen NJW 1960, 164.
[36] Although the BGH seems to have previously disagreed with that contention by stating that §§ 33 and 16 have nothing to do with each other, see BGH NStZ 1987, 20. This interpretation is difficult to reconcile with the purpose and systematic position of § 33; therefore, the view of Sch/Sch-Lenckner/Perron, § 33, Mn. 6 is better.

A person who exceeds the limits of self-defence out of confusion, fear or terror shall not be held criminally liable.

§ 33 is, according to the majority view and the courts, not applicable to the 'extensive excess' and the 'putative excess', which follow the general rules on mistake of fact and law explained earlier.[37] § 33 thus only covers the 'intensive[38] excess' and is almost unanimously considered to be an excusatory defence, although its mere wording does not make that conclusion cogent.[39] The purpose behind § 33 is to exonerate the defendant if she has made these errors of judgment in a psychologically stressed state of mind that did seriously affect her full self-control,[40] because[41] she felt threatened.[42] If these criteria are fulfilled, recourse to the subsidiary liability principles of § 16 or 17 is precluded with the consequence that D cannot be held liable for negligent offences, either. In a way, it is an extension of the risk attribution that is based on the fact that D is being attacked unlawfully by V, which already led to the omission of a general proportionality requirement in § 32 as opposed to § 34. The scope of the provision is restricted to the so-called 'asthenic' states of fear, terror and confusion; it cannot be extended[43] by analogy to the so-called 'sthenic' states of rage, hate, indignation, etc, even if they reach a similar severity; D will in the latter cases have to rely on the general rules, but under these the subsidiary liability may also be excluded.[44] If D provoked the attack against which she then acted in (excessive) self-defence, the application of § 33, according to more recent opinion,[45] is now tied to the question of whether she retained any right of self-defence at all as explained in chapter five on justificatory defences above; if so, § 33 may still apply in principle, yet a meticulous examination will be required whether D actually really acted out of fear, etc, which may be especially problematic if there is evidence of a *deliberate* provocation by D in order to attack V.[46]

[37] BGH NJW 1962, 309; BGH NStZ 1983, 453; 1987, 20; 2002, 141; 2003, 599; BGH NStZ-RR 2002, 204.
[38] This also has the consequence that just like § 32, § 33 is in principle not applicable to third-party collateral damage; see RGSt 54, 36; differently BGH NStZ 1981, 299 for public interest protections.
[39] RGSt 56, 33; BGHSt 3, 198; BGH NStZ 1981, 99; NStZ 1995, 77.
[40] Despite this basic principle, the majority view appears to be prepared to countenance the idea of an intentional excess as being covered by § 33 as well; see, eg BGHSt 39, 139. Lenckner and Perron rightly point out that this concept is hardly imaginable if the state of mind required by § 33 is reached, see Sch/Sch-Lenckner/Perron, § 33, Mn. 6.
[41] There must be causality between the perception of the attack, the frightened state of mind and the loss of control by D: BGH NJW 1991, 505; 2001, 3202. This does not exclude situations where other motives accompany the states of mind mentioned in § 33 (motive cluster) as long as the latter are the dominant ones or at least co-causal; see for the latter standard BGHSt 3, 198; BGH NJW 2001, 3202 and for the debate in the literature Sch/Sch-Lenckner/Perron, § 33, Mn. 5.
[42] BGH NJW 1991, 505; 2001, 3202.
[43] RG JW 1932, 2432; BGH NJW 1969, 802.
[44] Sch/Sch-Lenckner/Perron, § 33, Mn. 4.
[45] The BGH in earlier times tended to exclude § 33 altogether in cases of provocation: BGH NJW 1962, 308.
[46] BGHSt 39, 133; BGH NJW 1995, 973; BGH NStZ-RR 1997, 194.

Duress

We remember that necessity under § 34 in its traditional interpretation did not allow for justification in cases where the legal interests involved were of roughly equal value and where the means used were disproportionate. What if there is a danger to D's life or limb, or freedom, that cannot be otherwise averted, but § 34 is not available? D may be threatened by V into committing a serious offence or be pressured by circumstances to act in a manner that will expose him to criminal liability. German law regulates[47] these questions of duress on the level of guilt[48] by the excusatory defence of § 35, which reads:

> (1) A person who, faced with an imminent danger to life, limb or freedom which cannot otherwise be averted, commits an unlawful act to avert the danger from himself, a relative or person close to him, acts without guilt. This shall not apply if and to the extent that the offender could be expected under the circumstances to accept the danger, in particular, because he himself had caused the danger, or was under a special legal obligation to do so; the sentence may be mitigated pursuant to § 49(1) unless the offender was required to accept the danger because of a special legal obligation to do so.

> (2) If at the time of the commission of the act a person mistakenly assumes that circumstances exist which would excuse him under subsection (1) above, he will only be liable if the mistake was avoidable. The sentence shall be mitigated pursuant to § 49(1).

The concept of duress had previously been contemplated, for example, in cases of defendants who had:

a) been involved in the machinations and atrocities of the NS-regime;[49]
b) been spying for or against totalitarian governments;[50]
c) killed violent relatives that posed a constant serious threat;[51]
d) committed perjury to avoid bodily harm or worse;[52]
e) killed a person under threat of being killed themselves if they did not;[53] or
f) committed sexual intercourse with their mother/son under threat of force from the mother's husband.[54]

The wording of § 35 makes it clear that duress only protects D if he tries to avert a danger to his life, limb and personal liberty or that of a relative or person who is close to him;[55] the prevailing opinion rejects the possibility of analogies with

---

[47] As was set out above, the question of duress has a wider application in negligence offences.
[48] Sch/Sch-Lenckner/Perron, § 35, Mn. 1–2.
[49] BGHSt 2, 251; 3, 271; 18, 311; BGH NJW 1964, 370; 72, 834.
[50] BGH ROW 1958, 81; BGH MDR 1956, 395.
[51] RGSt 60, 318; BGH NJW 1966, 1823.
[52] BGHSt 5, 371.
[53] RGSt 64, 30.
[54] BGH GA 1967, 113.
[55] This encompasses the persons listed as relatives in § 11(1) No 1, where the actual existence of a close personal relationship is irrelevant, as well as any person with whom D has such a close relationship as long as it is reciprocated by the other, which excludes the 'secret love' and ex-girlfriends or boyfriends, regardless of whether D still has feelings for them; note, however, that the ex-husband

regard to other protected interests, such as property,[56] because the rule under § 35 is an exception from the general principles laid out under necessity and its commands to abide by the law instead of deciding for oneself what is right. § 35 indeed presupposes an unlawful act and its concession to human frailty in cases where virtually no one can be expected to deny the demands of human nature militates against an excessive interpretation.

'Life' in the context of § 35 also covers that of the unborn child.[57] 'Limb' in principle only covers acts against bodily integrity in a holistic understanding, but not mental harm. It must be of a level of seriousness comparable to a threat to life, thus merely transitory and lighter dangers may be excluded.[58] Finally, 'freedom' means physical freedom or freedom of movement as covered in § 239,[59] not the general freedom of action or personal choice under article 2 GG.[60] This restriction is also based on the idea that the degree of seriousness required by comparison with dangers to life and limb will not normally be reached otherwise. There may be difficult cases that are on the borderline, though, such as, for example, 16-year-old D killing or seriously wounding her despotic Kurdish father V as the, in her view, only available remedy against a forced marriage that is meant to take place in a week's time, because she is penniless and her father keeps her passport, etc so she cannot escape by merely running away: D cannot rely on necessity nor § 35, as none of the protected interests are involved; what is threatened is her freedom to choose her own husband, an essential part of her human right to privacy. Should it make a material difference that in the case of D's disobedience, V will seriously beat or even kill her, or send her back to Turkey or Iraq, thus triggering the elements required by § 35? When will that danger materialise and thus become imminent in the meaning of § 35?

The danger and its imminence within the context of § 35 are, in principle, similar if not identical to the concept as used in § 34,[61] and reference can be made to what was said in the chapter on justificatory defences; as with § 34, human agency

---

or -wife are still relatives within the meaning of § 11, yet no close relationship is required for them. See Sch/Sch-Lenckner/Perron, § 35, Mn. 15.

[56] See Sch/Sch-Lenckner/Perron, § 35, Mn. 4.

[57] Sch/Sch-Lenckner/Perron, § 35, Mn. 5.

[58] Sch/Sch-Lenckner/Perron, § 35, Mn. 6–7.

[59] '§ 239 Unlawful imprisonment

(1) Whosoever imprisons a person or otherwise deprives him of his freedom shall be liable to imprisonment of not more than five years or a fine . . .

(3) The penalty shall be imprisonment from one to ten years if the offender

1. deprives the victim of his freedom for more than a week . . .'

[60] Sch/Sch-Lenckner/Perron, § 35, Mn. 8–9.

[61] However, Sch/Sch-Lenckner/Perron, § 35, Mn. 11, propose to use an objectivised ex-ante view for all elements of the evaluation, the diagnostic and prognostic ones, in contrast to what they advocate for necessity, as was set out in the chapter on justificatory defences above, see Sch/Sch-Lenckner/Perron, § 34, Mn. 13 with references to the debate. This is because § 35 as opposed to § 34 does not grant a right to interfere based on the *danger* itself—with the attending severe consequences for the defence of the interest infringed by the action based on necessity—but because of the *psychological stress* caused to D.

is not required as a cause of the danger; § 35 thus covers both of the English common law concepts of duress and duress by circumstances. As in § 34, the reaction by D must be capable of ending the danger and at the same time be the least intrusive means, as is evident from the use of the words 'which cannot otherwise be averted'. These elements of proportionality already carry in themselves connotations of '*Zumutbarkeit*', ie of the question of whether D can legitimately be expected to undergo the danger; it is strictly speaking not necessary to have recourse to the criteria set out in § 35(1) 2nd sentence, such as, for example, whether D caused the danger or is under an obligation to suffer it. The law expects people to take measures which the average morally guided person would take under the circumstances without asking for heroism;[62] D must not simply choose the path of least resistance,[63] but must make every effort to evade the danger.[64] This may include other avenues that are fraught with risk, possibly and depending on the circumstances even to the level of endangering one's own life[65] otherwise. The courts have, for example, held that the following scenarios were *outside* of what could be legitimately expected of D:

a) recourse to only temporarily effective police or judicial protection in situations of a permanent danger;[66]
b) continuing to live in a dilapidated house that can collapse any moment, or face homelessness;[67]
c) litigating a divorce or the institutionalisation of a cruel and violent husband if during the proceedings the violence would continue;[68] and
d) immediately leaving the former GDR and giving up one's entire livelihood instead of serving as an informer to the state security service.[69]

Compare to this, however, the following cases where the courts required D to suffer serious danger to himself rather than actively avert it:

a) an SS officer feigning the execution of a criminal order or 'going underground' instead of carrying out an order to commit murder;[70] and
b) insubordination by a soldier instead of aiding murder.[71]

If one looks at these cases, one may be able to discern a certain pattern—that in the first list of cases, D in substance was faced with the danger without having previously and voluntarily associated with the potential source of the danger, whereas in the cases of the SS officer and the soldier in the context of the time (Nazi terror regime), there was a primary and *a priori* collaboration with the dangerous source,

---

[62] BGH MDR 1951, 537.
[63] BGH NJW 1972, 834.
[64] BGHSt 18, 311.
[65] BGH NJW 1952, 113 and the further references at Sch/Sch-Lenckner/Perron, § 35, Mn. 14.
[66] RGSt 60, 322 (killing a violent relative) and 66, 226 (perjury).
[67] RGSt 59, 69 (arson).
[68] BGH NJW 1966, 1825 (murdering husband).
[69] BGH MDR 1956, 395.
[70] OGHSt 2, 228.
[71] BGHSt 2, 257 (in the context of the so-called 'Röhm-Putsch' under the Nazi regime).

ie the Nazis, and their general political agenda, even if D may not have subscribed to the use of violence; however, because D was fundamentally and willingly part of the 'machine' in the first place, so to speak, he was under a duty to suffer greater danger than if he had not been. This may in effect be a parallel to the English case law on duress and prior voluntary association with criminal groups, which also leads to a serious restriction on D's ability to rely on duress.[72]

As is the case with the justificatory defences, § 35 requires a subjective element of finality, namely that D act *with the purpose* of averting the danger; the wording and substance of the defence exclude acting in the mere knowledge of the facts that support it as a sufficient subjective element; as with § 33 it is enough if the purpose is part of a motive cluster.[73] The courts also require D to exert due diligence as to possible other avenues and the proportionality elements,[74] yet Lenckner and Perron are correct when they point out that it is difficult to see how omitting this exercise of diligence should make a difference if in fact D arrives at the right conclusion; where it may make a difference is with the question about the avoidability of an error under § 35(2).[75]

According to the structure of the law, if the criteria of § 35(1) 1st sentence are met, D acts without guilt and this privilege is then excluded by the second sentence related to legitimately expected alternative options. Yet, as we saw above, the proportionality elements within the phrase 'cannot otherwise be averted' already include the same connotations, so the function of the second sentence is not as important as the wording might suggest. It merely highlights some examples of the general principle, and it is not exhaustive, either, meaning that there may be reasons why D has to suffer the danger other than the ones mentioned expressly (as is made clear by the use of the words 'in particular').

The first alternative, that D cannot rely on duress if she caused the danger herself, is worded unfortunately because the element of 'causing' the danger would also apply in the case of witness D who makes a truthful incriminating statement in court and then is threatened by the accused to withdraw her testimony in the next hearing or face grave consequences.[76] The mere causation element must thus be augmented by an element of moral blameworthiness, ie whether D caused the danger knowingly or recklessly *and* without good reason in that she would have had to realise that she would not then later escape the materialising danger unless she herself caused harm or damage to others.[77]

---

[72] See the House of Lords decision in *Hasan* [2005] UKHL 22, as per Lord Bingham at [38]:

'The policy of the law must be to discourage association with known criminals, and it should be slow to excuse the criminal conduct of those who do so. If a person voluntarily becomes or remains associated with others engaged in criminal activity in a situation where he knows or ought reasonably to know that he may be the subject of compulsion by them or their associates, he cannot rely on the defence of duress to excuse any act which he is thereafter compelled to do by them.'

[73] BGHSt 3, 275.
[74] BGHSt 18, 311; BGH NStZ 1992, 487.
[75] Sch/Sch-Lenckner/Perron, § 35, Mn. 16–17.
[76] Example used by Sch/Sch-Lenckner/Perron, § 35, Mn. 20.
[77] Sch/Sch-Lenckner/Perron, § 35, Mn. 20.

The BGH recognised this blameworthiness in the attempt by D, who had previously fled into West Germany without his family, to bring his family out of the former GDR, because D had to realise that armed border guards would in all likelihood try to stop him and them by the use of (deadly) force. D and his family when trying to flee through a tunnel dug for that purpose happened upon a GDR soldier who stopped them and wanted to check their identity. The soldier neither knew that D carried a gun nor had he already trained his own rifle on D. D shot him in order to complete the escape with his family. The BGH refused D the avenue of § 35 and even on the appeal by a relative of the soldier revised D's conviction by the trial court from murder under § 212 to aggravated murder under § 211 because D had acted insidiously[78] by shooting the unsuspecting soldier without warning. Given that D and his family were exercising the fundamental human right of freedom of movement and to a joint family life, and seeing that the case law of the BGH itself had always characterised the GDR border regime as a serious violation of that human right which even made the statutory GDR law partially void under the *Radbruch* formula, it is difficult to see where D acted unreasonably, even though he went back to the GDR and thereby exposed himself to danger, and whether the fact that he carried the gun made that much of a difference. The consequence of the BGH's view would be that D's family would have had to stay in the GDR and make the futile attempt of obtaining a permit to leave the GDR through the usual administrative channels,[79] thereby possibly inviting the unwelcome attention of the state security police which was not unlikely given that D was a so-called 'republic deserter' (*Republikflüchtling*).

The second alternative requires D to suffer the danger if he is under a legal obligation to do so. This should not be confused with the material duty to act vis-à-vis a specific person as used in the context of omission offences; what is meant here are those cases where a person has taken over[80] a position or office based on which she is generally obliged by the law regulating the exercise of that office to protect

[78] BGH NJW 2000, 3079. However, the BGH gave D the benefit of § 17 and accepted that he had been in a tragic situation which, although not enough to warrant the application of § 35 as an excusatory defence, had a heavy impact on sentencing, combined with the fact that the offence had happened 40 years ago. D was given a one-year suspended sentence.

[79] Turned on its head, if D *had* been shot by the soldier, the BGH's argument could almost lead one to say that D was acting in knowing self-endangerment which might even relieve the soldier of liability for shooting her. Because of the informed and deliberate *novus actus* through human agency (the *soldier* was in full control of the situation, not D) one would probably not reach that conclusion, yet the same reasoning would become more difficult if it was not a soldier but a minefield that D had to walk across in order to cross the border, if D knew of that fact: here it is definitely *only* D who is in control of the events and who is knowingly risking life and limb.

[80] The rule also applies to persons who have to suffer certain infringements of their rights on the basis of official legal acts, such as prisoners who have been convicted and sentenced, or car drivers who may be subjected to a legitimate taking of a blood sample under § 81a StPO. See Sch/Sch-Lenckner/Perron, § 35, Mn. 24. § 35 remains a problem, however, for the case of D who has been imprisoned (maybe even for life) after a fully lawful and fair trial and after exhaustion of all appeals, but who is in fact innocent. German law would probably countenance giving D the benefit of duress if she tried to escape from prison and, eg took one of the prison guards hostage for that purpose. See for references to the legislative *travaux préparatoires* Sch/Sch-Lenckner/Perron, § 35, Mn. 26.

individuals and the common good, such as, for example, police officers, firemen, soldiers, civil servants, doctors and medical personnel of hospitals, sailors, flying staff in airplanes, etc.[81] The exact scope of the obligation must be found through reference to the purpose of the respective office and the dangers typically connected with its exercise; there is no general duty identical to all of these positions.[82]

In the case of third persons with whom D has a special close relationship or who are relatives of his, the special obligation can have harsh consequences: if D is under one of these obligations and the dangers he is meant to accept under it also involve T who is his daughter, the duty to suffer the danger takes precedence, which in effect imposes on T a burden of suffering that danger, too, or at least expecting no privileged help from D. An example to clarify this: D is a fireman and is called to a fire which threatens several persons inside a house, one of whom is his 10-year-old daughter T, whom he knows is visiting there. He cannot find her immediately, but there are other inhabitants that (only) he can reach easily and take to safety. D is not covered by § 35 if he searches the house for T instead of rescuing the others.

Conversely, if it is T who is under a special obligation, D will not be able to rely on § 35 if she tries to keep T out of harm arising from the obligations. An example would be that of T, a professional soldier in the German Armed Forces on his way to a trouble region in Afghanistan, when T's mother D commits an act under § 109[83] to prevent him from having to go.[84] The law recognises some of these difficulties in the context of specific offences such as perjury[85] or assistance in avoiding punishment or prosecution.[86] Yet, under general principles of interpretation, the fact that there are specific rules for some scenarios militates in favour of a restrictive construction of § 35.

[81] See the examples listed at Sch/Sch-Lenckner/Perron, § 35, Mn. 23.
[82] BGH NJW 1964, 730.
[83] '§ 109 Avoiding draft by mutilation

(1) Whosoever through mutilation or by other means, renders himself or another person with that person's consent, or causes himself or another person to be rendered unfit for military service, shall be liable to imprisonment from three months to five years.
(2) If the offender causes the unfitness only for a certain period of time or for a certain type of duty, the penalty shall be imprisonment of not more than five years or a fine.'

[84] See on this Sch/Sch-Lenckner/Perron, § 35, Mn. 27–9.
[85] '§ 157 Duress

(1) If a witness or an expert has perjured himself or given false unsworn testimony, the court in its discretion may mitigate the sentence (§ 49(2)) or in the case of unsworn testimony order a discharge, if the offender told a lie in order to avert from a relative or himself a danger of being punished or subjected to a custodial measure of rehabilitation and incapacitation.
(2) The court in its discretion may also mitigate the sentence (§ 49(2)) or order a discharge if a person not yet competent to take an oath has given false unsworn testimony.'

[86] '§ 258 Assistance in avoiding prosecution or punishment

. . .

(5) Whosoever by the offence simultaneously intends to avoid, in whole or in part, his own punishment or being subjected to a measure or that a sentence or measure imposed on him be enforced shall not be liable under this provision.
(6) Whosoever commits the offence for the benefit of a relative shall be exempt from liability.'

D may also have to suffer the danger if it can be legitimately expected for other reasons, because the two alternatives mentioned are, as we saw, only examples and not an exhaustive list. Examples for further reasons include:

a) duties to act arising from the categories explained in the context of omissions liability;
b) duties to suffer an infringement of one's own rights based on another person's acting in the exercise of a justificatory defence such as self-defence or necessity;
c) if the harm to another is out of proportion to that threatening D;
d) the degree of the danger to D; and
e) if the chances of success of the rescue action are questionable and there is a high likelihood that it may cause further harm.[87]

Note the harsh sentencing rule that the possible reduction of the sentence under § 49(1) does not apply if D had to suffer the danger; his difficult position may only be considered as a general sentencing factor within the regular sentencing scale. If at the time of the commission of the act D mistakenly assumes that circumstances exist which would excuse him under § 35(1), ie he assumes that there is a danger, or he does not know that he caused it himself or is under an obligation to suffer it, he will not be liable if the mistake was unavoidable. Otherwise, his sentence will be mitigated pursuant to § 49(1). If D otherwise exceeds the ambit of the permissible reaction under § 35(1), he will not be exempt from liability; § 33 does not apply by analogy. Errors by D about the fact that an emergency exists at all or its actual circumstances, for example that D wrongly thinks he may have caused it, are not regulated in § 35; the same applies to a mistake about the legal boundaries of § 35 (for example, if D thinks that danger to property was sufficient). Their treatment is controversial: while the second sort is generally seen as irrelevant, the first category may in some cases benefit from the general principle underlying the mitigation made possible by § 35(2) 2nd sentence, 2nd alternative.[88] If only one of several participants to an offence acts under duress, § 29 states that this will not affect the liability of the others, but it may have an impact on their sentencing.

Supra-legal Duress?

Although not yet recognised by the courts, the prevailing opinion in the literature supports the recognition of a defence of so-called supra-legal duress (*übergesetzlicher entschuldigender Notstand*). This is meant to cover cases that are not within the remit of either § 34, because the interests cannot be quantified, such as, for example, human lives, or of § 35, the latter because the danger is to legal interests not covered in § 35 or to persons other than relatives and close friends, etc. The cases envisaged by the proponents of the supra-legal duress idea are to a large

---

[87] See on all of these with references to case law and literature Sch/Sch-Lenckner/Perron, § 35, Mn. 33–5.
[88] See for these problems the references at Sch/Sch-Lenckner/Perron, § 35, Mn. 38–45.

extent based on conflicts of conscience and religious freedom. The development of this concept arose partially from the post-war euthanasia trials, where, for example, doctors had been forced to decide whether to cooperate to a certain extent with the NS authorities in the concentration camps in the selection of mentally ill patients who were destined to be killed, and to save as many of them as possible, or to refuse to participate in the selection and risk that colleagues without similar scruples would take their place and apply a much harsher practice. The courts tried to acknowledge the dilemma of the doctors who participated by holding that there was a general exemption from liability (*Strafausschließungsgrund*)[89] or by arguing a mistake of law.[90] It is clear that in such cases one moves at the limits of what the administration of criminal justice is capable of doing in supporting and affirming the societal moral consensus, yet one will also understand the need of relatives or of survivors for a judicial closure to their indescribable ordeals.[91] Especially in the case of human lives, the development of this concept is a direct consequence of the traditional refusal in German case law and literature to subscribe to the idea that lives can in extreme cases be counted.[92] Manuel Ladiges has recently argued in a very perceptive paper that it is time to reconsider this stance[93] based on the 9/11 scenario and similar cases where a choice *has* to be made in practice; in it he mentions the current German Minister for Defence, Franz Josef Jung, who despite the above-mentioned judgment of the BVerfG on the Air Traffic Security Act and the general restrictions it placed on the use of the military in such situations, maintains that he would order the use of military force to shoot down even a commercial plane, especially if there were only terrorists on board, and was vilified for this in the political arena. Given that the German politicians have at the time of writing still not come up with a sorely needed replacement for the quashed legislation, I feel his stance at least deserves more moral respect than the dithering and procrastination of those who conveniently hide behind the BVerfG and simply wait until the next incident; what their reaction would be if and when a major loss of life occurs as in New York on that day and no action to shoot the plane down was taken is open to question. I have addressed some of these issues in chapter five under necessity; for the intricate discussion in the German literature in detail, the interested reader must be referred to the commentaries[94] for reasons of space.

---

[89] OGHSt 1, 335; 2, 126.

[90] BGH NJW 1953, 513.

[91] For a fascinating and deeply moving account of those times, the unimaginable suffering of the victims on the one hand, and an unusually forgiving attitude towards his previous oppressors on the other, see the book by the American Judge on the International Court of Justice, Thomas Buergenthal, who as a child survived the German concentration camps: *Ein Glückskind* (Frankfurt, Fischer Verlag, 2007).

[92] See the arguments at Sch/Sch-Lenckner, Vorbem §§ 32 *ff*, Mn. 116.

[93] See his article online at <http://www.zis-online.com/dat/artikel/2008_3_220.pdf> accessed 30 June 2008.

[94] Sch/Sch-Lenckner, Vorbem §§ 32 *ff*, Mn. 115–21.

Insanity

D will also be acting without guilt if he can successfully plead the full defence[95] of insanity. Insanity under § 20, as already alluded to, is a different concept from the one used in England and Wales, and it is closely linked to the defence of diminished responsibility under § 21, which again contrasts with the English position in that it applies to all offences across the board, but as a mere sentencing factor. It is therefore helpful to present both provisions together and merely address a few specific issues on § 21 under a separate heading.

§ 20 Insanity

Any person who at the time of the commission of the offence is incapable of appreciating the unlawfulness of their actions or of acting in accordance with any such appreciation due to a pathological mental disorder, a profound consciousness disorder, debility or any other serious mental abnormality, shall be deemed to act without guilt.

§ 21 Diminished responsibility

If the capacity of the offender to appreciate the unlawfulness of his actions or to act in accordance with any such appreciation is substantially diminished at the time of the commission of the offence due to one of the reasons indicated in § 20, the sentence may be mitigated pursuant to § 49(1).

The rule with adult offenders is that their sanity will be assumed unless there are facts that give rise to some doubt. This, to repeat, does not mean that D is under any burden of proof, evidential or probative, with regard to establishing his insanity or diminished responsibility. It is the task of the prosecution and, more to the point, the court, under § 244(2) of the Code of Criminal Procedure, to clear up the question regarding D's alleged insanity. The level needed to establish it is a balance of probabilities to the degree that the court cannot safely exclude the possibility that D was insane at the time of the offence. As in England, deciding such issues will in the

---

[95] However, in cases of dangerous offenders, certain measures of rehabilitation and incapacitation may be ordered: see, eg:

'§ 63 Mental hospital order

If a person has committed an unlawful act in a state of insanity (§ 20) or diminished responsibility (§ 21) the court shall make a mental hospital order if a comprehensive evaluation of the offender and the act leads to the conclusion that as a result of his condition, future serious unlawful acts can be expected of him and that he therefore presents a danger to the general public.

§ 64 Custodial addiction treatment order

If a person has an addiction to alcohol or other drugs and is convicted of an unlawful act committed while he was intoxicated or as a result of his addiction, or is not convicted only because he has been found to be insane or insanity cannot be excluded on the evidence, the court shall make a custodial addiction treatment order if there is a danger that he will commit future serious unlawful acts as a consequence of his addiction.

Such order shall not be made unless ab initio there is a sufficiently certain prospect of success that the person can be healed by way of custodial addiction treatment or that a relapse into addictive behaviour and the commission of serious unlawful acts caused by that addiction can be prevented for a substantial period of time.'

majority of cases require the aid of an (in Germany: court-appointed) expert. Another major difference to the English approach that needs to be pointed out again at this stage is the fact that intoxication is not a separate defence, but a subcategory of §§ 20 and 21, and at least within the defence of § 20 it is entirely irrelevant whether or not the intoxication was voluntary; as we will see under § 21, the voluntariness may have a consequence for the sentencing, but not for the establishment of diminished responsibility as such. Similar comments can be made for acts based on extreme provocation which would fall under a separate defence in English law.

The basic structure of both defences is that the criteria set out in § 20, to which we will turn presently, must lead to D's being incapable either of appreciating the unlawfulness of her actions or of acting in accordance with any such appreciation.

These two states, which are reminiscent of the *M'Naghten Rule*,[96] cannot occur cumulatively.[97] If D cannot appreciate the unlawfulness in the first place, it is illogical to say that he cannot act in accordance with that appreciation as well. The two criteria are the actual central problems of the defence, because based on the expert evidence with regard to the mental states the court must decide, again maybe with the aid of an expert, whether or not these criteria are met; judicial experience leads to the realisation that in the majority of all cases the answer is more likely to be one of reasonable doubt than of positive affirmation, although strictly speaking the very question of whether D could appreciate the unlawfulness or act on that appreciation is considered to be a question of law based on a comparison of the normal standards of behaviour with the abnormal, which as such would exclude the use of the *in dubio pro reo* principle.[98] While it is true that one is comparing standards, it does not necessarily follow that they are normative in the sense of legal-normative standards, or whether they are not more like mere brackets of expected behaviour within an empirical framework based on an average drawn from the cases actually studied by psychological science or psychiatry. One might thus at least argue that it is a mixed question of fact and law.

§ 20 lists the following categories of mental disturbances in the wider meaning that can be a basis for a claim of insanity in law:

a) a pathological mental disorder (*krankhafte seelische Störung*);
b) a profound consciousness disorder (*tiefgreifende Bewußtseinsstörung*);
c) debility (*Schwachsinn*); or
d) any other serious mental abnormality (*schwere seelische Abartigkeit*).

It is generally irrelevant whether the disturbance is permanent, intermittent or temporary, as long as it affected the offender at the time of his actions that are the basis of the criminal liability.[99] In fact, some of them may only be imaginable in a temporary fashion, for example, those based on alcohol and drug abuse or extreme affect. In principle, these four categories, particularly the first one, are meant as

---

[96] *M'Naghtens Case* (1843) 10 Cl & Fin 200.
[97] Consistent case law of the BGH: BGHSt 21, 27; BGH NStZ 1982, 201; 1991, 529; 2000, 578.
[98] Sch/Sch-Lenckner/Perron, § 20, Mn. 43.
[99] Sch/Sch-Lenckner/Perron, § 20, Mn. 5 for the first category.

disturbances that start from a 'biological' basis, for example, a disease or illness (*krankhaft*), disorder or abnormality, and have their impact on the 'mental' level, yet how far this dichotomy, if there is one at all, can actually be maintained is open to question. The wording of § 20, especially the last category, is wide enough to catch all the relevant mental states.[100] One has to remember that § 20 is concerned with making psychological phenomena usable for the legal process; as with causation, for example, the meaning of the concepts need not and sometimes cannot be the same in both law and science. It is, for example, also recognised that medical and psychiatric research has not yet found a physical cause for many of the disturbances that occur in the daily practice of the courts, and that even in medical science there is no consensus as to what constitutes an 'illness' within the meaning of the word *krankhaft*.[101] The topic is extremely wide and as far as the psychiatric side is concerned it would merit a book on its own. For the purpose of obtaining an impression in the context of an introduction to the general principles it may, however, be best to give examples for each of the categories.

*Pathological Mental Disorder (*Krankhafte Seelische Störung*)*[102]

Exogenous Psychosis

This refers to physical cerebral traumata; infection-based psychosis; genuine epilepsy; dementia; cerebral arteriosclerosis or cerebral atrophy; and cerebral damage caused by excessive substance abuse.

Endogenous Psychosis

This refers to schizophrenia and manic depression.

*Profound Consciousness Disorder (*Tiefgreifende Bewußtseinsstörung*)*[103]

Affect

An explosive reaction based on an extreme emotional state where no deliberate decision-making occurs anymore, for example, extreme rage, hate, shock, panic or fear. Some instances of battered-woman syndrome and generally provocation can be caught under this category. The question of whether affect is excluded as a defence if it had been caused by D is controversial; the prevailing opinion would appear to do so, yet the courts have recently become more reluctant in their approach.

---

[100] See Sch/Sch-Lenckner/Perron, § 20, Mn. 1 and 5.
[101] Sch/Sch-Lenckner/Perron, § 20, Mn. 9–10.
[102] See the references to case law and literature at Sch/Sch-Lenckner/Perron, § 20, Mn. 11–11a.
[103] See the references to case law and literature at Sch/Sch-Lenckner/Perron, § 20, Mn. 12–17.

Intoxication[104]

As previously mentioned, the question of whether D voluntarily intoxicated himself is irrelevant for insanity. As far as the concept of the *actio libera in causa* (D himself, while in a state of full mental control, causes the state of insanity to occur either in the knowledge of or with negligence with regard to a potential offence occurring in that state) is still applicable after the landmark decision of the BGH[105] in which the court doubted the constitutionality of that judge-made institution, D can still be liable even if he acted in a state of insanity.[106] The main criterion for insanity by intoxication is in practice the blood-alcohol concentration determined by an expert. If the value is 3.0 and more, the courts will as a rule accept the defence unless there are other factors that justify the assumption that despite that high level of alcohol, D was still capable of understanding what he or she was doing or of acting on that understanding. This may be a factor with defendants who are used to drinking large amounts of alcohol. A level of 2.0 and above will usually lead to diminished responsibility, and in between those two the circumstances of the individual case will determine the outcome of whether § 20 or 21 will apply. For intoxication by drugs other than alcohol, no such simple measure exists and the courts will refer to the question of whether D was on overdose or in withdrawal; during the normal saturation phase the use of drugs is generally considered to be irrelevant.

Debility (Schwachsinn)[107]

This category is a special case of the fourth and covers solely the retarded development of intelligence in its different stages of idiocy, imbecility and moronity.

---

[104] Note that in certain circumstances D may be liable under § 323 a for putting himself in a drunken state, *not* for the offence committed while drunk:

'§ 323a Committing offences in a senselessly drunken state

(1) Whosoever intentionally or negligently puts himself into a drunken state by consuming alcoholic beverages or other intoxicants shall be liable to imprisonment of not more than five years or a fine if he commits an unlawful act while in this state and may not be punished because of it because he was insane due to the intoxication or if this cannot be excluded.

(2) The penalty must not be more severe than the penalty provided for the offence which was committed while he was in the drunken state.

(3) The offence may only be prosecuted upon request, authorisation or upon request by a foreign state if the act committed in the drunken state may only be prosecuted upon complaint, authorisation or upon request by a foreign state.'

[105] BGHSt 42, 235.

[106] See on the discussion regarding the *actio libera in causa* the references to case law and literature at Sch/Sch-Lenckner/Perron, § 20, Mn. 33–42.

[107] See the references to case law and literature at Sch/Sch-See the references to case law and literature at Sch/Sch-Lenckner/Perron, § 20, Mn. 18.

Other Serious Mental Abnormality (Schwere Seelische Abartigkeit)[108]

Under this heading, we find all those mental states that are not caught by the other three categories and especially those which do not fall under the meaning of *krankhaft* within the first category, but are of a similar gravity. Examples include personality disorders, neuroses, deviations and perversions, alcoholism and drug addiction (as opposed to actual alcohol and drug use during a specific offence, which falls under the second group).

Diminished Responsibility

§ 21 is based on the same structure as § 20, with the only difference that D's capabilities of appreciation or acting on the same must not be excluded, but merely severely impaired. All of the above on the different categories within § 20 also applies, therefore, to § 21. It is not a material defence in the strict meaning of the word, but a sentencing provision that leads to a *facultative* shift in the sentencing scale according to § 49(1) within the discretion of the judge. It applies to all offences. Compared to the English approach under *Majewski* for intoxication, it is interesting to see that while the law does not require it, the courts have regularly used the fact that D was voluntarily intoxicated as a reason to deny the mitigation under § 49(1),[109] especially if D had a proclivity of committing offences while intoxicated and if he was aware of that.[110] Note that none of this applies without further consideration if D suffered from chronic alcoholism or other disorders that had an impact on his freedom of choice or which combined with the use of alcohol led to the state of § 21.[111]

---

[108] See the references to case law and literature at Sch/Sch-Lenckner/Perron, § 20, Mn. 19–24.
[109] BGHSt 43, 77.
[110] BGHSt 34, 33; BGH NStZ 2004, 495; 2005, 151 and with slight modifications BGH NJW 2004, 3350.
[111] Sch/Sch-Lenckner/Perron, § 21, Mn. 20 with further references.

7

Attempts

German criminal law recognises liability for attempt in certain cases. As was mentioned in chapter two, under § 23(1) the attempt of a *Verbrechen* is always punishable, that of a *Vergehen* only if the Special Part states so explicitly. As § 23(3) makes clear, the liability also extends to impossible attempts. Attempts under German law are not inchoate offences[1] in their own right as under English law, because an offender can withdraw from an attempt, with some exceptions, with the consequence of a full acquittal unless in the course of the attempt he already completed another, possibly lesser included offence, such as, for example, causing bodily harm to V in the course of a later abandoned murder attempt. The dispute about the underlying rationale for attempt liability is still not quite settled: older theories operated from the point of view of the endangerment of the attacked interest,[2] whereas others see D's hostile attitude towards the law (*rechtsfeindliche Gesinnung*) as the doctrinal basis;[3] a third and intermediate opinion stresses the impression D's actions make on society as a whole[4] and accepts a reason for penalisation if the actions are capable of shattering society's trust in the existence of the legal order. Not many answers to practical questions will depend on which view one follows, but it may have an impact on interpretation in some areas. Today it is commonly accepted that an attempt can be committed by omission.[5] The general law relating to attempts is regulated in §§ 22 to 24:

---

[1] One might argue that the so-called *Unternehmensdelikte*, as was mentioned in the chapter on the *Tatbestand*, have a similar function as the English inchoate offences. Interestingly, it is accepted that some of these offences which often penalise merely preparatory acts that would otherwise under general rules not even rise to an attempt on the legal interest they are meant to protect, can be attempted themselves, as was decided by the BGH for the offence of § 96, treasonous espionage, in BGHSt 6, 387. § 96 reads as follows:

> '§ 96 Treasonous espionage; spying on state secrets
>
> (1) Whosoever obtains a state secret in order to disclose it (§ 94) shall be liable to imprisonment from one to ten years.
> (2) Whosoever obtains a state secret which has been kept secret by an official agency or at its behest in order to disclose it (§ 95) shall be liable to imprisonment from six months to five years. The attempt shall be punishable.'

[2] Compare, eg RGSt 68, 340.
[3] RGSt 1, 441; 8, 203; 34, 21 and BGHSt 11, 268.
[4] See for an overview Sch/Sch-Eser, Vorbem § 22, Mn. 22, who claims that this view is now the majority opinion.
[5] OGHSt 1, 359; and for derivative omission offences BGHSt 38, 358; 40, 270; BGH NStZ 1997, 485.

§ 22 Definition

A person attempts to commit an offence if he takes steps which will immediately lead to the completion of the offence as envisaged by him.

§ 23 Liability for attempt

(1) Any attempt to commit a felony entails criminal liability; this applies to attempted misdemeanours only if expressly so provided by law.
(2) An attempt may be punished more leniently than the completed offence (§ 49(1)).
(3) If the offender due to gross ignorance fails to realise that the attempt could under no circumstances have led to the completion of the offence due to the nature of its object or the means by which it was to be committed, the court may order a discharge, or mitigate the sentence as it sees fit (§ 49(2)).

§ 24 Withdrawal

(1) A person who of his own volition gives up the further execution of the offence or prevents its completion shall not be liable for the attempt. If the offence is not completed regardless of his actions, that person shall not be liable if he has made a voluntary and earnest effort to prevent the completion of the offence.
(2) If more than one person participate in the offence, the person who voluntarily prevents its completion shall not be liable for the attempt. His voluntary and earnest effort to prevent the completion of the offence shall suffice for exemption from liability, if the offence is not completed regardless of his actions or is committed independently of his earlier contribution to the offence.

There are now a number of special withdrawal provisions tied to specific offences or categories of offences in the Special Part that do not completely match the general rules and additionally allow the court to consider a reduction in sentence, for example, §§ 83a,[6] 264(5),[7] etc. For reasons of space, we will not look closely at these here, but restrict ourselves to the more important principles of the General Part,[8] also

[6] Relates to offences of treason:

'§ 83a Preventing completion of offence

(1) In cases under § 81 and § 82 the court in its discretion may mitigate the sentence (§ 49(2)) or order a discharge if the offender voluntarily gives up the further commission of the offence and averts or substantially lessens any danger known to him that others will continue with the commission or if he voluntarily prevents the completion of the offence.
(2) In cases under § 83 the court may proceed according to subsection (1) above if the offender voluntarily gives up his plan and averts or substantially lessens a danger known and caused by him that others will further prepare or continue with the commission or if he voluntarily prevents the completion of the offence.
(3) If the danger is averted or substantially lessened or the completion of the offence is prevented regardless of the contribution of the offender his voluntary and earnest effort to avert or lessen the danger or to prevent the completion of the offence shall suffice.'

[7] Relates to offence of subsidy fraud:

'(5) Whosoever voluntarily prevents the granting of a subsidy on the basis of the offence shall not be liable pursuant to subsections (1) and (4) above. If the subsidy is not granted regardless of the contribution of the offender he shall be exempt from liability if he voluntarily and earnestly makes efforts to prevent the subsidy from being granted.'

[8] See for a brief discussion and further references Sch/Sch-Eser, § 24, Mn. 116–21.

bearing in mind that the relationship between the General Part and those specific withdrawal provisions is partly controversial. As we will see in chapter eight, there is a special rule for conspiracy-like constellations of attempted participation in §§ 30 and 31, which will be treated there.

The Definition of Attempt

§ 22 provides that an attempt occurs if D 'takes steps which will immediately lead to the completion of the offence as envisaged by him'. This phrase contains two important statements: first, that there must be a degree of imminence about D's actions leading to the commission of the offence; and, secondly, that it is D's plan or expectation of the course of his actions that defines the attempted act, in other words, his subjective horizon is of great importance. This shows also in the practical application of attempt law when courts start the examination of whether an attempt was committed not with the *objektiver Tatbestand* or *actus reus*, but with the intent of the offender. The intention of the offender decides whether she has begun with the execution of the offence or is about to do so because an attempt by definition requires absence of the full *actus reus* so one only has the state of the offender's mind to rely on in order to determine what offence was going to be committed and how. An example: D wants to appropriate V's handbag and in order to do so she moves close behind V in a queue at the counter of a self-service restaurant. If she intends to rip the bag from V's hands while they are both standing in the queue, she will be attempting a robbery, if she plans to wait for a moment of carelessness on V's part when she puts down the bag to pay for her food and then to grab the bag, she will be attempting a mere theft. Until the moment when she actually does something, we have only her intention to tell us about the attempted offence.

Bearing in mind what we just said about the importance of the intention, we will have to begin with an objective part of the concept of attempt, the lack of full completion of the offence—otherwise there would be no reason to talk about attempt. The full *Tatbestand* may not be completed for objective or subjective reasons:[9] D may try to shoot V but misses her, or she may try to steal a wrist-watch she believes belongs to her brother V, whereas in reality it belongs to herself. The subjective side of the *Tatbestand* may be missing because D is mistaken about the actual causal chain that brought about a certain result. Finally, even if the *Tatbestand* has been completed, D may still only be liable for attempt if, for example, on the second tier of unlawfulness, he objectively found himself in a situation of self-defence, but did not act out of its knowledge or the will to defend, ie he lacked the subjective element of self-defence. Similar considerations may apply for the defence of consent.[10] As we will see later, if D's intended actions do not constitute

---

[9] See Sch/Sch-Eser, § 22, Mn. 6–9.
[10] See on the latter BGHSt 4, 199.

a recognised criminal offence at all, but D believes they do, we speak of an imaginary offence (*Wahndelikt*) as opposed to an impossible attempt, where D's intended actions could in theory be an offence, but for certain reasons the completion of the offence is not feasible; only the second of the two may entail criminal liability under German law. The differentiation between them is, however, not always easy.

Once we have established that a full offence has not been committed, we need to turn our attention to the intention of the offender in a twofold manner: first, there must be an unconditional[11] decision to act (*Tatentschluss*); and, secondly, of course, we need to ascertain the scope and object of that decision and any necessary other subjective offence elements.[12] In effect, this is equivalent to the *mens rea* required for the full offence.[13] D's intention must, on the cognitive side, cover all the elements of the offence, including criteria that increase the punishment.[14] There is no requirement that D acted deliberately and with planning; spontaneous ad hoc knowledge will be sufficient.[15] If D is to be held liable for the attempted murder of his daughter from drowning by omitting to exert all his diligence and efforts to save her, the court must be sure that he thought that she could still be saved in the first place.[16] On the volitive side, D must have the requisite degree of

[11] Qualms and reservations of the offender or the need to get a final push may negate that decision: RGSt 16, 135; 68, 341; 70, 203; BGH NStZ-RR 2004, 361. This scenario must, however, be distinguished from situations where D himself is fully prepared and ready to go ahead, but waits for a certain event to occur before he does so, ie an external condition such as, for example, V leaving her house so D can enter and search the house for the object he wants to steal; see BGHR § 22 Ansetzen no 25, BGH NJW 1991, 1963. The latter category also covers those cases where D enters a house in order to steal when he makes the decision what to steal dependent on what he finds. Indeed, merely examining an object as to whether it can be an adequate object for the theft can be sufficient to establish the decision to act, although it will depend on objective factors whether D has also already begun to put it into practice, see BGHSt 12, 306; 21, 17; 22, 80 and the text below.

[12] For example, for D to be liable for attempted aggravated murder under § 211, she needs to have the intent to kill V *and* act out of at least one of the subjective criteria mentioned in § 211, for example, bloodlust. If those criteria are missing, she will only be guilty of attempted murder under § 212.

[13] See for the doctrinal debate as to how far the subjective element in attempt and the intention for the offence overlap, Sch/Sch-Eser, § 22, Mn. 12–13.

[14] BGH NJW 1999, 1505.

[15] Sch/Sch-Eser, § 22, Mn. 14–15.

[16] Compare also the gruesome case of BGH NStZ 1997, 485: D, in a drunken state, had had an altercation with his partner V; V fled into the bathroom of their flat and hid herself in a niche of the room. D then pushed her down into a sitting position in that niche so that several parts of her body touched the central heating attached to the wall, which was running at its full temperature of about 80°C in the boiler. D then tore off the thermostat to prevent V from turning down the temperature and left V in her plight. A few hours later, D tried to free V who by now could not help herself anymore, and to refit the thermostat, but to no avail. Instead of going for help he just went to bed. The next morning he found her in the same position, by now she was fatally hurt due to the heat she had been exposed to all night, which D apparently realised. An expert had testified at the trial that V could not have been saved anymore at that time. D, however, went out of the house and only a few hours later could V be extricated from the corner after a neighbour who had heard V's cries had insisted and pleaded with D to let help into the flat. V died two days later. The BGH quashed the conviction for bodily harm causing death and false imprisonment on the appeal by the prosecution and remanded the case to the trial court for retrial on the issue of what D's knowledge or assertions were at all times and whether he might not have been liable for attempted murder by omission depending on whether he thought that V might die unless he did something, even if only under conditional intent.

intent demanded by the offence in question;[17] this may be as little as conditional intent, or *dolus eventualis*.[18] This is different from the approach of English law where the parallel problem of recklessness in attempt has been solved in so far as recklessness can only apply to cognitive elements, but not to volitive ones which require full intent.[19]

D must, as § 22 says, take 'steps which will immediately lead to the completion of the offence'; this is the German equivalent to 'more than merely preparatory' under English and Welsh law, and as is the latter, so is the German formula fraught with definitional difficulties. The only thing that one can be certain of these days[20] is that this sort of imminence does not require that one of the elements of the *Tatbestand* has already been fulfilled.[21] Indeed, in the case of murder, such a restrictive approach would make an attempt conceptually impossible, because the only element is causing V's death. For the debate as to what is meant by D's '*unmittelbares Ansetzen*' (being on the immediate verge of committing the offence), the general rule appears to be that the closer D's actions come to causing the actual result intended by him, the more likely it is that the courts will find it to be sufficient. However, even an act that would normally qualify as constituting an element of an offence may not be sufficient if the temporal relationship to the final result is too tenuous: if D untruthfully tells V that he is a wealthy businessman in order to gain V's trust, which he intends to exploit later by making a fraudulent business proposition to V, then this first deception will not be sufficient to constitute *unmittelbares Ansetzen* for the fraud under § 263 intended by the business proposition.[22] In case of so-called *mehraktige Delikte* or combined offences,[23] which require several successive acts by D, it will usually be enough if D fulfils the first act but does not manage to carry out the full offence. In rape, for example, it is sufficient for D to be liable under attempt if he uses force against V in order to subdue her even if after that he does not succeed in having intercourse with her.[24] There have been several theories put forward to arrive at a satisfactory definition of when D's acts come close enough to the critical threshold,[25] with the somewhat disappointing, if not in such a highly doctrinal context actually comical, result that

---

[17] For example, the special intention to shield an offender from prosecution or punishment in § 258, see OLG Hamm NJW 2004, 1189.

[18] RGSt 61, 160; BGHSt 22, 332; 31, 378; BGH NStZ 1985, 501;1997, 485.

[19] See, eg *Khan* [1990] 2 All ER 783 (CA).

[20] See for the older view, eg RGSt 70, 157: deception offences can only be attempted once the offender has engaged in the act meant to deceive the victim.

[21] BGHSt 37, 297; 48, 35 and the discussion at Sch/Sch-Eser, § 22, Mn. 24–45.

[22] OLG Karlsruhe NJW 1982, 59; BGHSt 37, 294.

[23] For the so-called result-qualified offences and codified sentencing factors (*Regelbeispiele*), the prevailing view is now that D must have begun with the execution of the entire *Tatbestand*, which means that merely fulfilling an element that increases the sentence will not be enough if D does not also cross the threshold for the basic offence; an example is BGH NStZ 1995, 339, where the court rejected an aggravated offence attempt based on D carrying a firearm if D had to cross another 200 metres to his car to get the weapon. See generally Sch/Sch-Eser, § 22, Mn. 58.

[24] Similar arguments can be made for robbery as a combination of use of force and theft. Compare RGSt 69, 327.

[25] See Sch/Sch-Eser, § 22, Mn. 24–45.

the courts now even employ a formula like '*Jetzt geht's los!*', ie 'Here we go!', and similarly more or less circuitous phrases in order to describe when D is passing the threshold.[26] Yet, for our purposes it may be more useful to employ an illustrative approach and see what the courts have or have not accepted as constituting *unmittelbares Ansetzen*—we will find that the vague immediacy or imminence qualifier has also found its way into some of the case law definitions and that clear dividing lines rarely exist.

The courts have held that D had crossed the threshold to attempt liability in the following cases:

a) pulling out a gun with the intention of shooting immediately[27] or pointing the gun at V, even if it was not yet cocked;[28]
b) pursuing V with a weapon;[29]
c) asking V to be let into the house in order to carry out a clandestine theft (notorious cases of tricking old people)[30] or ringing the bell on V's door whom D intends to rob;[31]
d) lying in wait in V's corridor or rooms if D thinks that V will appear at any moment;[32]
e) a pick-pocket in a crowd putting his hand between people in order to reach into their pockets;[33]
f) fixing steel girders to railroad tracks in order to block the rail traffic;[34]
g) checking in luggage that contains illegal drugs in order to import them at the destination, unless there is a delay between check-in and departure of several days,[35] similarly nearing a border customs office by car or even having passed the last exit from the motorway before the border;[36]
h) closing a contract to obtain illegal drugs unless the drugs are not going to be handed over directly;[37] and
i) installing an ignition-triggered explosive device in V's car if D knows that the driver of the car will show up very soon.[38]

---

[26] eg BGHSt 26, 203; 28, 164; 37, 297; 40, 268; 48, 36. It is actually very difficult to explain this concept because it is highly abstract and the use of other words that merely are another way of saying the same thing is not the same as breaking the concept down into its constituent parts if there are no words for them. This will apply to any language to more or less the same degree, given that German is already a highly complex and diverse language—yet we still do not manage to achieve an acceptable result.
[27] BGH NStZ 1993, 133.
[28] RGSt 59, 386; 77, 1. RGSt 68, 336 even accepted the act of merely grabbing the gun.
[29] RG JW 1925, 1495.
[30] BGH MDR 1985, 627.
[31] BGHSt 26, 201; 39, 238.
[32] RGSt 77, 1.
[33] BGH MDR 1958, 12.
[34] BGHSt 44, 34.
[35] BGH NJW 1990, 2072.
[36] OLG Düsseldorf MDR 1994, 1235; BGHSt 36, 249.
[37] BGHSt 40, 31.
[38] BGHSt 44, 91.

The courts have rejected an attempt in the cases below:

a) poisoning a guard dog on the grounds of V's estate if D intends to enter into V's house at another location of the estate;[39]
b) merely lying in wait for V, unless D expects her to appear within a few moments;[40]
c) HIV-positive D asking V for unprotected intercourse;[41]
d) disposing of an insured object in order to declare it as stolen to the insurance company later;[42]
e) ringing the bell at V's door if D first intends to establish homosexual contacts or merely wants to find out whether V is at home, before robbing V later as intended;[43]
f) if D prepares the location of a bank for a robbery meant to take place the next day,[44] or bank robbers parking the getaway car in front of the bank without having got out the guns and put on their masks;[45] and
g) entering a supermarket with a hidden gun, and before putting on the mask.[46]

These examples show that the temporal element, combined with the question of whether D still needs to take another decision before embarking on a certain course of action, play a large role in deciding whether or not the Rubicon to attempt liability has been crossed.

Omission offences pose a special problem in the context of the *unmittelbares Ansetzen*, as opinion is divided about when D crosses the threshold. One view puts the emphasis on the last possibility of saving the endangered interest, which brings attempt liability close to that of the full commission. Another view stresses the relevance of the first possibility to save V, as, for example, in the case where D for the first time withholds food from her daughter V in order to starve her to death;[47] this does, however, jar with the case law set out above where a protracted temporal element can exclude the *unmittelbares Ansetzen*.[48] It would appear more and more that the courts tend to subscribe to a conciliatory position between the two that refers to the point in time when the protected legal interest is actually endangered, because only then is D obliged under general principles of omission liability to act to save V.[49]

The general principles also become more complicated if it is not just one, but several persons who engage in criminal activity. When do they cross the threshold

[39] RGSt 53, 218.
[40] BGH MDR 1973, 728.
[41] BayObLG NJW 1990, 781.
[42] BGH NJW 1952, 430.
[43] BGH GA 1971, 54.
[44] BGH NStZ 2004, 38.
[45] BGH MDR 1978, 985.
[46] BGH NStZ 1996, 38.
[47] Apparently in this vein BGHSt 40, 271.
[48] See for the debate and further references Sch/Sch-Eser, § 22, Mn. 47–8.
[49] See the general discussion in BGHSt 38, 360; 40, 271 and the further references at Sch/Sch-Eser, § 22, Mn. 50–51.

to attempt liability and what effect does the *unmittelbares Ansetzen* of one of them have on the other accomplices? One will have to distinguish[50] between the cases of principal by proxy where D uses T as an instrument, joint principals where D1–D^n act on the basis of a common plan, and finally secondary participation in the form of aiding, where D intentionally assists P in her actions. A principal by proxy will now probably be seen as engaging in more than merely preparatory actions as soon as the agent T has been sent on his way, D basically having relinquished control over the instrument, if and when the release of the agent leads to an endangerment of the targeted interest.[51] The situation is different for joint principals where, based on the mutual attribution of the actions of each single accomplice to all others on the basis of the common agreement, attempt liability will be triggered for all of them as soon as the first accomplice begins with the *unmittelbares Ansetzen* on the basis of the common plan.[52] If D merely aids P, his actions providing assistance will be treated as marking the beginning of the attempt by P, even if P has not done anything herself yet, if and when D is acting on the basis of a common agreement with P, as they will then be treated similarly to joint principals. Without such an agreement, D cannot conceptually aid P until P begins with the *unmittelbares Ansetzen* herself[53] because there is no such thing as attempted aiding, only aiding P in her attempt.

Impossible Attempts and Imaginary Offences

An impossible attempt, or *untauglicher Versuch,* is an attempt that could under no circumstances have led to success; this is in contrast to the fact that many attempts fail or that the best-laid plans do sometimes go astray. An attempt may be impossible because of the qualities of either object, means or subject of the action meant to complete a criminal offence, and it bears mentioning that while the first two of these categories are accepted as leading to liability despite impossibility, the latter is controversial,[54] also because of the wording of § 23(3), which does not mention the subject, but the prevailing opinion appears to be that this category is also to be included based on doctrinal reasons.[55] The impossible attempt must be distinguished from the imaginary offence or *Wahndelikt:* while both are based on errors by the offender, the former is aimed at a result that could in theory constitute an existing criminal offence, while the latter is aimed at a result that does not, and it will not incur criminal liability.[56] Put another way and somewhat simplified, an

---

[50] See for a deeper analysis of the different types the chapter on complicity.
[51] See the discussion at Sch/Sch-Eser, § 22, Mn. 54–4a.
[52] BGHSt 36, 249; 39, 237; 40, 301 and the discussion at Sch/Sch-Eser, § 22, Mn. 55–5a.
[53] Sch/Sch-Eser, § 22, Mn. 55b.
[54] See for a discussion of the rationale behind punishing impossible attempts, Sch/Sch-Eser, § 22, Mn. 60–67a.
[55] Since RGSt 72, 112.
[56] RGSt 42, 93; 64, 239; 66, 126; BGHSt 8, 268.

impossible attempt is based on a misconception about facts, whereas an imaginary offence is based on a misconception about the law; this simple distinction breaks down, of course, when we look at normative offence elements, but it nevertheless helps as a rule of thumb. An attempted abortion, for example, may be impossible because the woman is not pregnant (object) or because D wrongly hopes that by giving her laxatives the pregnancy will be terminated (means). D may mistakenly assume that he is a civil servant for the purpose of the bribery offences and by accepting a bribe commit an impossible attempt of these offences. A *Wahndelikt* may be based on the wrong assumption that a certain behaviour has been penalised, as, for example, D, a lesbian, thinking under the old § 175 on homosexual acts that lesbian relationships were also criminal (which they were not). It may also arise from an error about the existence or scope of a defence, for example, if D thinks that self-defence is only a defence if life or limb is threatened.[57] The really problematic cases are those where D mistakenly extends the meaning or scope of a normative element of an existing offence, because in those cases both consequences are possible. An example from the law on forgery of documents, § 267, which is in principle not concerned with the question of whether the document's contents are incorrect, but with the question of whether the author of the document (*Aussteller*) has been misrepresented: if D mistakenly assumes that a forged written declaration allows conclusions as to its author, he will commit an impossible attempt of § 267; however, if he thinks that merely forging the content of an otherwise genuine document is forgery, his actions will constitute an imaginary offence.[58] Reverse errors also play a role in derivative omission offences, where the courts have accepted that the concept of impossible attempts can apply. For example, if D is mistaken about facts that could give rise to a duty to act and does not act, he will commit an impossible attempt; however, if he knows the real facts but wrongly assumes that he is obliged to act on that basis, it will be an imaginary offence.[59] The doctrinal difficulties arising from trying to distinguish[60] between the two categories[61] have led some to call for a clear distinction by saying that any reverse error of law in this context should be treated as an imaginary offence.[62] Finally, § 23(3) states that if the offender due to gross ignorance about the causal facts and circumstances of the case fails to realise that the attempt could under no circumstances have led to the completion of the offence due to the nature of its object or the means by which it was to be committed, the court may order a discharge, or mitigate the sentence as it sees fit under § 49(2). Note that this category does not cover the so-called '*irrealer Versuch*' or supernatural attempt, where D tries to use mystical, magical or divine powers to harm V, for

---

[57] See Sch/Sch-Eser, § 22, Mn. 79–81.

[58] BGH JZ 1987, 522 and Sch/Sch-Eser, § 22, Mn. 83.

[59] BGHSt 16, 155; 19, 299; 38, 356; 40, 256; BGH NStZ 1997, 485.

[60] These reverse errors can, of course, also occur in combined fashion; see See Sch/Sch-Eser, § 22, Mn. 92.

[61] See the case law examples at Sch/Sch-Eser, § 22, Mn. 90, which show that the courts have at times taken contradictory stances on similar problems.

[62] See the references at Sch/Sch-Eser, § 22, Mn. 89.

example, through the invocation of the devil, praying for the death of V, voodoo practices, etc.[63] In these scenarios, there is as far as the law is concerned no attempt at all because D is trying to use causal factors that are outside the realm of the human perception and logic, and most of all, human control.[64] Supernatural attempts are per se not punishable.

Withdrawal—Failed, Finished and Unfinished Attempts

Unlike the law of England and Wales, German law allows an offender to withdraw from an attempted offence with the consequence of a full acquittal for the attempted offence if she fulfils several criteria, as set out in § 24. The reasons for allowing someone to withdraw from an attempt with this consequence are controversial, ranging from paving the way for the offender's reintegration into society (*goldene Brücke*) back into legality, to *actus contrarius* approaches that see the reason for extinguishing criminal liability in the fact that just as much as an attempt may show that D defies the law, the withdrawal can be evidence that he embraces the societal order again.[65] Depending on which theory one wishes to follow, the character of the withdrawal and its position within the tripartite structure changes; it can transmogrify from a factor extinguishing guilt to one of negativing the general unlawfulness element, to a change in the offence as a whole. These days, the prevailing opinion is that the withdrawal is none of those and that it is not a defence as such, but stands outside the tripartite hierarchy as a personal reason, also within the meaning of § 28,[66] for exemption from punishment (*persönlicher Strafaufhebungsgrund*).[67] § 24(1) distinguishes between two different fundamental types of attempt when establishing the criteria for withdrawal, namely unfinished and finished attempt (*unbeendeter* and *beendeter Versuch*). Roughly speaking, the former is the case when D has not yet done all that he needs to do to set the causal chain in motion, for example, when D points the gun at V, cocks it but then does not pull the trigger, as opposed to where D has done everything and now only needs to wait for the result to occur, for example, when D has

---

[63] See, eg RGSt 33, 321.

[64] Sch/Sch-Eser, § 23, Mn. 13–13a. For attempts this is easy enough to accept. It would, however, be highly interesting if there ever was a case in which D could demonstrate in front of witnesses that by sticking needles into a voodoo doll representing V she could cause V pain in the regions that correspond to those of the doll or even kill her. If one generally denies the causal character of such actions, D would have to be acquitted of murder even if to all appearances it was her voodoo practice that killed V.

[65] See for a discussion of the different models Sch/Sch-Eser, § 24, Mn. 2–5.

[66] See the chapter on complicity.

[67] BGHSt 7, 299; Sch/Sch-Eser, § 24, Mn. 4. This could lead to the consequence that while criminal punishment as such may be extinguished, measures of rehabilitation and incapacitation that only require an unlawful act could still be imposed. However, the courts have rejected this by holding that the withdrawal is evidence that D is no longer a danger to society; see BGHSt 31, 132; BGH DRiZ 1983, 183.

put a primed time-bomb on a plane and the plane has taken off. In all cases, the withdrawal must be voluntary. If an attempt fails and D realises that, then in principle there can be no withdrawal because desisting after *recognised* failure is no longer voluntary and in some cases there may be no possibility of repeating the failed efforts anyway. So much for the basics, but, of course, things are more complex than that because here, as in the definition of attempt in the first place, the *subjective view of the offender* is determinative, not whether the attempt is *actually* finished, unfinished or has failed, which is clear from § 24(1) 2nd sentence (see below).

Very much depends in this context on the plan that D had for the execution of the offence; it will determine whether according to his view the attempt is finished or failed. In this context, we now also speak of the 'withdrawal horizon' (*Rücktrittshorizont*). As seen by the prevailing modern opinion, an attempt has failed if in D's own view it can no longer be carried out successfully, because otherwise one could include *ab initio* impossible attempts within the concept of failed attempt, thus denying D the chance to withdraw from an impossible attempt, which appears to be unfair.[68] Failed attempts occur in the following main categories:

a) D recognises that the goal of the attempt can no longer be reached. This is obvious if successful completion is physically impossible, for example, if the necklace is not in V's dresser as D had hoped, or V is unexpectedly not present at the scene of the crime or has fled from D.[69] Some argue that legal impossibility should also be included in this category, for example, if D wants to steal V's car and V unexpectedly consents to D's taking it, or D wants to rape V and she unexpectedly consents to intercourse.[70] The latter is, however, controversial, and the BGH has not subscribed to it arguing that in these cases it is already questionable whether D gives up his plan at all.[71]

b) D recognises that while he could still physically carry on, the completion of the offence has become pointless or undesirable for other reasons. Examples from the case law include that of D intending to rape V, whom he thinks is a total stranger but then discovers that she is a school mate;[72] the amount of money hoped for by D for setting up a business and which was to be obtained by theft is not reached by far;[73] the object of the theft is damaged and now unusable;[74] the intended rape victim V is having her period.[75]

As far as the withdrawal horizon of D and its function in deciding whether an attempt is finished or unfinished is concerned, the debate has been controversial

---

[68] See for the development Sch/Sch-Eser, § 22, Mn. 7–8.
[69] Compare the case law of BGH NStZ 1993, 40; BGH NStZ-RR 2004, 361; BGH StV 1999, 596.
[70] Sch/Sch-Eser, § 24, Mn. 9.
[71] BGHSt 39, 246.
[72] BGHSt 9, 48.
[73] BGHSt 4, 56; BGH NJW 1959, 1654.
[74] RGSt 45, 6.
[75] BGHSt 20, 280.

and complicated for some time and still is,[76] yet it is for all practical purposes now settled in the jurisprudence of the courts based on a so-called *Gesamtbetrachtung* or holistic approach[77] that emphasises the point in time when the decision to withdraw is made rather than a comparison with the plan of D when he initially set out to commit the offence. The courts thus have overall become more withdrawal-friendly in their approach as long as D's actions are part of a coherent event (*einheitlicher Lebensvorgang*), meaning that there must be close temporal and spatial proximity between the acts already performed and those being given up or still capable of being carried out to achieve the result.[78] Based on this case law,[79] the following basic principles apply:[80]

a) An attempt is considered as *unfinished* as long as D after the last act of his efforts at the implementation of the offence when the withdrawal happens has, in his view, not done everything necessary to achieve his goal, but thinks, even if mistakenly, that by simply continuing to act directly at that point in time he could reach it. This also applies to cases where D pursued a further objective by his actions over and above the completion of the offence, and by the mere attempt he has already achieved that objective, for example if D intends to kill V, who is a policeman following him after a bank robbery, in order to facilitate his flight, yet by merely pointing the gun in V's direction he makes V desist from further pursuit: D has thus reached his extraneous goal of getting away, yet this, according to the jurisprudence, will not preclude him from withdrawing from the attempted murder by merely ceasing to attack V any further.[81]

b) An attempt is considered as *finished* if D at the time of the withdrawal decision must clearly consider the possibility that no further action from his part is needed in order to achieve the intended result.

c) An attempt is considered as *failed* if either there is clearly no chance that the result will occur soon or if D has no immediate possibility of carrying out the offence to completion by other means.

If several persons are involved, the question as to when an attempt is finished or unfinished is answered as follows: for joint principals, § 24(2) contains a definitive

---

[76] See Sch/Sch-Eser, § 24, Mn. 18a–24.

[77] See for a discussion of the development Sch/Sch-Eser, § 24, Mn. 13–17c with references to the development of the case law.

[78] BGHSt 34, 57.

[79] See the exposition in BGHSt 39, 227; BGH NStZ 1993, 399.

[80] As set out in Sch/Sch-Eser, § 24, Mn. 18.

[81] In the case of result-qualified offences, the fact that by the mere attempt of the basic offence the serious consequence has already been caused, for example, if robber D by merely applying force already causes V's death before taking the money, does not preclude D from withdrawing from the offence of robbery causing death under § 251; see BGHSt 42, 158. Omission offences also distinguish between finished and unfinished attempts, with an unfinished attempt occurring if D thinks that simply performing the omitted act will prevent the result from happening, whereas the attempt is finished if D assumes that the omitted act is no longer capable of being performed, as long as there is any chance of averting the result, because if there is not, then the attempt has failed. See Sch/Sch-Eser, § 24, Mn. 30 with further references.

provision which we will examine below. For principals by proxy, the distinction is made on the basis of the relationship to the agent; if the agent is innocent or acting under compulsion, the attempt will be finished for P as soon as the agent is sent on her way, if the agent is neither innocent nor acting under compulsion, then the degree of execution by the agent and her ensuing chance of withdrawal is also determinative for P.[82]

Withdrawal from *unfinished* attempts by positive act[83] merely requires the cessation by D of any activity intended to accomplish the commission of the offence[84] if in his view further action is still possible. However, D must entirely desist from carrying out the plan, a mere pause—for example, in order to wait until the unexpectedly present owner has left the house—will not suffice; conversely, the fact that D pauses will not normally deprive him of the chance to withdraw after that, unless the pause was caused by circumstances that render the attempt a failed one.[85] D, according to the prevailing view,[86] must desist not only from the specific act needed to carry out the plan, but from the execution of the plan to attack the identified object altogether.[87] If D's attempt is *finished*, § 24(1) 1st sentence requires positive acts in order to avert the completion of the offence in a threefold manner: D must exert endeavours to prevent the result from occurring,[88] he must do it deliberately to break the causal chain, not merely by accident,[89] and finally his acts must show that he wishes to desist from the commission of the offence entirely, ie he must choose a means of averting the result that has reasonable prospect of success and does not leave it to chance whether the result is avoided; D is not required, however, to choose the optimal means.[90] His efforts must be causal in preventing the result *and* actually prevent it.[91] § 24(1) 2nd sentence offers a relaxation from the strict causality requirement in cases where the offence is not completed regardless of D's efforts—because the attempt was, for example, *ab initio* impossible or has failed[92]—and where D *is not aware* of that fact, but believes that the completion is still possible: here D will be able to withdraw if he exerts due diligence to avert the result.[93]

The withdrawal in both alternatives must be voluntary. This is clearly not the case if and when D realises that the attempt has failed or was impossible. The BGH requires that D is still fully capable of deciding of her own free will to carry on or

---

[82] Sch/Sch-Eser, § 24, Mn. 31–6.
[83] In cases of omission offences the nature of the scenario requires positive action to avert the result.
[84] BGH NJW 1984, 1693.
[85] BGHSt 35, 187; BGH NStZ 1988, 70; BGH NStZ-RR 2005, 70; RG JW 1936, 324.
[86] See for the debate Sch/Sch-Eser, § 24, Mn. 39–40.
[87] BGHSt 7, 279; 33, 142; 39, 247.
[88] BGHSt 31, 46.
[89] BGH MDR 1978, 279; BGH NJW 1989, 2068.
[90] BGHSt 31, 50; 33, 301; 44, 204; 48, 151; BGH NStZ 1999, 300; BGH NStZ-RR 1997, 194.
[91] Sch/Sch-Eser, § 24, Mn. 60–66 with references to case law and literature.
[92] Again, the importance of the offender's own personal view cannot be stressed enough, as this provision shows.
[93] Sch/Sch-Eser, § 24, Mn. 68–71 with references to case law and literature.

desist when she thought that she could go on.[94] It is not necessary that D act out of ethically praiseworthy motives.[95] The measure against which voluntariness is to be determined is the view of the offender at the time the decision is made,[96] which may be inferred from external circumstances and reasonableness arguments based on general experience; the voluntariness is not excluded by D's reacting to external stimuli, such as the victim's pleading for mercy, etc, but it is if external factors, or his internal reaction to external circumstances, eliminate D's choice.[97] Traditionally, the distinction is often made on the basis of the so-called Frank's Formula (*Frank'sche Formel*), named after a well-known academic of the time. Frank's formula states that a withdrawal is voluntary if D thinks 'I do not wish to carry on even if I could', whereas it will be involuntary if she says 'I cannot carry on, even if I wanted to'.[98] Elimination of choice may be caused if the act has become objectively impossible either by external factors or because D on embarking upon the commission of the offence becomes frightened, ashamed, overly nervous, etc. This also applies if D has been discovered in the act or thinks he has been.[99]

If several persons have been involved in an attempt, § 24(2) states that the withdrawing participant can go free from *attempt* liability in three distinct categories:

a) if he voluntarily prevents the completion of the offence, he will not be liable for the attempt;
b) his voluntary and earnest effort to prevent the completion of the offence will suffice for exemption from liability, if the offence is not completed regardless of his actions; or
c) if despite his best efforts, it is committed independently of his earlier contribution to the offence.

This rule contains a personal characteristic within the meaning of § 28(2),[100] according to which special personal characteristics that aggravate, mitigate or exclude punishment shall apply only to the accomplices (principals or secondary participants) in whose person they are present. This is an exception to the general rule for joint principals that their actions based on a common plan are attributed to all of them mutually. The rule under § 24(2) establishes a harsh regime for participants if the offence is completed and their actions are still even partially causal for the completion: even if they have tried all they could to prevent its commission, they remain fully liable and any credit for their remorse can only go to sentencing,

---

[94] BGHSt 7, 299; 21, 216; 35, 187.
[95] BGHSt 35, 186; 39, 320.
[96] BGHSt 35, 186.
[97] Sch/Sch-Eser, § 24, Mn. 44–57.
[98] Sch/Sch-Eser, § 24, Mn. 44 and 46.
[99] For case law examples, see the references in Sch/Sch-Eser, § 24, Mn. 57.
[100] Sch/Sch-Eser, § 24, Mn. 73.

which is without effect[101] when there is a mandatory minimum sentence as the life sentence in aggravated murder under § 211.[102] § 24(2) does not apply, either, in order to save D from liability for completion of the offence if he has succeeded in removing any causality of his own actions before the completion, because then he will not be liable for that under general principles of complicity: § 24(2) merely addresses the question of whether he will then still be liable for the attempt.[103] Similar points apply where the causality is removed in the attempt stage, unless it is a case of the special withdrawal rule under § 31[104] or when D succeeds in the preparatory phase to convince the accomplice not to go on with the commission[105] or to make sure that a previous contribution by himself is neutralised and the ensuing attempt made impossible, for example, when D secretly replaces the live ammunition in the gun P borrowed from him for the murder of V with blanks.[106] In all of these cases, D may escape liability under general rules, rather than under § 24(2). D must act voluntarily, and what was said above for single perpetrators applies accordingly. The above-mentioned principles apply *mutatis mutandis* also to principals by proxy, where in relation to P the agent is seen as a separate participant for the purposes of § 28(2) and his withdrawal takes effect for P only if P has in some way caused it[107] so that it also appears to be an emanation of his will. An example from recent German history is provided by the shootings of GDR citizens trying to flee the country by border guards, where the soldiers were under instructions to arrange medical care for the wounded victims.[108]

Effects of Withdrawal

The general rule of § 24 leads to a full acquittal from the charge based on the attempted offence; however, as mentioned above, modern legislative technique

---

[101] It may help in avoiding the additional stigma that the court classifies the offender's guilt as particularly serious within the meaning of § 57a(1)1st sentence, no 2:

'(1) The court shall grant conditional early release from a sentence of imprisonment for life under an operational period of probation, if

1. fifteen years of the sentence have been served;
2. the particular seriousness of the convicted person's guilt does not require its continued enforcement . . . '

[102] BGHSt 28, 348; 37, 293.
[103] BGHSt 28, 348.
[104] BGHSt 32, 133 and the chapter on accomplices below.
[105] RGSt 47, 351; 55, 106; BGHSt 28, 348. However, if P only pretends to agree to drop the plan and then goes on nevertheless to commit the offence, D will remain liable for the completed offence; RGSt 55, 106.
[106] Sch/Sch-Eser, § 24, Mn. 83–4.
[107] RGSt 39, 41; 56, 211.
[108] See BGHSt 44, 204.

tends to create specific withdrawal provisions in the Code's Special Part that normally take precedence over § 24 and often only allow the judge to mitigate the sentence or to order a discharge whilst retaining the conviction as such.[109] The law provides for a withdrawal from factually completed offences in certain cases, yet the scope of their application to similar offences where such withdrawal provisions are absent is unclear;[110] the overall picture lacks coherence and may be viewed as unfair to certain individual classes of offenders. § 24 does not cover any offences that may have been completed in the course of the attempted offence, for example, bodily harm caused in the course of a murder attempt.[111] This applies also to lesser included offences that merely penalise an endangerment rather than a full result, if the particular mode of endangerment has been neutralised by the withdrawal.[112]

---

[109] Sch/Sch-Eser, § 24, Mn. 107–8. However, the relationship between § 24 and offences that penalise mere preparatory acts can be such that a withdrawal from the attempt covers also the offence based on the preparatory acts, as for example, § 30; see BGHSt 14, 378. The issue is controversial and problematic, see Sch/Sch-Eser, § 24, Mn. 117–21.

[110] Sch/Sch-Eser, § 24, Mn. 116 with examples and references to the case law.

[111] BGHSt 1, 156; 7, 300; 16, 123; 17, 1; 41, 14; BGH NJW 1995, 1437.

[112] BGHSt 39, 128; see critically Sch/Sch-Eser, § 24, Mn. 110.

8

Forms of Participation—
Principals, Aiders and Abettors

The principle on which the descriptions of almost all criminal offences build is that of the sole perpetrator. Yet, in reality many of the worst crimes are committed, in fact can only be committed, by several persons who participate in a common scheme of some sort or other. Some of these persons may be the driving force behind the activities, others may merely take instructions or orders, or wish to help. Others yet do not wish to be seen at the scene of the crime and stay in the background as organisational masterminds. Criminal law as a system of state reaction to the degree of personal guilt in law-breaking must provide for differing answers and liabilities depending on the type of participation in criminal behaviour. One traditional way of approaching this task is to create distinct categories of offenders based on the kind of involvement. German criminal law knows of five basic categories of participation in a criminal offence, depending on the level and degree of involvement:

a) principal by proxy (*mittelbare Täterschaft*);
b) independent multiple principals (*Nebentäterschaft*);
c) joint principals acting on a common plan (*Mittäterschaft*);
d) abetting (*Anstiftung*); and
e) aiding (*Beihilfe*).

These concepts, as well as the preliminary stages of attempted participation— a conspiracy-like offence—and the rules on withdrawal from participation are regulated in §§ 24(2), 25–31. It is helpful to remember the terminological structure, shown in Figure I below.

These distinctions apply only to criminal offences of the level of *Vergehen* and *Verbrechen*. In the lowest category of offence, the *Ordnungswidrigkeiten*, the law has abandoned the division between principals and secondary participants and adopted the so-called *Einheitstäterbegriff* or unified perpetrator concept in § 14(1) OWiG. This concept considers anyone a principal whose actions helped cause the result or establish the *actus reus* elements of the offence, regardless of the actual weight of their contribution. There have been calls to extend the *Einheitstäterbegriff* to the Criminal Code as well, but so far without success, because the concept is regarded as too crude an instrument to justify the imposition of the

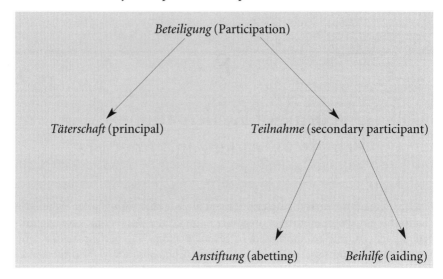

Figure I—Terminological Structure

The position as principal offender can be further sub-categorised as shown in Figure II.

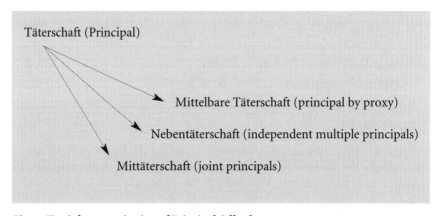

Figure II—Sub-categorisation of Principal Offender

serious consequences under criminal law proper.[1] For the purposes of this chapter, we will therefore neglect it.

Another qualification needs to be made at this point, and that is that German law does not know of secondary participation in the field of offences based on

---

[1] See Wessels/Beulke, AT, 181; Sch/Sch-Cramer/Heine, Vorbem. §§ 25 *ff.* Mn. 11–12.

negligence; in this area only the figure of the principal offender exists;[2] anyone involved in the commission of a negligent offence other than the direct principal offender can be guilty only if under general rules related to negligence he or she fulfils all criteria leading to liability. There are those academic commentators who argue that at least employing the concept of joint principals could be acknowledged as feasible within the ambit of negligence, but this, as shall become clear based on the explanations below, is in stark contrast to the law at this time. The extent to which the concept of principal by proxy can be used in the context of negligence is also highly controversial. For an introduction to the principles of the law as it presently stands, an analysis of this complex debate is unnecessary.[3]

Let us first examine the core provisions regulating the concept of participation:

§ 25 Principals

(1) Any person who commits the offence himself or through another shall be liable as a principal.
(2) If more than one person commit the offence jointly, each shall be liable as a principal (joint principals).

§ 26 Abetting

Any person who intentionally induces another to intentionally commit an unlawful act (abettor) shall be liable to be sentenced as if he were a principal.

§ 27 Aiding

(1) Any person who intentionally assists another in the intentional commission of an unlawful act shall be convicted and sentenced as an aider.
(2) The sentence for the aider shall be based on the penalty for a principal. It shall be mitigated pursuant to § 49(1).

§ 28 Special Personal Characteristics

(1) If special personal characteristics (§ 14(1)) that establish the principal's liability are absent in the person of the secondary participant (abettor or aider) their sentence shall be mitigated pursuant to § 49(1).
(2) If the law provides that special personal characteristics aggravate, mitigate or exclude punishment this shall apply only to the accomplices (principals or secondary participants) in whose person they are present.

§ 29 Separate criminal liability of the accomplice

Each accomplice shall be liable according to the measure of his own guilt and irrespective of the guilt of the others.

Obviously, the first alternative of § 25(1), sole perpetration, needs no further elaboration. The second alternative comes closest to this mode of committing offences and we shall turn to it now.

---

[2] Sch/Sch-Cramer/Heine, Vorbem. §§ 25 *ff.* Mn. 7a and 112–17.
[3] See for references and further reading Sch/Sch-Cramer/Heine, Vorbem. §§ 25 *ff.* Mn. 7a and 112–17.

Principal by Proxy (*Mittelbare Täterschaft*)

The basic provision is § 25(1) 2nd alternative, committing the offence through another. This variant of the concept of principal is concerned with scenarios where the principal uses another person as an instrument to commit an offence. He controls the situation because he has superior knowledge or superior powers in relation to the agent. This rule would seem to assume, *e contrario*, that the instrument is in principle not criminally liable himself (innocent agent) because if he were the situation would be one of either joint principals or secondary participation. As we will see, this does not, however, preclude scenarios where the agent himself commits an offence, even if it is congruent with the liability of the principal.

A person can become an instrument for a variety of reasons, with potentially differing consequences. Jurisprudence and commentators have acknowledged the following categories:[4]

a) The agent is not fulfilling either the *actus reus* or *mens rea* of the offence. Example: P asks A to take V's car and bring it to P's house; he tells A that the car is his own and V had borrowed but not returned it despite P's demands. In reality, the car is V's. Here A lacks the *mens rea* for the *actus reus* element 'property belonging to someone else'.

b) The agent lacks a specific *mens rea* component or has the *mens rea* for a different offence. Example: P tells A that he only wants to borrow V's car for a short ride and return it immediately afterwards. A has the necessary *mens rea* for all the *actus reus* elements of theft, but lacks the additional intention to appropriate the car for himself or P.

c) The agent is acting objectively lawfully (*rechtmäßig*) under an accepted defence. Example: A, a police constable, is told untruthfully by P that V has just stolen a handbag from her. A pursues V and arrests her. A is acting under his power to arrest persons suspected of an offence.

d) The agent is acting without personal guilt (*schuldlos*) under an accepted defence. Examples: P forces A to commit an armed bank robbery by holding his wife and children hostage, threatening to kill them; A is acting under duress (*Nötigungsnotstand*). P is telling A, who suffers from a mental illness amounting to insanity in the legal sense, to kill V. Alternatively: P tells elderly A that the approaching V is about to attack her with a knife, A hits V over the head with a large stick. Although A is not acting in self-defence, he may be acting without guilt or intent because of his error.

e) The agent lacks criminal capacity. Example: P asks A, a 10-year-old child, to steal a packet of cigarettes. A, even if she thinks she is committing an offence, is not criminally liable as she is under 14.

---

[4] See the references at Sch/Sch-Cramer/Heine, § 25, Mn. 6–60.

Identity of Agent and Victim

The concept of principal by proxy also covers the unusual scenarios where agent and victim are one and the same person, and the agent is acting within the first category mentioned above. These cases occur when the agent is hurting or trying to kill herself, as in the famous, and bizarre, *Sirius* case, which was decided in 1983 by the BGH:[5]

In 1973 or 1974, the defendant met the victim at a disco. She suffered from an emotionally and intellectually retarded personality development. They struck up a friendship, in which sexual contacts remained largely irrelevant; the conversations centred on psychology and philosophy: these sometimes ran into long hours. The defendant became the confidant and indeed teacher and counsellor in all matters of life. He was always there for her and she trusted him blindly. During their philosophical talks he told her that he was from the planet Sirius, the Sirians being on a much higher plane of philosophical sophistication than mankind. He had been sent to Earth with the task of saving a few 'valuable' humans and to ensure that after their bodies had fully decayed their souls could go on to live on other planets or indeed, on Sirius. In order to achieve this she did have to advance spiritually and philosophically. When the defendant realised that she believed him he decided to exploit her financially. He pretended that he could speed up her passage to a higher level if she donated a large sum of money to the monastery of a monk well known to him, who would then meditate on her behalf. The woman took out a bank loan and gave the money to the defendant who used it for his own purposes. When she kept asking him about the monk's efforts, he finally told her that the monk had informed him that her own consciousness had built up a blockade against her progress; this could only be removed by the total destruction of her old body and by acquiring a new one.

When the defendant realised that she still believed his ruse, he decided to exploit her further. She would, he said, after killing herself wake up in a new body as an artist in a 'red room on Lake Geneva'; she would, however, also need money in her new life. She should take out a life insurance for cases of accident and nominate him as the irrevocable beneficiary, and then feign an accident. He would hold the insurance in trust for her until she woke up in Geneva and then transfer the money to her. The victim did as she was told. The plan was that she should kill herself by dropping a running hairdryer in the bath while she was in it, after having left some clues in her flat that would indicate that she did not intend to commit suicide[6] and which would point to an accident. However, the plan failed as the current was not strong enough to kill her. The defendant called her flat to check whether she was dead and was surprised when she took up the receiver; he continued over three hours and 10 phone calls to give her instructions to continue her efforts to kill herself. When this did not lead to the desired result, he desisted. The victim never

---

[5] BGHSt 32, 38.
[6] This would have voided the insurance.

considered her actions as attempted suicide and indeed thought suicide to be an immoral concept. She saw the whole affair as a passage to another life. The defendant was fully aware that only because she was totally enslaved to him did she agree to these actions.

The defendant was convicted of attempted murder as a principal by proxy. The BGH first reiterated that the line between murder and mere participation in another's suicide was not a clear one and unlike the cases of insanity or duress, the treatment of a suicide based on a deception on the part of the principal could not be defined in the abstract. It depended on the manner and scope of the error caused. If the principal by deception hides from the agent the fact that the latter is about to cause his death and deliberately sets this causal chain in motion, then he will be the principal of the offence of (attempted) murder, having made the agent an instrument against himself by using his superior knowledge of the facts and steering the agent based on that. The BGH concluded that such had been the case in the present appeal, where the accused had intended all along to get hold of the money of the victim by telling his fabricated story and exploiting the sheer gullibility of the woman. The obvious objection that the victim knew she was going to have to kill herself in order to be 'reborn' in a different body in that red room on Lake Geneva and thus was not in error about the central fact that she was causing her death got short shrift from the BGH, because in the court's view she did not view this as a final termination of her life, but rather as a fleeting and immediate transition to another form of *earthly* life, as opposed to the usual religious connotation of a life in the hereafter.

Hierarchical Structures

Recent German history has provided the basis for deciding whether someone can be a principal by proxy even though the agent is himself committing a full offence. This was the case of the border killings during the time of the German Democratic Republic (GDR). The GDR border guards were under orders from the Party Central Committee and under law to shoot at and if necessary kill GDR citizens trying to flee across the inner-German border. After reunification, some members of the government and central committee were prosecuted for their involvement in establishing these orders. The trial court found them guilty of merely abetting murder because the guards had been entirely responsible and criminally liable for their own actions, but on appeal the BGH held[7] that the accused had been acting as principals by proxy. The court had already held earlier that the border guards could be principals in their own right and not just as secondary participants to the actions of the GDR high command.[8]

The BGH embarked on an in-depth review of the history of the concept and of the case law and literature on the topic which it would be too long to reproduce

[7] BGHSt 40, 218 at 232.
[8] BGHSt 39, 1 at 31.

here. It came to the following conclusions, based on the legal principle of 'control over the act' (*Tatherrschaft*), which set out the principles for the liability of superiors in a hierarchical structure:

a) If and when a person acts without being under the influence of any error and is otherwise not subject to a defence negating his mens rea or guilt (*uneingeschränkt schuldfähig*), then the so-called '*Hintermann*', ie literally the person 'standing behind' that person, translatable to some extent as 'mastermind' or, if one wanted to coin a new word as I did in my translation of the German Criminal Code,[9] as 'hinterman', cannot normally be liable as a principal by proxy, but merely for aiding and abetting. This is especially the case if and when the direct perpetrator completely controls the act and the situation, both factually and legally, and also wants to exercise that control.

b) However, there are groups of cases when the independently liable direct perpetrator is acting based on a contribution by the *Hintermann*, which will as a matter of course *almost automatically* lead to the offence intended by the *Hintermann* being committed. This can be the case when the *Hintermann* uses the framework conditions prevalent in certain organisational power structures or hierarchies within which his actions regularly set in motion certain trains of events (*regelhafte Abläufe*). Such frameworks exist within, for example, organisational structures of the state, in business and business-like enterprises such as organised crime rings (Mafia), and the military chain of command. If the *Hintermann* knowingly utilises these circumstances, especially if he exploits the unreserved preparedness of his subordinate to commit the offence as such, then he will have control over the act and as such be liable as a principal by proxy. In practice, he will usually have a much stronger control because of these structures than is required for other groups of principals by proxy. The *Hintermann* in these cases possesses the overriding will to control the act and he knows that the framework conditions make any resistance of the direct perpetrator to his plans highly unlikely. To treat the *Hintermann* as a mere secondary participant and not as a principal would not do justice to the importance of his contribution. This solution also has the added advantage of doing away with the necessity of deciding whether the direct perpetrator was acting in good or bad faith, which may be difficult in the individual case.

Effect of Errors of the Agent

A final group of cases that will be considered here is the effect that an error of the agent will have on the liability of the principal. *Beulke* uses two instructive examples:[10]

---

[9] *The German Criminal Code—A Modern English Translation* (Oxford/Portland, Hart, 2008).
[10] Wessels/Beulke, AT, 196.

Example 1: P, a doctor, asks nurse A to give patient V1 in room 1 an injection; unknown to A the syringe contains a hardly detectable lethal poison. A, who is extremely short-sighted, gets confused about the room numbers and gives the injection to patient V2 in room 7.

Example 2: P asks A, whom he knows to be legally insane, to kill V1 and gives him a photo of V1 to help A identify her. However, A kills V2 who he thought was V1 at the time he fired the shot.

Will the irrelevant mistake of A in both cases, as far as P is concerned, also be treated as an irrelevant mistake of identity or as a so-called *aberratio ictus*, an accident possibly caused by P's negligence? German law no longer subscribes to a pure idea of transferred malice as does, for example, the law of England and Wales,[11] where the physical and social identity of the victim is irrelevant for, for example, a murder charge. The question may be raised whether P should be treated, in both cases, like A, ie whether the mistake by A is also an irrelevant mistake of fact for him, or whether in relation to V2 his acts fall under negligent manslaughter liability whereas vis-à-vis V1 he is liable of attempted murder. Some would treat both cases as an *aberratio ictus*, whereas other commentators[12] would differentiate between both scenarios based on the degree to which P left the actual identification of the victim *in situ* to A or not. In the first example, they would argue that P told A clearly whom to give the injection to with the consequence of an *aberratio*, whereas in the second example, the identification of the victim was much more left to A by P, ie P was taking a bigger risk, with the consequence that A's mistake should be treated as if P himself had made the mistake about the social, not physical, identity of V2, which for a direct perpetrator is an irrelevant mistake of fact (*error in persona*). Whether one finds that distinction cogent is open to question. If the defining parameter is the risk taken by P in letting an agent loose that he cannot fully control, then it is difficult to see why the first and second examples should make that much of a difference, or why any difference in degree of that risk should be relevant at all.

Multiple Independent Principals (MIP)
(*Nebentäterschaft*)

Strictly speaking, cases of MIP are not part of the category that is normally covered by the concepts of participation in another's offence, because the MIP neither

---

[11] See chapter four on the subjective component of the *Tatbestand*.

[12] See Wessels/Beulke, AT, 196 at fn 82: Beulke states that the *aberratio* solution was the one followed by the prevailing opinion in the literature, whereas Sch/Sch-Cramer/Heine, § 25, Mn. 51–3 wish to see the scenario treated in the same way as in the case of abetting, see below, and refer to the criterion of how much freedom of choice was left to the agent. According to them, an irrelevant error in *persona vel obiecto* by the agent is also irrelevant for the principal. This is in keeping with the constant jurisprudence of the courts, as will be explained below when we look at abetting.

share any common plan, nor do they use one another as agents or aid and abet each other. They embark on the commission of an offence vis-à-vis the same victim entirely independently and are only liable for their own individual acts. Just a few words need to be said here. The largest field of application of this concept is that of crimes committed by negligence or recklessness rather than intent. The respective actions of the MIP normally only become important as factors in the causal chains started by each of them.

An example: P1 and P2 are V's sons and stand to inherit a large sum on V's death. Unbeknown to P2, P1 tries to poison V with a slow-acting lethal substance over a long period of time to avoid detection; V has already been subjected to such an amount of the poison that she will die within 24 hours. P2, without P1's knowledge, has asked insane A to kill V by running her over with his car, which A does. V dies immediately of the injuries suffered before the poison can take effect. The causal chains are completely independent. The chain set in motion by P1 has been broken by the act of A acting as an innocent agent of P2. P2 is thus guilty of murder as a principal by proxy; P1 is guilty of attempted murder.

Because MIP is largely irrelevant for the purposes of the doctrine of deliberate participation in another's offence, we will not delve into it any deeper.

Joint Principals (*Mittäterschaft*)

Set out in § 25(2), this form of liability comes close to the English law concept of a joint criminal enterprise (JCE), but with a few important differences. Just like in a JCE, there needs to be a common plan subscribed to by all persons taking part in the commission of the offence. However, unlike English law after section 8 of the Accessories and Abettors Act 1861, German law still attaches a lot of weight to the distinction between principals and secondary participants, as will be seen below when we look at aiding and abetting under §§ 26 and 27. The consequence of liability under § 25(2) is that every participant is treated as a principal, with the consequence that in sentencing, an aider under § 27(2) gets a statutory discount even on mandatory minimum sentences, whereas a joint principal under § 25(2) and an abettor, who for the purpose of sentencing is to be treated as a principal under § 26, normally do not. This makes it necessary to establish first the criteria by which joint principals are distinguished from aiders *and* abettors, because as we will see below, the actual basis for abettor liability is distinct and separate from that of a principal; only the punishment is the same.

Distinguishing Joint Principals from Secondary Participants

For the majority of academic commentators, just like in the category of principal by proxy, the defining criterion for the distinction between joint principals and secondary participants today is the *Tatherrschaft*, the control over the act. As long as one of the participants in the offence offers a contribution that *has an impact* on how the common plan is shaped or enforced, and as long as he wants to influence the actual mode of commission, then he will be classified as a joint principal. If his actions do and are merely meant to support the acts of the other(s), but not to influence the mode of planning or commission of the offence, he will more likely be classified as a secondary participant. As always, there is no clear line, and mere planning support away from the scene of the crime or presence as a getaway driver may be sufficient.

The courts, and mainly the BGH, traditionally have adhered to the so-called subjective theory, ie the distinction made mainly on the basis of the offender's *mens rea*, that is, based on whether D wants the offence 'as his own' (*animus auctoris*) or merely wants to support someone else's actions (*animus socii*). In earlier times, this distinction had created bizarre consequences, as is best exemplified by the famous *Stashynskij* case,[13] which became the more or less leading case of the modern[14] subjective theory. Stashynskij was a KGB assassin who in 1957 had committed two murders of exile dissidents to the Soviet regime, on the direct orders of the head of the KGB. On the day the Berlin Wall was being built in 1961, he fled to West Berlin with his wife and was immediately taken into custody and then tried for the murders. The trial court quite obviously wanted to avoid the mandatory life sentence for murder and treated Stashynskij, who after all had had full operational control over the events *in situ*, as a mere aider of the head of the KGB in Moscow, who was said to have been the real principal, thus making the application of § 27(2) possible. Stashynskij was sentenced to eight years' imprisonment. The BGH upheld the judgment and coined the above-mentioned two categories. The BGH was widely criticised for this obvious attempt at result-driven and inconsistent[15] jurisprudence that was patently *contra legem* with regard to the clear wording of § 25(1). Quite clearly, the idea at the time, after all at the height of the Cold War, was to be able to give agents from the USSR and other Eastern Bloc countries an incentive to defect and divulge information about their actions, etc without the fear of facing life in prison. Overall, one can say that the subjective theory as practised by the BGH arose out of post-war trials where atrocities committed by the *Wehrmacht*, SS and in concentration camps had to be tried, and in some cases the courts may have felt that treating the people who did the shooting

---

[13] BGHSt 18, 87.

[14] There had been a precursor case, the so-called *Bathtub Case*, decided in 1940 by the *Reichsgericht* in RGSt 74, 84. In that case, the sister of the mother of a newborn child had drowned the baby in a bathtub merely for her sister's sake, without wanting the result herself. The court treated the sister as an aider and the mother as the principal, based on the application of the extreme subjective theory.

[15] The decision was also in stark contrast to previous case law of the BGH, as in the so-called *Case of the Murder of the Fellow Soldier* (*Kameradenmordfall*) in BGHSt 8, 393, from 1956, when the BGH stated that a person who kills another with his or her own hands is to be treated as a principal, even if he or she did the act in the presence, under the influence and merely for the sake of a third person. The decision expressly gave up the full subjective approach taken by the *Reichsgericht* in the *Bathtub Case*, RGSt 74, 84.

as principals did not do justice to their actual role and position in the hierarchy.[16] In more recent years,[17] the BGH has come around to an approach which combines paying lip service to the subjective theory approach with a more objective evidential test: the court will now base its decision as to whether or not the accused had the *animus auctoris* on the scope of the accused's objective influence and control over the offence as shown by the evidence. The BGH thus merely treats the substantive concept of who is a principal as a question of inferring the necessary *mens rea* from the objective evidence, which in effect makes it almost congruent to the academic majority approach of *Tatherrschaft*.

The Common Plan and the Objective Contribution of the Joint Principals

The consequence of establishing that offenders have acted as joint principals according to a common, that is mutually communicated and agreed, plan is that the factual contributions by each of them to the commission of the offence are attributed to all others without the need to establish the commission of a full offence as such by one of them. The principle behind the German concept of JCE is thus not accessory liability to someone else's offence, as in aiding and abetting under §§ 26 and 27, but an attribution of blame to all participants for all acts committed by any of them because of the common plan, as long as their actions further the commission of the offence. The common plan and the influence on the planning or commission of the crime raise everybody to the level of a principal *eo ipso*. Put another way, this means in practice that as soon as two or more people agree beforehand on the commission of a certain crime and on a division of labour to achieve that end, they are more likely to be found liable as joint principals than as mere secondary participants, although there is no legal presumption to that effect. Only if it is clear that one of them is the absolute mastermind who is directing the subordinate activities of the others entirely according to his own discretion, will a court accept that those others are merely aiding him. The common plan is the foundation for the cooperation of the participants as equal partners in crime, as it were, their individual acts combining to a whole that provides the factual basis for the offence in the legal sense. This, according to the jurisprudence of the BGH,[18] must be mirrored in the agreement entered into by the several accused. Each of them must see his actions as furthering those of the others and theirs as furthering his, as part of a common whole, not merely to assist another in the execution of that other's plans. The court infers this intention, which will not often be evident as such, from the objective participation in the execution of the crime and

---

[16] See, eg the decisions of the BGH in 4 StR 32/40 of 13 February 1951 and 3 StR 333/51 of 5 July 1951.
[17] See, eg BGHSt 28, 346; 35, 347 (*Case of the 'Cat King'*); 40, 218; 45, 270; BGH Wistra 2001, 420; BGH NStZ-RR 2002, 74; BGH JZ 2003, 575.
[18] BGH NStZ 1988, 406.

from the interest of the individual members of the operation in its outcome.[19] The greater the interest and the part played by an offender, the more likely he will be taken to be a joint principal.

The agreement between the joint principals can be established during the commission of a crime; premeditation is not necessary.[20] This raises the interesting question of whether a successively joining offender can be held liable for acts that were committed before he joined. The law is not quite settled and much will depend upon the circumstances of the individual case.[21] There is, however, agreement that liability for acts which were completely terminated at the time of the joining is excluded.[22]

As was already indicated above, the actual contribution of each participant must reach a certain, albeit difficult to define in the abstract, level of functional control over the commission of the offence. Contrary to the opinion of some commentators in academic writing, and as we already saw with regard to principals by proxy in hierarchical structures, it is not necessary that the contribution be made during the execution stage, but it may be given in the planning phase or even, as a successive partner, in the period between the actual completion of the *actus reus* (*Vollendung*) and the factual end of the commission of the offence (*Beendigung*).

An example: P1 goes to a liquor store to steal a bottle of whisky. He takes it off a shelf and hides it in his long coat. The shop owner V becomes suspicious of P1 when he passes the counter and only pays for a packet of crisps. When he walks out of the door, he calls after him to stop. P1 quickly gives the bottle to his friend P2, who just happens to come along, saying that they will drink it together if he helps him hide it from V. P2 immediately agrees and puts it behind a bin near the door. Both then go to V and P1 turns out his pockets. The *actus reus* of theft, under German law, is complete at the very latest when P1 walks past the counter and out the door, but the bottle as the object of the theft is not secured before P1 and P2 walk away from the store again and pick up the bottle. P2's help was crucial for the factual completion of the offence, but irrelevant for the *actus reus*.[23]

The Limits of Mutual Attribution

It is necessary to point out that there are certain limits to the attribution of acts to the joint principals. This applies to elements of the *actus reus* of an offence, such as certain qualities of the offender, as well as to *mens rea* elements such as specific intentions. The rule is that if one of the participants lacks a certain quality necessary for the specific offence, or a certain *mens rea* element such as a distinct

---

[19] BGHSt 47, 383; BGH StV 2003, 279; BGH NStZ-RR 2004, 40.

[20] BGH NStZ 1985, 70.

[21] See references in Wessels/Beulke, AT, 186 at fn 33.

[22] BGH GA 1977, 144. BGH NStZ 1997, 272.

[23] There may be a separate liability of P2 for handling stolen goods under § 259 StGB or assisting an offender in retaining the profits of his crime under § 257 StGB, but both of these pre-suppose that P2 was not already a party to the theft.

Opinion is divided about whether the instigating act must be communicated to the principal or whether § 26, as the English law concept of procuring, also covers cases where the principal is unaware that he or she is being manipulated into the offence. The prevailing opinion appears to wish to leave open the concept for such non-communicated causal actions by the abettor.[30] However, it appears to be agreed that the actions of the abettor must significantly increase the likelihood that by being exposed to them the principal will commit the offence. Doubtful cases, as mentioned by Roxin,[31] would be that of a thief who leaves a number of £50 notes on his trail to slow down any pursuers (he might be liable for abetting theft[32] of the notes by the pursuers) or that of a person leaving open a window in the hope that someone would burgle the house, or, finally, that of a man telling his best friend, whom he knows to have a temper, that his wife has an affair with another man, whose name and address he gives him. These examples show that it all very much depends on the circumstances and the context, as is also made clear by another case decided by the BGH:[33] D had raped V and then asked P, who had been present during the rape but who had not yet decided whether he wanted to have intercourse against V's will with her himself, 'Do you want, too?' P then also raped V. The BGH accepted that abetting rape had taken place on D's part, but on the questionable basis that D had a 'conditional intent to abet'. Roxin[34] is right when he points out that the court first should have established whether a mere question can be an instigation at all. That could be the case if P was, for example, under peer pressure or if he wanted to be initiated in a gang and raping V was what was expected of him to show he was serious, etc.

Abetting—*Mens Rea*

As was indicated above, D needs to know about P's (intended) actions and he has to want to instigate or cause them to happen. The prevailing view would accept *dolus eventualis* as sufficient, ie full direct intent is not required.[35] The knowledge required from D about the offence to be committed must encompass the essential factual elements, but need not cover every detail.[36] The approach to the degree of detail in essence overlaps with the Court of Appeal's views in *Bryce*.[37] The rules about mistakes of fact and law and those about defences apply as they would with the principal P.[38] If D believes that P would be acting in self-defence if he hit V because D is under the honest impression that V is about to attack P himself, he

---

[30] See on the different schools of thought Roxin, AT II, 153; also Sch/Sch-Cramer/Heine, § 26 Mn. 12.
[31] Roxin, AT II, 153.
[32] Under English law terminology. German law knows of a different concept for appropriation without taking away, namely under § 246 StGB, *Unterschlagung*.
[33] BGH GA 1980, 183.
[34] Roxin, AT II, 155.
[35] Sch/Sch-Cramer/Heine, § 26 Mn. 16; BGH NJW 1998, 2835.
[36] BGHSt 42, 138.
[37] (2004) 2 Cr App Rep 592.
[38] Sch/Sch-Cramer/Heine, § 26 Mn. 19.

would be lacking intent with respect to the principal offence because of an error about facts underlying a recognised defence (*Erlaubnistatbestandsirrtum*)—P's actions would then not be unlawful and D would not have the intent to instigate an unlawful act. Equally, D must want the offence to be completed, not merely to be unsuccessfully attempted; otherwise he will not incur criminal liability. The most important application of this principle is that of the *agent provocateur*.[39] While the courts[40] draw the line between merely wanting the attempt to occur[41] (no liability) and contemplating the completion of the offence (liability), the criticism of academic commentary[42] objects that this delineation does not make any sense in the context of the vast and practically highly relevant category of the so-called *Tätigkeitsdelikte*, ie those, as pointed out above, which criminalise the mere conduct of the offender, without the need for an additional extraneous result. One major example of this category concerns drug-related offences. Finally, there is a substantial dispute about the consequences of police *agents provocateurs* who instigate an otherwise innocent and untarnished individual to commit an offence, if but for the abetting the person would never have contemplated the offence. The prevailing view today treats this as a factor to be considered in sentencing, whereas in the earlier debate there were voices which, for example, advocated a bar against prosecution based on arguments related to the concept of entrapment.[43]

If P's actions are less serious than those envisaged by D when instigating the offence, D is only liable for what was actually accomplished, provided it remains within the general category of offence that was contemplated by D and not something completely different. This is a direct consequence of the principle of limited dependence. Thus if D told P to rob V of her handbag, but P in the event only needed to pick it up when V was not watching, D would be liable of abetting theft. However, if he told P to steal V's handbag and P then went on to rape her, no liability would ensue, not even under § 30(1), as theft under § 242 is not a felony. Yet, if P exceeded D's instructions, liability may depend on whether there is a link between the offences based on the concept of (de facto) lesser included offences, which D's *mens rea* is taken to have included. If D tells P to steal V's money and P then goes on to rob her because she put up a resistance, there is no good reason not to hold D liable for abetting theft, as theft is a constituent lesser element in robbery under § 249 which is basically theft with the use of force, leaving aside the question about the exact quality of robbery as an independent qualification of theft. If there is no such link to a lesser included offence, there will be no liability.

---

[39] Sch/Sch-Cramer/Heine, § 26 Mn. 20.

[40] BGH GA 1975, 333; StV 1981, 549.

[41] This needs to be distinguished from the case where D wants P to complete the offence, but P's actions fail: D tells P to shoot V, P misses; in this case D is, of course, liable for abetting attempted murder.

[42] Sch/Sch-Cramer/Heine, § 26 Mn. 20.

[43] See on the development of the debate Sch/Sch-Cramer/Heine, § 26 Mn. 21.

Errors of the Principal and their Effect on the Abettor's Liability

Mistakes by D were already briefly addressed above. The general rules apply. However, what if P makes a mistake or his or her actions go wrong for another reason? Will the same rules apply as set out above for principals by proxy? According to the courts in constant[44] jurisprudence since the times of the *Preußisches Obertribunal*, the Prussian Superior Tribunal, caution is advisable:

If the error by P was an irrelevant mistake, for example of identity, D will be treated the same way and no reference to *aberratio ictus* will lie. The basis for this view is the famous *Rose-Rosahl* case decided in 1858 by the *Preußisches Obertribunal*:[45] The wood trader Rosahl from the town of Schiepzig promised Rose, a worker, to pay him a lot of money if he, Rose, were to kill the carpenter Schliebe from the neighbouring town of Lieskau. Rose, who knew Schliebe well, hid near the road between the two towns and when in the twilight he saw a man coming towards his place of ambush, he shot him, believing him to be Schliebe. In fact, it was the 17-year-old son of a church organist called Harnisch. While the error was obviously irrelevant for Rose, Rosahl—not without some justification if we remember the treatment of principals by proxy for errors of their agents advocated by some commentators described above—argued that from his point of view the whole thing had gone horribly wrong and he should only be held liable, if at all, under the principle of *aberratio ictus*, but not for abetting murder. The court rejected his argument and convicted for abetting murder by simply declaring the error also as irrelevant in relation to D because there was no good reason to let the abettor benefit from a fact that was irrelevant to the principal. Ingeborg Puppe[46] has argued impressively that the objections from academic commentators who advocate the use of the *aberratio ictus* principle were based on a flawed understanding of the idea of limited dependence and the nature of the intent required, especially that the idea of a concretisation of the victim by the acts of the abettor or principal and the allegedly resulting focus on the identity of the intended victim was lacking in substance. In effect, this is a good example that both cases, mistaken identity and *aberratio ictus*, in essence fall under the general heading of transferred malice and reinforce the irrelevance of identity for the *actus reus* of the offence of murder. However, despite the long-standing and clear tradition of the jurisprudence, the debate in the German academic community has not yet found its end.[47]

Note that if the principal merely misses the target, the rules of *aberratio ictus* will apply to him or her and the abettor.

[44] See recently in the so-called *Hoferbenfall* (*Case of the farm heirs*) BGHSt 37, 218, with a very similar set of facts as *Rose-Rosahl*.
[45] GA 1859, 322.
[46] *Strafrecht Allgemeiner Teil im Spiegel der Rechtsprechung*, vol 2 (Baden-Baden, Nomos, 2005) 172–6.
[47] See the references to the different approaches summarised at Sch/Sch-Cramer/Heine, § 26, Mn. 23.

exclusion only applies to those who have the qualities. The wife of a civil servant who helps him in accepting bribes by setting up a bank account in the Cayman Islands for the payments because he does not speak English, and who administers the finances generally, cannot be a joint perpetrator to the bribery offence because she lacks the quality of being a civil servant (*Sonderdelikt*), which is a quality that *establishes* liability within the meaning of § 28(1). She is therefore a mere aider under § 27, even if under general principles of joint perpetratorship she has a control over the affairs of her husband that would qualify for full or partial functional control. The effect of § 28(1) is that her sentence must be reduced under § 49(1) as long as she has the necessary *mens rea* regarding the offence of her husband and her own support for it.

§ 28 only applies to characteristics of the offender, not of the offence. Thus, for example, regardless of how one views the relationship between § 212 and § 211 (separate offences or qualifications of each other), § 28 never applies to alternatives that describe the modus of commission, such as, for example, 'by stealth or cruelly or by means that pose a danger to the public' in § 211. The general rules apply for these offence-related elements. The effect of § 28 is thus a potential shift in the applicable provision including the ensuing sentencing frames for the participant. A joint perpetrator in an aggravated murder under § 211, if one follows the prevailing opinion in literature, is treated under § 28(2): if D1 kills V out of greed, but D2 merely wants to help his friend D1 without earning any money out of the offence, D1 will be guilty of aggravated murder under § 211, whereas D2 will be guilty of murder under § 212. The difference is that D1 receives a mandatory life sentence, whereas D2's sentencing range begins at five years.

§ 28 covers qualities that adhere to a person permanently by nature, such as sex, age or being someone's relative, but also those that may be merely temporarily assigned, for example, whether someone is a civil servant, a judge or a soldier, whether he or she has been specifically entrusted with the care for a certain matter (for example, in the context of § 266). It may also refer to mere circumstances, such as the withdrawal from an attempt.[61] Care must be taken not to confuse personal characteristics with offences that can only be directly committed by the principal, so-called '*eigenhändige Delikte*', such as, for example, perjury under § 154—only the witness can give the false testimony, yet this fact forms the basis for the definition of the offence in the first place. These are not cases for § 28, but they follow the general rules.[62]

The relationship between §§ 28 and 29 is controversial. § 29 states:

> Each accomplice shall be liable according to the measure of his own guilt and irrespective of the guilt of the others.

The prevailing opinion in the literature and the courts interpret this as meaning that § 29 covers only the third stage of the tripartite structure, which means

---

[61] See for more Sch/Sch-Cramer/Heine, § 28, Mn. 11 *ff.*
[62] Sch/Sch-Cramer/Heine, § 28, Mn. 19, and § 25, Mn. 45–8.

that only *general* guilt-related issues such as, for example, an error of law (§ 17), excessive self-defence (§ 33), duress (§ 35) and insanity as well as diminished responsibility (§§ 20 and 21), are covered by § 29; any other *specific and typified* elements are said to fall under § 28.[63] A minority applies § 29 to the latter category as well, although there is no uniform view of which typified elements fall under that category.[64] This can have consequences if one accepts such elements—which establish liability—as 'carelessly' within § 315c(1) no 2 or 'maliciously' in § 90a(1) no 1 as representing typified elements of guilt, because if the participant does not possess these qualities, § 29 could mandate absolution from any liability as an element of guilt is lacking, whereas § 28(1) would merely order a mitigation of sentence. The minority view is fraught with additional doctrinal problems that make its application undesirable.

The law of homicide, as previously addressed several times, holds a specific problem in that the courts, and especially the BGH, treat §§ 211 and 212 as separate offences, which means that the elements of both offences *establish* liability: they do not increase or reduce it. We will return to take a closer look at that problem in chapter nine below.

Attempted Participation or Conspiracy—§§ 30 and 31

German law does not recognise an inchoate offence category of conspiracy, yet the need to cover certain preparatory acts and stages of criminal behaviour has led to a similar concept, which is, however, more closely modelled on the general concept of attempts. Nevertheless, it has been called conspiracy here to preserve crispness of expression. Its ambit is regulated in §§ 30 to 31, which contain a specific rule on withdrawal:

§ 30 Conspiracy

(1) A person who attempts to induce another to commit a felony or abet another to commit a felony shall be liable according to the provisions governing attempted felonies. The sentence shall be mitigated pursuant to § 49(1). § 23(3) shall apply mutatis mutandis.

(2) A person who declares his willingness or who accepts the offer of another or who agrees with another to commit or abet the commission of a felony shall be liable under the same terms.

§ 31 Withdrawal from conspiracy

(1) A person shall not be liable under § 30 if he voluntarily

1. gives up the attempt to induce another to commit a felony and averts any existing danger that the other may commit the offence;

---

[63] See the references at Sch/Sch-Cramer/Heine, § 28, Mn. 2–3.
[64] Sch/Sch-Cramer/Heine, § 28, Mn. 4–5.

2. after having declared his willingness to commit a felony, gives up his plan; or
3. after having agreed to commit a felony or accepted the offer of another to commit a felony prevents the commission of the offence.

(2) If the offence is not completed regardless of his actions or if it is committed independently of his previous conduct, his voluntary and earnest effort to prevent the completion of the offence shall suffice for exemption from liability.

German law recognises liability for these preparatory acts only in the cases of felonies, not misdemeanours. Both the instigator and the willing recipient of the exhortation to commit a felony may be liable. The law allows for liability even in cases of impossible attempts, but gives the court a wide discretion to order a discharge or reduce the sentence, as the reference to § 23(3) in § 30(1) signifies, if the offender acted in gross ignorance of that fact. § 31 extends to the co-conspirators the chance of withdrawing with the consequence of an acquittal from the charge under § 30. The law is a variation on the general withdrawal rule for multiple offenders in § 24(2), which is treated in the chapter on attempts. Because of its specific relationship to § 30, we shall examine its implications here. A good example for the problems this provision entails is given by a decision of the BGH of 14 June 2005:[65]

A was in financial trouble because his divorced wife W demanded a large sum of money from him. He thought that the new partner (P) of his ex-wife W was behind all of this and came to the conclusion to have P 'removed' by a hired killer. A friend helped him make contact with a man who called himself 'N', but who was, in fact, a police agent working undercover. On 30 March 2004, A told N that he wanted a 'full disposal' of P—just scaring him away would not be enough. He then filled N in on the details as to how the murder could be committed, ie that P was often at home alone because W's father was in hospital at the time and she visited him very often. When N asked about the payment, A handed him €4,000 and promised a further €8,000 on completion of the deal. N pretended to be prepared to kill P, but asked A for more information, such as the address of W and the layout of the house, etc. A then agreed to meet N a second time and show him the house. At that second meeting when he showed N the house, A told N that he had received a letter from W's solicitors setting out the claim by W and modalities of a settlement. A told N that he was first going to see whether a settlement could be reached, but if it could not, then the 'whole thing should go through'. Because of this, he told N he could keep the down payment of €4,000. However, because W's father would by then be out of hospital, the murder would become more difficult to commit, and they would need a silencer and possibly would have to drug P in the process of getting him away from the house, but the actual modalities were left to N. A told N that he would contact him, should the plan go through. On 23 April 2004, A was arrested without having contacted N again. A was sentenced by the trial court to three and a half years' imprisonment on a conviction for attempted

[65] Docket No 1 StR 503/04. The text is a modified version of my case comment on that decision in (2006) *Journal of Criminal Law* 70 135–8.

176

procurement, or conspiracy, to murder. He appealed the conviction on the grounds that he had withdrawn from the attempt and thus not committed any offence. The BGH dismissed the appeal, holding that A had not withdrawn effectively from the attempt to procure N into killing P, because § 31 required the honest and sincere, as well as voluntary, effort on the part of the procurer to prevent the crime from being committed, even if it was not carried out for other reasons. A did not fall into that category. The attempt had not been terminated after the second meeting, either.

To give a short recapitulation on the withdrawal issue: whether a withdrawal is successful depends on whether it is an 'unfinished' (*unbeendet*) attempt or a 'finished' (*beendet*) one. An unfinished attempt leaves some acts still to be performed, in the view of the offender, before the full result can occur: for example, if D points a loaded gun at V with his finger on the trigger, but then lowers the gun and lets V run away. In such a case, the voluntary abstention from further acts will be sufficient and D will not be liable for the attempted offence. A finished attempt occurs when D has done all that is needed in his view to bring about the full result, for example, when D puts a bomb with a timer on a plane and the plane takes off. In this case, D must prevent the full offence from happening, or if it does not happen for reasons unconnected to his efforts, he must at least make every effort in his powers to prevent the offence. Unfinished or finished, an attempt is always complete and withdrawal normally impossible when the attempt has miscarried (*fehlgeschlagen*) for other reasons, and any change of mind is no longer voluntary (D is being surrounded by the police before he can shoot V; D has been seen when he put the bomb on the plane and is being pursued by the police).

One could argue that A had voluntarily given up the further execution of the attempted procurement, as he had told N that he was only to go through with the murder if A contacted him again. The trial court and the BGH took a different stance based on A's (mistaken) view of the facts and the interplay of § 31 with the general provision of § 24, because in A's view he had successfully procured N to commit murder, although as the BGH said, the attempt had miscarried for objective reasons, which under §§ 24 and 31(1) would have meant that withdrawal was no longer possible. Because N was an undercover police agent, it could be argued that the offence was not carried out because of reasons unconnected to his efforts, as provided for under § 31(2) of the Criminal Code. The BGH indeed held that in order to obtain freedom from liability, he was to be treated as in the case where the full offence does not happen regardless of any preventative actions by the conspirator, but which still requires voluntary, honest and sincere efforts on his part to prevent the commission. Therefore, § 31(2) also appears to cover miscarried attempts and is an exception to the general doctrine under § 24. A's subsequent actions, such as showing N the house after the letter from W's solicitors, leaving N in possession of the down payment and asking him to be prepared should he contact him showed, however, that he had not really given up his intention to have P killed. A's attempt was not an impossible one, because in theory N could have been persuaded by the money to kill P, however unlikely that may have been. The BGH did not accept A's argument, either, that the attempt was ended voluntarily when he told N not to go ahead until he had heard from A to do so. The court viewed the chain of events as one continuous sequence, and if N had carried out the murder after getting the go-ahead from A, that would not have been a new procurement, but merely the continuation of the first one, the execution of which had merely been suspended. This reasoning can be supported on the basis that A left the €4,000 with N and did not demand the sum back, and that N, who was in A's view acting out of sheer greed, could have gone ahead with the murder in any case to 'earn' the remaining €8,000 or put pressure on A to pay the rest. The situation was thus still very dangerous and A's efforts were not sincere enough, although they could, based on A's view, have been voluntary.

9

Homicide Offences

Structural Overview

German law calls homicide offences 'offences against life', which includes abortion; the terms will be used interchangeably here. The main offences against life can be found in §§ 211 to 222. There are, however, many homicide offences in other sections of the Special Part in the form of result-qualified offences where D causes death by committing a non-homicide basic offence, as, for example, § 227 on bodily harm causing death. We have seen that in these cases it is a question of the link between basic offence and aggravated result under § 18 whether D will be held liable for the result. We shall not address the issue in depth again in this chapter. After a few general observations, we shall examine the individual offences in turn, pointing out the more problematic issues in brief. This chapter, as the other two on sexual offences and property offences, is meant to be a mere introduction and its object cannot be treated at the same length for reasons of space. The offence of genocide previously found in this chapter (§ 220a) has now been moved to the separate Code of International Criminal Law (*Völkerstrafgesetzbuch*); because of all the additional problems of international crimes, these will not be treated here.[1]

The first basic distinction in comparison with English law, which has been addressed earlier but bears repeating, is that German law under § 222 knows of a form of negligent homicide that does not require gross negligence:

§ 222 Negligent manslaughter

Whosoever through negligence causes the death of a person shall be liable to imprisonment of not more than five years or a fine.

§ 18 is a testament to the fact that German law does not recognise constructive liability in homicide offences.

The intentional homicide offences, §§ 211, 212, 213 and 216, present a problem as far as their structural doctrinal relationship is concerned. They read as follows:

---

[1] See on this Werle, *Principles of International Criminal Law* (The Hague, TMC Asser Press, 2005), Mn. 238–65.

§ 211 Murder under specific aggravating circumstances

(1) Whosoever commits murder under the conditions of this provision shall be liable to imprisonment for life.
(2) A murderer under this provision is any person who kills a person for pleasure, for sexual gratification, out of greed or otherwise base motives, by stealth or cruelly or by means that pose a danger to the public or in order to facilitate or to cover up another offence.

§ 212 Murder

(1) Whosoever kills a person without being a murderer under § 211 shall be convicted of murder and be liable to imprisonment of not less than five years.
(2) In especially serious cases the penalty shall be imprisonment for life.

§ 213 Murder under mitigating circumstances

If the murderer (under § 212) was provoked to rage by maltreatment inflicted on him or a relative, or was seriously insulted by the victim and immediately lost self-control and committed the offence, or in the event of an otherwise less serious case, the penalty shall be imprisonment from one to ten years.

§ 216 Killing at the request of the victim; mercy killing

(1) If a person is induced to kill by the express and earnest request of the victim the penalty shall be imprisonment from six months to five years.
(2) The attempt shall be punishable.

Despite the sequence of these provisions, which should normally be a strong indicator as to what is the basic norm, what is a qualification, etc, the courts and the commentators disagree as to the relationship between §§ 212 and 211 and the ensuing consequences for the other forms of intentional homicide. The BGH has traditionally held[2] that because of the different substance of both provisions, §§ 211 and 212 are two separate offences that are not to be considered in a relationship of basic or qualified norm. The literature, however, views them precisely thus; opinion is divided about whether § 211 is the basic norm and § 212 a less serious case, or § 212 the basic norm and § 211 an aggravated form. The literature view is to be preferred; it has at least systematic interpretation on its side because, first, § 211 is the first offence to be mentioned and, secondly, § 212 talks about a person who is not a murderer under § 211. That the majority view still sees § 212 as the basic norm is of secondary importance, as the only real application of the different views is in § 28 on participation and complicity, where the view of the BGH leads to the application of § 28(1) and that of the commentators, regardless of which model, to § 28(2).[3] A similar problem arises in the context of § 216 on mercy killings, which the prevailing opinion in the literature[4] views as a privileged form of § 212, whereas the BGH[5] regards it as a separate offence as well; as we saw

[2] And still does: see BGHSt 36, 233.
[3] See Sch/Sch-Eser, Vorbem §§ 211 *ff*, Mn. 5.
[4] Sch/Sch-Eser, Vorbem § 211 ff., Mn. 7. *Eser* himself, however, sides with the BGH on this issue.
[5] BGHSt 2, 258.

above, the fact that § 216(2) makes a statement about attempt liability militates in favour of the BGH's view because it would strictly speaking be unnecessary to do so if it was a mere variation on the felony of § 212. § 213—and § 212(2) for that matter—are mere sentencing provisions in relation to § 212(1); note that § 213 does not apply to § 211 as it makes clear reference only to § 212. § 218 on abortion is a separate issue, because § 212 in principle only applies to life after the stage covered by abortion, so conceptually there can hardly be an overlap. § 221 finally contains an offence that primarily consists of actually, and not merely abstractly, endangering someone's life; it may be questionable, however, whether strictly doctrinally speaking it belongs to the homicide offences at all or whether it is not more akin to offences against the person, because many other offences that have a basic offence coupled with a lethal result under § 18 could be seen as falling under the same category:

§ 221 Abandonment

(1) Whosoever

    1. places a person in a helpless situation; or
    2. abandons a person in a helpless situation although he gives him shelter or is otherwise obliged to care for him,

and thereby exposes him to a danger of death or serious injury shall be liable to imprisonment from three months to five years.

(2) The penalty shall be imprisonment from one to ten years if the offender

    1. commits the offence against his own child or a person entrusted to him for education or care; or
    2. through the offence causes serious injury to the victim.

(3) If the offender causes the death of the victim the penalty shall be imprisonment of not less than three years.

(4) In less serious cases under subsection (2) above the penalty shall be imprisonment from six months to five years, in less serious cases under subsection (3) above imprisonment from one to ten years.

Beginning and End of Life for the Purposes of Homicide Offences

The homicide offences only apply to persons who have passed the threshold of the beginning of full human life, which generally equates to the born human. A person is considered to be born once the dilating pains begin, which was supported under the previous law of § 217 which punished the killing of a child 'within the act of birth' as murder and established a sentencing privilege for the mother if she killed the baby due to the psychological stress situation during birth. This was no longer covered under abortion. If the birth is effected by Caesarian section, the equivalent point in time is the opening of the uterus. Whether the child has the capacity to survive is irrelevant as long as he or she is alive at the moment of the offence and lives independently of the mother; generally[6] any reduction in the span of life is sufficient for the completion of a homicide offence.[7]

In this context, it can be difficult to determine the nature of acts committed in the pre-natal stage, the effects of which manifest themselves in death only after V's birth: is D guilty of murder or abortion? One might put the emphasis on the time of the commission of the act or on the point of death. German doctrine rejects both extreme views and opts for a stance between the two: the nature of the offence is determined by the time when the effects of the act begin to manifest themselves in the child and thus start the chain of causation towards the lethal result in V. An example is that of D infecting V's mother with a virus while she is still pregnant with V. If the virus is transmitted to V while V is still connected to the mother by, *and through* the umbilical cord, then it would be a case of abortion, which also means that if it was done negligently, D would escape any criminal liability. If the virus is transmitted from the infected mother only when she holds the newborn child to her breast directly after birth, D would be liable for murder or negligent homicide of V depending on his *mens rea*. It is obvious that this little difference in time may make a big difference in sentence; in the case of intentional infection between a few years and a mandatory life sentence, should D's behaviour qualify under § 211, or a discretionary one under § 212(2).[8]

The law must define when human life ends to make sure when liability for murder ends if actions are taken that impact on the body of V. It is in these times also highly relevant due to the necessities and increased possibilities of modern medicine: organ transplants, for example, are only permissible once V has died. This decision is even more difficult than the one about the beginning of life, where at least one can refer to an overt biological process, yet the end of life has yet to be evidenced by similarly clear indicators. There appears to be agreement that for the purposes of the law the brain death is the relevant point in time, yet the exact definition is anything but clear.[9] Similar problems arise with regard to the evidence required to establish brain death, which is why the German legislator has so far not acted on demands to provide a legal definition of death and has left it to the current state of the art in medicine to provide that function.[10] While this is, of course, problematic because medical doctors may have an interest in certifying death at an early stage in order to be able to begin with transplant operations, etc, it is difficult to see where the alternative could lie.

---

[6] See generally on the constitutional issues surrounding sanctity of life, BVerfGE 39, 1: 88, 203.
[7] BGHSt 10, 292; 31, 348; 32, 194; OLG Karlsruhe NStZ 1985, 315.
[8] See for a discussion Sch/Sch-Eser, Vorbem §§ 211 *ff*, Mn. 15, who also cites that example.
[9] See the references at Sch/Sch-Eser, Vorbem §§ 211 *ff*, Mn. 19.
[10] Sch/Sch-Eser, Vorbem §§ 211 *ff*, Mn. 19a.

Euthanasia

Another area that needs general consideration is that of euthanasia in the wider meaning of assisted dying. As should be obvious from § 216, German law does not subscribe to the view that anyone can dispose of their life as they see fit;[11] life is excepted from human decision-making and acceding to V's desire to die and be killed leads to D's criminal liability with a mere reduction in sentencing. This applies in principle certainly to any form of active euthanasia, even if it is meant to end excruciating pain and suffering. However, with the problems of modern medicine and the increased reach of palliative care, this basic principle has suffered several exceptions. At the end of a person's life, palliative care, even if it leads to a decrease or loss of consciousness, but does not shorten life, is clearly permitted.[12] Although initially controversial, the scenarios which would be regulated under the double-effect doctrine in English law, ie where the palliative care also shortens life, have become almost universally recognised as being exempt from criminal liability, the reasoning being similar in part to English law, but with an increasing preparedness[13] to situate the problem in the field of necessity or related principles.[14] At the beginning of life, based in part on the horrible events during the country's darkest period from 1933 to 1945, German law does not recognise the idea of the active 'destruction of life unworthy to live' (*Vernichtung lebensunwerten Lebens*) in the meaning of eugenics;[15] yet the problems connected to the birth of severely disabled neonates and the question of whether they may be left to die by not providing medical support rather than actively killed are far from having been solved,

---

[11] BGHSt 46, 285.

[12] Sch/Sch-Eser, Vorbem §§ 211 *ff*, Mn. 23.

[13] German law has not yet taken the step as, eg Dutch law, that introduced legislation in 2001 to cover assisted dying. See *Wet van 12 april 2001, houdende toetsing van levensbeëindiging op verzoek en hulp bij zelfdoding en wijziging van het Wetboek van Strafrecht en van de Wet op de lijkbezorging (Wet toetsing levensbeëindiging op verzoek en hulp bij zelfdoding)* available at <http://wetten.overheid.nl> accessed 2 July 2008. Previously, the Dutch courts had based their approval on necessity. See the decision by the *Hoge Raad*, the Dutch Supreme Court, judgment of 9 November 2004, Case no 02641/03 and my comment in (2005) *Journal of Criminal Law* 401 for the full facts. The *Hoge Raad* held that the following criteria had to be met under the old law:

> —Was there, according to the prevailing medical opinion, unbearable suffering, *and* was the patient without hope of recovery or at least improvement?
> —Was there no other acceptable way of treating the patient?
> —Had at least one other, independent doctor been consulted?
> —Had there been consultations with other persons directly involved in the care of the patient?
> —Was the act of euthanasia done in accordance with diligent medical practice?
> —Had the coroner been notified of the death as being the result of unnatural causes?

[14] Sch/Sch-Eser, Vorbem §§ 211 *ff*, Mn. 26.

[15] Sch/Sch-Eser, Vorbem §§ 211 *ff*, Mn. 24. *Eser* is right to point out that despite the general revulsion of the system to the idea of eugenics, similar ideas seem to have crept into the civil law liability of doctors for the additional costs of so-called 'wrongful life', ie bringing up severely disabled children that were, for example, conceived because of a mistake by the doctor carrying out a sterilisation; see the case law of BGH NJW 1983, 1371; 1985, 568; 1994, 788.

with a tendency by some to make the support available from the state or the community to the burdened parents a decisive criterion; the less support the community is willing to provide for this exceptional burden, the more say the parents should have in whether or not to take up that burden. It should also be noted, as *Eser* correctly points out, that we are moving into the area of pure social eugenics and away from individual euthanasia.[16] Passive euthanasia, ie by omission, does in principle follow the general rules of liability for omission offences and § 323c, yet despite a duty to act there will be no liability if V consents or there is presumed consent[17] to non-intervention; the scope of § 216 is thus in the final analysis reduced in omission scenarios for public policy reasons. The will of the patient may have to be exercised by third persons such as guardians, etc, and in some cases a judicial certification will be necessary. If patients have made a will for such scenarios (*Patientenverfügung*), the courts[18] tend to view their effect generously, but much about them is still controversial.[19] The issue of unilateral cessation of treatment without consent or presumed consent of the patient because it appears no longer to serve purpose or ceasing treatment might even put the patient out of his or her misery is controversial;[20] the contours are unclear, yet the BGH has accepted in principle that there is no duty to maintain a patient's life at any cost.[21] No clear answer has been given by the courts, either, on the issue of 'cost-benefit' decisions and conflicting demands on restricted resources, such as respirators, etc. There appears to be consensus in the literature that if two or more patients need the same apparatus at the same time, the doctor has a certain discretion in choosing which one is to benefit; if a new patient is admitted and needs the instruments to which another patient has been previously connected, then the first patient normally takes precedence over the new. Economic factors will only in the rarest of circumstances be allowed to influence the decision.[22]

Suicide

Suicide attempts are not punishable, as the law talks about the killing of 'another' person. Consequently, secondary participation in an autonomous act of suicide does not make D liable, either, because there is no unlawful principal offence. The emphasis on the autonomy as the ability to understand the consequences of one's actions and to make a free, deliberate and informed choice is of the utmost importance, as we saw above in connection with the *Sirius* case, where D was liable

---

[16] Sch/Sch-Eser, Vorbem §§ 211 *ff*, Mn. 32a.
[17] BGHSt 40, 257.
[18] *Ibid.*
[19] Sch/Sch-Eser, Vorbem §§ 211 *ff*, Mn. 28–28b with references.
[20] Sch/Sch-Eser, Vorbem §§ 211 *ff*, Mn. 29.
[21] BGHSt 32, 379.
[22] Sch/Sch-Eser, Vorbem §§ 211 *ff*, Mn. 30.

for murder as a principal by proxy by using the victim as an unwitting instrument against herself. It must be noted that if V's suicide wish is not serious because of lack of autonomy, D will be guilty of murder under § 211 or 212, not 216. Lack of autonomy may be present even if V is not suffering from any of the conditions mentioned in §§ 20 and 21, but may be lacking because of deception, etc.[23] In contrast to the principles just explained, the courts have traditionally tended to state a general duty to avert a suicidal result if V has already set the causal chain in motion,[24] with the consequence that if D is under a duty to act, he may be liable for murder by omission, or otherwise under § 323c; this has been rightly criticised as inconsistent.[25]

Abortion

Abortion is regulated in an intricate system of provisions. It is addressed to the woman and to the doctor who performs the abortion, with the woman receiving special treatment because of her circumstances. This becomes evident for our purposes when looking at the provisions themselves.[26] The basic offence is found in § 218:

§ 218 Abortion

(1) Whosoever terminates a pregnancy shall be liable to imprisonment of not more than three years or a fine. Acts the effects of which occur before the conclusion of the nidation shall not be deemed to be an abortion within the meaning of this law.

(2) In especially serious cases the penalty shall be imprisonment from six months to five years. An especially serious case typically occurs if the offender

1. acts against the will of the pregnant woman; or
2. through gross negligence causes a risk of death or serious injury to the pregnant woman.

(3) If the act is committed by the pregnant woman the penalty shall be imprisonment of not more than one year or a fine.

(4) The attempt shall be punishable. The pregnant woman shall not be liable for attempt.

§ 218(3) and (4) reduce the sentencing scale and exempt the woman from attempt liability. The previously mentioned supra-legal state of necessity that was developed on the basis of an abortion case and found its more modern expression in § 34 on necessity has also made its way into more specific regulations about abortion that do partially go above and beyond the criteria set out in § 34. They can

---

[23] Sch/Sch-Eser, Vorbem §§ 211 *ff*, Mn. 33–44.
[24] See BGHSt 32, 367 for the development of the case law.
[25] Sch/Sch-Eser, Vorbem §§ 211 *ff*, Mn. 43.
[26] For an overview of the development and the problems of the individual provisions, see the commentary by *Eser* in Sch/Sch-Eser, Vorbem §§ 218 *ff*–219b.

be found in § 218a and have been the object of heated controversy since the 1970s between those opposed to free choice, who emphasise the right to life, and the free choice advocates. After German unification in 1991, the abortion law was reformed again in 1992 because the previous GDR had had a purely time-based rule (*Fristenlösung*), as opposed to the West German approach that, in a simplified manner of speaking, required the existence of certain indicators (*Indikationslösung*). The new law in § 218a(1) allows an abortion without these indicators up to the 12th week after conception and even systematically speaking excludes them from the *Tatbestand* of § 218, and even later in the old case of danger to the woman's health, § 218a(2). The woman's liability does in fact not start before the end of the 22nd week: see § 218a(4). § 218a(3) recognises the fact that the pregnancy is the result of a sexual offence as a specific reason for terminating it.

§ 218a Exception to liability for abortion

(1) The offence under § 218 shall not be deemed fulfilled if

    1. the pregnant woman requests the termination of the pregnancy and demonstrates to the physician by certificate pursuant to § 219(2) 2nd sentence that she obtained counselling at least three days before the operation;

    2. the termination of the pregnancy is performed by a physician; and

    3. not more than twelve weeks have elapsed since conception.

(2) The termination of pregnancy performed by a physician with the consent of the pregnant woman shall not be unlawful if, considering the present and future living conditions of the pregnant woman, the termination of the pregnancy is medically necessary to avert a danger to the life or the danger of grave injury to the physical or mental health of the pregnant woman and if the danger cannot reasonably be averted in another way from her point of view.

(3) The conditions of subsection (2) above shall also be deemed fulfilled with regard to a termination of pregnancy performed by a physician with the consent of the pregnant woman, if according to medical opinion an unlawful act has been committed against the pregnant woman under §§ 176 to 179, there is strong reason to support the assumption that the pregnancy was caused by the act, and not more than twelve weeks have elapsed since conception.

(4) The pregnant woman shall not be liable under § 218 if the termination of pregnancy was performed by a physician after counselling (§ 219) and not more than twenty-two weeks have elapsed since conception. The court may order a discharge under § 218 if the pregnant woman was in exceptional distress at the time of the operation.

The law requires a rigorous counselling and certification process and doctors may be criminally liable for neglecting their duties:

§ 218b Abortion without or under incorrect medical certification

(1) Whosoever terminates a pregnancy in cases under § 218a(2) or (3) without having received the written determination of a physician, who did not himself perform the termination of the pregnancy, as to whether the conditions of § 218a(2) or (3) were met shall be liable to imprisonment of not more than one year or a fine unless theoffence is punishable under § 218. Whosoever as a physician intentionally and

knowingly makes an incorrect determination as to the conditions of § 218a(2) or (3) for presentation under the 1st sentence above shall be liable to imprisonment of not more than two years or a fine unless the act is punishable under § 218. The pregnant woman shall not be liable under the 1st or 2nd sentences above.

(2) A physician must not make determinations pursuant to § 218a(2) or (3) if a competent agency has prohibited him from doing so because he has been convicted by final judgment for an unlawful act under subsection (1) or under § 218, § 219a or § 219b or for another unlawful act which he committed in connection with a termination of pregnancy. The competent agency may provisionally prohibit a physician from making determinations under § 218a(2) and (3) if an indictment has been admitted to trial based on a suspicion that he committed unlawful acts indicated in the 1st sentence above.

§ 218c Violation of medical duties in connection with an abortion

(1) Whosoever terminates a pregnancy

1. without having given the woman an opportunity to explain the reasons for her request for a termination of pregnancy;
2. without having given the pregnant woman medical advice about the significance of the operation, especially about the circumstances of the procedure, after-effects, risks, possible physical or mental consequences;
3. in cases under § 218a(1) and (3) without having previously convinced himself on the basis of a medical examination as to the state of the pregnancy; or
4. despite having counselled the woman with respect to § 218a (1) pursuant to § 219,

shall be liable to imprisonment of not more than one year or a fine unless the act is punishable under § 218.

(2) The pregnant woman shall not be liable under subsection (1) above.

The counselling as such is not open-ended, as § 219(1) 1st and 2nd sentences makes clear: it serves to protect unborn life and is meant to encourage the woman to continue the pregnancy.

§ 219 Counselling of the pregnant woman in a situation of emergency or conflict

(1) The counselling serves to protect unborn life. It should be guided by efforts to encourage the woman to continue the pregnancy and to open her to the prospects of a life with the child; it should help her to make a responsible and conscientious decision. The woman must thereby be aware that the unborn child has its own right to life with respect to her at every stage of the pregnancy and that a termination of pregnancy can therefore only be considered under the law in exceptional situations, when carrying the child to term would give rise to a burden for the woman which is so serious and extraordinary that it exceeds the reasonable limits of sacrifice. The counselling should, through advice and assistance, contribute to overcoming the conflict situation which exists in connection with the pregnancy and remedying an emergency situation. Further details shall be regulated by the Act on Pregnancies in Conflict Situations.

(2) The counselling must take place pursuant to the Act on Pregnancies in Conflict Situations through a recognised pregnancy conflict counselling agency. After the

conclusion of the counselling on the subject, the counselling agency must issue the pregnant woman with a certificate including the date of the last counselling session and the name of the pregnant woman in accordance with the Act on Pregnancies in Conflict Situations. The physician who performs the termination of pregnancy is excluded from being a counsellor.

In certain cases, the law also punishes advertising one's services and the distribution of substances for an abortion:

§ 219a Advertising services for abortion

(1) Whosoever publicly, in a meeting or through dissemination of written materials (§ 11(3)), for material gain or in a grossly inappropriate manner, offers, announces or commends

1. his own services for performing terminations of pregnancy or for supporting them, or the services of another; or
2. means, objects or procedures capable of terminating a pregnancy with reference to this capacity,

or makes declarations of such a nature shall be liable to imprisonment of not more than two years or a fine.
(2) Subsection (1) No 1 above shall not apply when physicians or statutorily recognised counselling agencies provide information about which physicians, hospitals or institutions are prepared to perform a termination of pregnancy under the conditions of § 218a(1) to (3).
(3) Subsection (1) No 2 above shall not apply if the offence was committed with respect to physicians or persons who are authorised to trade in the means or objects mentioned in subsection (1) No 2 or through a publication in professional medical or pharmaceutical journals.

§ 219b Distribution of substances for the purpose of abortion

(1) Whosoever with intent to encourage unlawful acts under § 218 distributes means or objects which are capable of terminating a pregnancy shall be liable to imprisonment of not more than two years or a fine.
(2) The secondary participation by a woman preparing the termination of her own pregnancy shall not be punishable under subsection (1) above.
(3) Means or objects to which the offence relates may be subject to a deprivation order.

§ 211—the Special Elements of Aggravated Murder

As we have already seen, German law reserves the mandatory[27] life sentence for especially heinous acts of intentional homicide, with the 'normal' murder having

[27] The constitutionality of the mandatory life sentence for murder had been challenged in the BVerfG and the court upheld it under the condition that the convicted person must have a chance of regaining his or her freedom through parole (which led to the introduction of § 57a) and that the elements of § 211 be interpreted restrictively. See BVerfGE 45, 187.

a scale from five to 15 years, and in especially serious cases not caught by § 211, a discretionary life sentence. § 211, as § 212, requires intent to kill which may normally be conditional intent or *dolus eventualis* for the mere act of killing as opposed to the special elements. Note that German law allows for the mitigation of the mandatory sentence in line with general sentencing provisions such as § 49, and according to the BGH also in cases of wholly exceptional situations where the harshness of the mandatory life sentence would be entirely inappropriate; the court then applies § 49(1) No 1 by analogy.[28] Let us refresh our memory about what these heinous acts are according to § 211(2). A murderer under this provision is any person who kills a person:

a) for pleasure;
b) for sexual gratification;
c) out of greed; or
d) otherwise base motives;

e) by stealth; or
f) cruelly; or
g) by means that pose a danger to the public; or

h) in order to facilitate or to cover up another offence.

I have listed these elements in three distinct clusters because only the first and third are relevant as personal characteristics within the meaning of § 28, because only they relate to the person and mind of the *offender*. The second group describes heinous modes of commission of the *offence* that follow the general rules of secondary participation and complicity set out above. The courts have traditionally treated the elements of all three clusters as a final and conclusive list of what makes murder into an offence under § 211. They have tried to restrict their application by a narrow interpretation of their prerequisites.[29] The literature tends to comprehend these elements as mere typifications of the especially heinous nature of § 211 offences and consequently wants to allow the judge to reject a verdict under § 211 if despite the fact that one of the elements has been fulfilled, the act is for other reasons not within the general bracket of seriousness as required by § 211.[30] The elements are—briefly—defined as follows:

[28] BGHSt 30, 105.
[29] BGHSt 30, 105.
[30] Sch/Sch-Eser, § 211, Mn. 9–10b.

a) 'For pleasure' means that the victim did not give D any reason to kill him or her; that D's purpose was killing for killing's sake and expressed a fundamental disdain for human life; it does not necessarily require some sort of emotional gratification for D. It requires direct intent: *dolus eventualis* is not enough.[31]

b) 'For sexual gratification' is fulfilled if the act of killing as such gives D sexual gratification; it may, however, be enough if D kills V in order to commit necrophilic acts on the corpse or if during the commission of a rape D has *dolus eventualis* with regard to V's death. Whether D reaches gratification is irrelevant, as long as he desires to attain it, and not merely to become sexually aroused—the latter might be an otherwise base motive.[32]

c) 'Out of greed' requires that D's assets increase, either in reality or at least in his or her imagination, by the death of V, such as, for example, in the case of a murder with the intent to rob V, or in the case of the hired contract killer. D's desire for material gain must be deplorable by general standards, a striving for gain at any cost without regard for human life.[33]

d) D is acting out of 'otherwise base motives' if compared to the previous three elements the nature of D's motivation, according to the moral views of society, is an expression of deepest moral depravity and utterly deplorable. Examples are killing V because she refused to have intercourse with D, killing V in order to become sexually aroused (as opposed to achieving gratification), killing one's spouse in order to enjoy fully an adulterous relationship with another partner, killing a daughter in order to save the family honour, discriminatory killing of V because of her affiliation with a certain ethnic or religious group, etc.[34]

e) 'By stealth' requires D to act in an insidious manner, by intentionally exploiting the fact that V, at the time of the attack, is not expecting an attack (*Arglosigkeit*) and his or her consequent defencelessness (*Wehrlosigkeit*), and all of this with hostile intention. The classic cases are the shot in the back when V turns away from D, D lying in wait in an ambush and killing V when he or she passes by. It includes persons who are asleep, because they are said to take their *Arglosigkeit* with them into their sleep, but not those who are unconscious, because the victim must at the time of the attack at least be generally capable of forming a view about whether or not an attack might be imminent. Hostile intention can exclude such motivations as wanting to spare the victim shame that he or she would otherwise be exposed to, pity for a terminally ill patient, etc.[35]

f) D acts 'cruelly' if he intentionally causes V more pain and suffering, physical or mental, than is necessary to kill him or her. D must act with an unfeeling and

---

[31] BGHSt 34, 49; BGH NJW 1994, 2629.
[32] BGHSt 7, 353; 19, 105; BGH NStZ 2001, 598; BGH NJW 1982, 2565.
[33] See the many references at Sch/Sch-Eser, § 211, Mn. 17.
[34] Compare Sch/Sch-Eser, § 211, Mn. 18–20.
[35] Sch/Sch-Eser, § 211, Mn. 21–6.

merciless attitude. The cruelty need not necessarily be in the act of killing, such as, for example, in particular horrendous or protracted means of execution like being hung, drawn and quartered as in the Middle Ages, but may already occur in the preparation phase, if the victim has to countenance the offender's slow preparations—and D wishes him or her to do so as part of his or her plan to kill him or her—even if the actual method of killing is quick and painless, such as a shot to the head.[36]

g) A killing 'by means that pose a danger to the public' requires D to use a means that when used is no longer controllable and poses a danger to a larger, indeterminate group of people apart from the intended victim(s). The classic example is the use of explosives in a public setting to kill a certain person such as a car bomb in a crowded parking lot or in the case of suicide bombers (where the criminal liability, of course, is usually that of the people who use them as (innocent) agents).[37]

h) The final element, 'in order to facilitate or to cover up another offence' requires D to kill V in order to be able to carry out a criminal offence (felony or misdemeanour) or in the case of (possible) detection in order to avoid third parties obtaining knowledge of his or her participation in it. The intent to kill can be *dolus eventualis*, but the intent to facilitate or cover up must be direct intent (*Absicht*). Classic examples are D shooting a night watchman in order to be able to enter the bank or shooting the policeman who is pursuing him or her. This is regardless of whether or not the participation of D has in fact been discovered, as long as he or she thinks that his or her discovery may be prevented. The application of this element becomes problematic the closer the offence whose discovery is to be prevented and the act of preventative killing are together, both in time and space. If they more or less spontaneously follow on from each other, it may be difficult to apply the condition, and regrettably the jurisprudence of the BGH until recent times has not been able to produce a clear method of delineation.[38]

§§ 211 and 28

The different approaches of the courts and the majority of academic commentators have consequences for the liability of homicide offenders that participate in another's actions under § 28. It is useful to have a look at that provision again:

[36] Sch/Sch-Eser, § 211, Mn. 27–8.
[37] Sch/Sch-Eser, § 211, Mn. 29.
[38] Sch/Sch-Eser, § 211, Mn. 31–5.

§ 28 Special personal characteristics

(1) If special personal characteristics (§ 14(1)) that establish the principal's liability are absent in the person of the secondary participant (abettor or aider) their sentence shall be mitigated pursuant to § 49(1).
(2) If the law provides that special personal characteristics aggravate, mitigate or exclude punishment this shall apply only to the accomplices (principals or secondary participants) in whose person they are present.

The BGH views the elements of § 211 as establishing liability which is mainly based on the fact that it sees §§ 211 and 212 as separate and not linked offences; consequently, it applies § 28(1). The literature sees §§ 211 and 212 in a relationship of basic offence and qualification, leading to the application of § 28(2). Remember that the elements of the second cluster do not fall under § 28 at all, but follow the general principles of accessory liability, most notably that of double intent.[39] Clusters one and three fall under § 28. The following problematic scenarios related to those elements can occur, with acute issues related to fair labelling and sentencing:

a) P fulfils one of the elements of the first or third cluster, D does not, but knows of P's element. The BGH will hold D liable for participation in § 211 with a reduction in sentence under § 49(1);[40] the literature view will only apply § 212 to D, but § 211 to P—§ 28(2) in other words effects a shift in the *Tatbestand* and not just the sentence, much like the traditional English approach to murder under provocation and diminished responsibility, where the *charge* shifts to one of (voluntary) manslaughter.
b) P fulfils no element, but D does. The BGH must apply § 212 to both P and D because § 28(1) only orders the reduction in sentence in the case of their absence in the person of the secondary participant; the presence of an element

---

[39] The case of the secondary participant D having an element of the second cluster, which is absent in P, leads to liability of D based on § 212, with a potentially added charge of conspiracy under §§ 30 and 211 and a sentence increase under § 212(2); see Sch/Sch-Eser, § 211, Mn. 51.

[40] § 49 reads as follows:

'§ 49 Special mitigating circumstances established by law

(1) If the law requires or allows for mitigation under this provision, the following shall apply:

1. Imprisonment of not less than three years shall be substituted for imprisonment for life.
2. In cases of imprisonment for a fixed term, no more than three quarters of the statutory maximum term may be imposed. In case of a fine the same shall apply to the maximum number of daily units.
3. Any increased minimum statutory term of imprisonment shall be reduced as follows:

—a minimum term of ten or five years, to two years;
—a minimum term of three or two years, to six months;
—a minimum term of one year, to three months;
—in all other cases to the statutory minimum.

(2) If the court may in its discretion mitigate the sentence pursuant to a law which refers to this provision, it may reduce the sentence to the statutory minimum or impose a fine instead of imprisonment.'

with D is not a ground for shifting the *Tatbestand* into the more serious level. The literature view would convict D on the basis of § 211, because for § 28(2) it makes no difference whether P has one of the elements.

c) P has one element and D has a different one. The literature again has no problem in holding both liable under § 211 as it does not matter under § 28(2) which element they both fulfil. The BGH, however, has enormous difficulties with this scenario, as the strict interpretation of its view would lead to D being punished on the basis of § 212, not § 211, because for § 28(1) the element of P is determinative of D's liability. Faced with this undesirable situation in which D clearly deserves to be punished and labelled under the more serious provision of § 211, the BGH has developed the vehicle of the so-called 'crossed murder elements' (*gekreuzte Mordmerkmale*) and refuses D the sentence reduction under § 28(1) if D's element is a base motive comparable to that of P.[41] While doctrinally questionable, the desirability of this solution from a public policy point of view can hardly be doubted.

---

[41] See on all this Sch/Sch-Eser, § 211, Mn. 42–55.

10

Sexual Offences

Recent Reform History

In recent times, much like in the law of England and Wales, the German legislature has engaged in what one might almost term a 'reform frenzy' intended partially to allay the public's fear of crime, which was, of course, legitimate to some extent. The general thrust has been to increase the severity of the law. The law has become complicated and convoluted in the extreme because the reforms lacked coherence and were introduced in a piecemeal manner. The reform that laid the foundation for the present shape of the sexual offences legislation began in the 1970s. The ideology behind that development was decriminalisation of behaviour that was at worst considered immoral (the law was previously entitled: Crimes against morality—*Verbrechen und Vergehen gegen die Sittlichkeit*), but did not involve personal harm to any person and their sexual self-determination (*sexuelle Selbstbestimmung*), which was made the new guiding principle of penal legislation in this area. As the provisions set out below show, this idea was not fully implemented, as some offences such as, for example, incest in § 173, that might generally qualify as a sexual offence in the wider meaning, are really offences based on public policy considerations on the protection of the moral views of society and to some extent concerns about genetic consequences of such acts. Some commentators have criticised the use of the label of self-determination in the context of offences against children and immature juveniles, where some have doubted the capacity of the victims to form the necessary intellectual understanding in order to exercise that self-determination. In the 1990s, further major reform packages were implemented, among others the law on human trafficking and sexual exploitation of 1992, as well as the 1994 law on the stay of the statute of limitations for some sexual offences.

The largest of the recent reforms began in the late 1990s with the 33rd Criminal Law (Amendment) Act 1997 and the Sixth Criminal Law (Reform) Act 1998. The former involved a re-conceptualisation of the offences of rape and sexual assault, which were moulded into one basic offence where the force and threat aspect of rape was extended to sexual assault in general, which to some raised issues of fair labelling. It also abolished the restriction of the concept of rape to female victims and especially extended the application of the rape offence to marital violence, whereas previously the law had employed the label of rape only to forced extra-marital intercourse, marital violence having previously been caught, even if not to the same extent as today,[1] under § 240, the general norm on forcing somebody else to do, suffer or omit an act. During the preparatory discussions there had been arguments for allowing some kind of safety valve such as prosecution on request, or a reconciliation clause, in order to enable the parties to the conflict to keep the state out of their private affairs if they thought the problems could be solved without public intervention; however, because of the obvious potential for abuse by the offender or maybe even the victim's family who might want to 'encourage' the victim to use those clauses in order to avoid shame or dishonour to the family, they were not implemented in the end. The Sixth Criminal Law (Reform) Act 1998 amended some of the new legislation again and was generally concerned with harmonising the sentencing frames for the offences among themselves and in comparison to non-sexual offences; normally that meant an increase in severity. Another major motivation was the improvement of the protection of children and of persons with a disability, addicts or resident in an institution, against sexual abuse. Both reforms have been criticised as being poorly drafted and contradictory in parts, as well as lacking a golden conceptual thread.

In 2001, the law on prostitution was reformed, which had mainly to do with abolishing the previous civil law rule that contracts for the services of prostitutes were void under § 138 BGB because they violated public policy, which had meant that prostitutes could not sue their customers if they declined to pay. It also restricted the criminal liability for pimping or facilitating services of prostitutes to clearly exploitative situations to avoid penalisation of what are now commonly termed voluntary sex workers. The Sexual Delinquency (Amendment) Act 2003 led to another increase in sentencing scales, based on highly publicised individual crimes that led the wider public to ask for more drastic measures and heightened the preparedness of people to subscribe to an attitude of increased punitiveness. It was a clear example of unprincipled and symbolic legislation because the alleged deterrent effect was in no way based on empirical evidence.[2] The most recent piece of reform legislation that is not *eo ipso* a sexual offence, but is connected to the area, is § 238 on stalking, which was introduced in 2007.

Because of the selective approach of the reforms and the ensuing lack of coherence, it is difficult to explain the offences in a structured manner without looking at each of them in turn. I therefore propose, as with the homicide offences, to reproduce the provisions themselves, as to a large part they are self-explanatory, and to offer some introductory comment on each group of offences. One general comment must be made at this point, and that is to refer to the general definitional clause of § 184f, which contains a *de minimis* bar on prosecution:

---

[1] See, eg BGH NStZ 1983, 72, which refused to accept an aggravated case under the old law if the wife could have left the joint dwelling. See now the explanation on § 240 below in this chapter, under § 240(4) 2nd sentence No 1.

[2] See on the foregoing in more detail and with further references Sch/Sch-Lenckner/Perron/Eisele, Vorbem. § 174 *ff*, Mn. 1–10, and at 11 for the transitional law related to German unification.

§ 184f Definitions

Within the meaning of this law

1. sexual acts and activities shall only be those which are of some relevance in relation to the protected legal interest in question;
2. sexual acts and activities in the presence of another shall be those which are committed in the presence of another who observes them.

Incest

As previously mentioned, this provision is meant to protect the family from what are still commonly perceived to be socially unacceptable sexual relationships:

§ 173 Incest

(1) Whosoever performs an act of sexual intercourse with a consanguine descendant shall be liable to imprisonment of not more than three years or a fine.

(2) Whosoever performs an act of sexual intercourse with a consanguine relative in an ascending line shall be liable to imprisonment of not more than two years or a fine; this shall also apply if the relationship as a relative has ceased to exist. Consanguine siblings who perform an act of sexual intercourse with each other shall incur the same penalty.

(3) Descendants and siblings shall not be liable pursuant to this provision if they were not yet eighteen years of age at the time of the act.

§ 173 does not require any force; it also covers purely mutual intercourse and even genuine love relationships. If the intercourse is forced within the meaning of rape, the victim may not, depending on the actual facts, be within the *actus reus* of § 173 at all, for example, if D uses *vis absoluta*; if V submits because of threats, the view appears to be that she is not able to rely on necessity, but will have the excusatory defence of duress.[3] V can only participate in D's offence if she exceeds what is called the scope of necessary participation (*notwendige Teilnahme*), ie what a victim normally has to submit to within the context of any given offence. Liability for victim participation is thus the doctrinal exception, not the rule as under the English *Tyrrell* principle.[4] Note that subsection (3) contains an exemption from liability (*Strafausschließungsgrund*) for siblings and descendants under the age of 18. In a recent case, the BVerfG[5] was called upon to declare § 173 unconstitutional and void as far as intercourse between brother and sister was concerned. The

---

[3] Sch/Sch-Lenckner, § 173, Mn. 7.

[4] See for an explanation of the rule and a critique of the recent UK reform legislation my article, 'The Sexual Offences Act 2003 and the Tyrrell Principle—Criminalising the Victims?' (2005) *Criminal Law Review* 701–13.

[5] Decision by the Second Senate of 26 February 2008, Docket No 2 BvR 392/07, available at <http://www.bundesverfassungsgericht.de/entscheidungen/rs20080226_2bvr039207.html> accessed 3 July 2008, with the dissenting opinion of Judge Hassemer at para 73.

majority rejected the challenge and declared the provision as still being within the legislative discretion of Parliament. Judge Hassemer, one of the foremost criminal law professors in Germany and the Vice-President of the Court, wrote a dissent which criticised the criminalisation as in conflict with the proportionality principle, by arguing that there were less intrusive and moreover more effective measures available to the state to deal with such cases.

Abuse of Trust Offences

As was mentioned in the historical overview, the protection of persons who are entrusted to the care of others, because they are vulnerable, from sexual attacks and exploitation has increasingly come into the sights of the criminal law. Vulnerability may arise from a young age and being put into an educational environment (§ 174, but see also § 180(3) below), institutionalisation (§ 174a), being confronted with official authority (§ 174b) or trusting in someone and consequently letting down one's guard in counselling and treatment relationships (§ 174c).

§ 174 Abuse of position of trust

(1) Whosoever engages in sexual activity

1. with a person under sixteen years of age who is entrusted to him for upbringing, education or care;
2. with a person under eighteen years of age who is entrusted to him for upbringing, education or care or who is his subordinate within an employment or a work relationship, by abusing the dependence associated with the upbringing, educational, care, employment or work relationship; or
3. with his biological or adopted child not yet eighteen years of age,

or allows them to engage in sexual activities with himself, shall be liable to imprisonment from three months to five years.

(2) Whosoever, under the conditions of subsection (1) Nos 1 to 3 above

1. engages in sexual activity in the presence of the person; or
2. induces the person to engage in sexual activity in his presence,

in order to obtain sexual gratification for himself or the person shall be liable to imprisonment of not more than three years or a fine.

(3) The attempt shall be punishable.

(4) In cases under subsection (1) No 1 above, or subsection (2) above in conjunction with subsection (1) No 1, the court may order a discharge under this provision if taking into consideration the conduct of the person the harm of the offence is of a minor nature.

§ 174a Sexual abuse of prisoners, patients and institutionalised persons

(1) Whosoever engages in sexual activity with a prisoner or a person detained by order of a public authority, who is entrusted to him for upbringing, education, supervision or care, by abusing his position, or allows them to engage in sexual activity with himself shall be liable to imprisonment from three months to five years.

(2) Whosoever abuses a person who has been admitted to an institution for persons who are ill or in need of assistance and are entrusted to him for supervision or care, by engaging in sexual activity with the person by exploiting the person's illness or need of assistance, or allows them to engage in sexual activity with himself shall incur the same penalty.

(3) The attempt shall be punishable.

§ 174b Abuse of official position

(1) Whosoever in his capacity as a public official charged with participation in criminal proceedings or proceedings with the aim of imposing a custodial measure of rehabilitation and incapacitation or detention imposed by a public authority, by abusing the dependency caused by the proceedings, engages in sexual activity with the person against whom the proceedings are directed or allows them to engage in sexual activity with himself shall be liable to imprisonment from three months to five years.

(2) The attempt shall be punishable.

§ 174c Abuse of a relationship of counselling, treatment or care

(1) Whosoever engages in sexual activity with a person entrusted to him for counselling, treatment or care because of a mental illness or disability including an addiction, or because of a physical illness or disability, and abuses the counselling, treatment or care relationship, or allows the person to engage in sexual activity with himself shall be liable to imprisonment from three months to five years.

(2) Whosoever engages in sexual activity with a person entrusted to him for psychotherapeutic treatment by abusing the treatment relationship or allows them to engage in sexual activity with himself shall incur the same penalty.

(3) The attempt shall be punishable.

Child Abuse Offences

As in almost any criminal jurisdiction, the law provides for strict rules regarding the sexual relationships with minors, and given the problem of violent child abuse and child pornography the severity increases if the activities go beyond the 'merely' sexual and enter the area of serious physical or mental abuse and even death as intended or accepted consequences of the sexual activity. Note that unless the law specifies a minimum age for the offender, the general rules apply: anyone over the age of 14 can be liable.

§ 176 Child abuse

(1) Whosoever engages in sexual activity with a person under fourteen years of age (child) or allows the child to engage in sexual activity with himself shall be liable to imprisonment from six months to ten years.
(2) Whosoever induces a child to engage in sexual activity with a third person or to allow third persons to engage in sexual activity with the child shall incur the same penalty.
(3) In especially serious cases the penalty shall be imprisonment of not less than one year.
(4) Whosoever

1. engages in sexual activity in the presence of a child;
2. induces the child to engage in sexual activity on their own person;
3. presents a child with written materials (§ 11(3)) to induce him to engage in sexual activity with or in the presence of the offender or a third person or allow the offender or a third person to engage in sexual activity with him; or
4. presents a child with pornographic illustrations or images, audio recording media with pornographic content or pornographic speech,

shall be liable to imprisonment from three months to five years.
(5) Whosoever supplies or promises to supply a child for an offence under subsections (1) to (4) above or who agrees with another to commit such an offence shall be liable to imprisonment from three months to five years.
(6) The attempt shall be punishable; this shall not apply to offences under subsection (4) Nos 3 and 4 and subsection (5) above.

§ 176a Aggravated child abuse

(1) The sexual abuse of children under § 176(1) and (2) shall entail a sentence of imprisonment of not less than one year if the offender was convicted of such an offence by final judgment within the previous five years.
(2) The sexual abuse of children under § 176(1) and (2) shall entail a sentence of imprisonment of not less than two years if

1. a person over eighteen years of age performs sexual intercourse or similar sexual acts with the child which include a penetration of the body, or allows them to be performed on himself by the child;
2. the offence is committed jointly by more than one person; or
3. the offender by the offence places the child in danger of serious injury or substantial impairment of his physical or emotional development.

(3) Whosoever under § 176(1) to (3), (4) Nos 1 or 2 or § 176(6) acts as a principal or secondary participant with the intent of making the act the object of a pornographic medium (§ 11(3)) which is to be disseminated pursuant to § 184b(1) to (3) shall be liable to imprisonment of not less than two years.
(4) In less serious cases under subsection (1) above the penalty shall be imprisonment from three months to five years, in less serious cases under subsection (2) above imprisonment from one to ten years.
(5) Whosoever under § 176(1) to (3) seriously physically abuses the child or places the child in danger of death shall be liable to imprisonment of not less than five years.

(6) Any period during which the offender was detained in an institution pursuant to an order of a public authority shall not be credited to the term indicated in subsection (1) above. An offence resulting in a conviction abroad shall be equivalent, under subsection (1) above, to an offence resulting in a domestic conviction if under German criminal law it would have been an offence under § 176(1) or (2).

§ 176b Child abuse causing death

If the offender in cases under § 176 and § 176a causes the death of the child at least by gross negligence the penalty shall be imprisonment for life or not less than ten years.

Sexual Assault and Rape

As I have pointed out elsewhere,[6] the German law on rape does not adopt the pure 'absence of consent' model to which England and Wales and many other common law jurisdictions subscribe. Rather, it requires the use of force or threat of force, or generally speaking, exploitative scenarios that by their very nature deny the victim freedom of choice.[7] Rape by mistaken consent is thus not an issue in German law, not even in the form as retained by the common law with regard to the nature or purpose of the act or the impersonation of a husband. The severity of the punishment is staggered according to the seriousness and dangerousness of the offender's conduct, such as carrying or actually using weapons to overcome the victim's resistance, or causing the victim's death.

§ 177 Sexual assault by use of force or threats; rape

(1) Whosoever coerces another person

1. by force;
2. by threat of imminent danger to life or limb; or
3. by exploiting a situation in which the victim is unprotected and at the mercy of the offender,

to suffer sexual acts by the offender or a third person on their own person or to engage actively in sexual activity with the offender or a third person, shall be liable to imprisonment of not less than one year.

(2) In especially serious cases the penalty shall be imprisonment of not less than two years. An especially serious case typically occurs if

---

[6] 'Mistaken consent to sex, political correctness and correct policy' (2007) *Journal of Criminal Law* 412.

[7] Compare to this the judgment of the European Court of Human Rights (ECtHR) of 4 December 2003 in *MC v Bulgaria* (Application no 39272/98), where the question was raised whether proof or force or threats required proof of physical resistance by the victim. Note that the German law does not require such resistance by the victim in the substantive sense; physical resistance may merely be one evidential indicator for the fact that force was being used or threatened.

1. the offender performs sexual intercourse with the victim or performs similar sexual acts with the victim, or allows them to be performed on himself by the victim, especially if they degrade the victim or if they entail penetration of the body (rape); or
2. the offence is committed jointly by more than one person.

(3) The penalty shall be imprisonment of not less than three years if the offender

1. carries a weapon or another dangerous instrument;
2. otherwise carries an instrument or other means for the purpose of preventing or overcoming the resistance of another person through force or threat of force; or
3. by the offence places the victim in danger of serious injury.

(4) The penalty shall be imprisonment of not less than five years if

1. the offender uses a weapon or another dangerous instrument during the commission of the offence; or if
2. the offender

   a) seriously physically abuses the victim during the offence; or
   b) by the offence places the victim in danger of death.

(5) In less serious cases under subsection (1) above the penalty shall be imprisonment from six months to five years, in less serious cases under subsections (3) and (4) above imprisonment from one to ten years.

§ 178 Sexual assault by force or threat of force and rape causing death

If the offender through sexual assault or rape (§ 177) causes the death of the victim at least by gross negligence the penalty shall be imprisonment for life or not less than ten years.

Vulnerable Persons—Physical or Mental Disabilities and Young Age

While §§ 174 to 174c require a position of trust, §§ 179 to 180 recognise that even in the absence of such a position, the mere exploitation of the fact that a person may be incapable of putting up a resistance is sufficient to warrant the criminal sanction. Note that § 180(3) is a bit out of place as it covers situations that properly belong to scenarios of V being in D's care or under his or her control as a superior, etc, the difference to §§ 174 to 174c being that here D uses his or her position to induce acts with or in front of third persons. The creation of an opportunity for sexual activity under § 180(1) No 2 is not an offence if it is done by the person who is in charge of the minor's education, ie parents, guardians, etc, and if in their view it is consistent with a liberal and responsible sexual education, unless they grossly overstep the bounds of what is generally acceptable.

§ 179 Abuse of persons who are incapable of resistance

(1) Whosoever abuses another person who is incapable of resistance

1. because of a mental illness or disability including an addiction or because of a profound consciousness disorder; or
2. is physically incapable,

and by exploiting the incapability to resist engages in sexual activity with the person or allows them actively to engage in sexual activity on his person shall be liable to imprisonment from six months to ten years.

(2) Whosoever abuses a person incapable of resistance (subsection (1) above), by inducing the person, under exploitation of the incapability of resistance, to engage actively in sexual activity with a third person or to allow a third person to engage in sexual activity with them, shall incur the same penalty.
(3) In especially serious cases the penalty shall be imprisonment of not less than one year.
(4) The attempt shall be punishable.
(5) The penalty shall be imprisonment of not less than two years if

1. the offender performs sexual intercourse or similar sexual acts with the victim which include penetration of the body, or allows them to be committed on himself by the victim;
2. the offence is committed jointly by more than one person; or
3. by the offence the offender places the victim in danger of serious injury or substantial impairment of his physical or emotional development.

(5) In less serious cases under subsection (5) above the penalty shall be imprisonment from one to ten years.
(6) § 177(4) No 2 and § 178 shall apply mutatis mutandis.

§ 180 Causing minors to engage in sexual activity

(1) Whosoever encourages a person under sixteen years of age to engage in sexual activity with or in the presence of a third person or whosoever encourages sexual acts of a third person on a person under sixteen years of age

1. by acting as an intermediary; or
2. by creating an opportunity,

shall be liable to imprisonment of not more than three years or a fine. The 1st sentence No 2 above shall not apply if the offender is the person responsible for the care of the minor unless the offender, if responsible for the care of the minor, grossly violates his duty of education.

(2) Whosoever induces a person under eighteen years of age to engage in sexual activity with or in the presence of a third person or to suffer sexual acts by a third person for a financial reward, or whosoever encourages such acts by acting as an intermediary, shall be liable to imprisonment of not more than five years or a fine.
(3) Whosoever induces a person under eighteen years of age who is entrusted to him for upbringing, education or care or who is his subordinate within an employment or a work relationship, by abusing the dependence associated with the upbringing,

educational, care, employment or work relationship to engage in sexual activity with or in the presence of a third person or to suffer sexual acts by a third person shall be liable to imprisonment of not more than five years or a fine.

(4) In cases under subsections (2) and (3) above the attempt shall be punishable.

Exploitative Behaviour—Prostitutes and Juveniles

As mentioned above, the increasing recognition of prostitution as a legitimate way of earning one's livelihood or generally as an activity that no longer carries the same moral opprobrium as it used to do, has led to a pruning of the previous law of prostitution offences as far as the protection *of the prostitute* is concerned (see below §§ 184d and e on the protection *from prostitution*). The liability is now based on exploitative factors that rob the person of their freedom of choice, such as personal or financial dependency and on the protection of minors. In the case of § 182, the legislature created a provision that is meant as a uniform protection law for the whole federation and which was necessary to effect a harmonisation with the law in the five new Member States after unification. It also takes into account that the repeal of the previous ban on male[8] homosexual activities in § 175 had come under criticism for those scenarios where the homosexual advances were made in an environment where the juvenile or minor did not have the complete freedom to choose whether or not he wanted to engage in the sexual activity. § 182 now covers both male and female homosexual and heterosexual activity if it fulfils the conditions of being exploitative within the meaning of the law.

§ 180a Exploitation of prostitutes

(1) Whosoever on a commercial basis maintains or manages an operation in which persons engage in prostitution and in which they are held in personal or financial dependency shall be liable to imprisonment of not more than three years or a fine.

(2) Whosoever

1. provides a dwelling or on a commercial basis an abode or a residence to a person under eighteen years of age for the exercise of prostitution; or
2. urges another person to whom he has furnished a dwelling for the exercise of prostitution to engage in prostitution or exploits the person in that respect,

shall incur the same penalty.

§ 181a Controlling prostitution

(1) Whosoever

1. exploits another person who engages in prostitution; or
2. for his own material benefit supervises another person's engagement in prostitution, determines the place, time, extent or other circumstances of the engagement

---

[8] Lesbian consensual homosexual activity had never been an offence.

in prostitution, or takes measures to prevent the person from giving up prostitution, and for that purpose maintains a general relationship with the person beyond a particular occasion

shall be liable to imprisonment from six months to five years.

(2) Whosoever impairs another person's personal or financial independence by promoting that person's engagement in prostitution, by procuring sexual relations on a commercial basis, and for that purpose maintains a general relationship with the person beyond a particular occasion shall be liable to imprisonment of not more than three years or a fine.

(3) Whosoever commits the offences under subsection (1) Nos 1 and 2 above or the promotion under subsection (2) above in relation to his spouse shall incur the penalty under subsections (1) and (2) above.

§ 182 Abuse of juveniles

(1) A person over eighteen years of age who abuses a person under sixteen years of age by

1. engaging in sexual activity with the person or causing the person to engage actively in sexual activity with him by taking advantage of an exploitative situation or for a financial reward or
2. by taking advantage of an exploitative situation inducing the person to engage in sexual activity with a third person or to suffer sexual acts committed on their own body by a third person,

shall be liable to imprisonment of not more than five years or a fine.

(2) A person over twenty-one years of age who abuses a person under sixteen years of age by

1. engaging in sexual activity with the person or causing the person to engage actively in sexual activity with him or
2. inducing the person to engage in sexual activity with a third person or to suffer sexual acts committed on their own body by a third person,

and thereby exploits the victim's lack of capacity for sexual self-determination shall be liable to imprisonment of not more than three years or a fine.

(3) In cases under subsection (2) above the offence may only be prosecuted upon request unless the prosecuting authority considers propio motu that prosecution is required out of special public interest.

(4) In cases under subsections (1) and (2) above the court may order a discharge under these provisions if in consideration of the conduct of the person against whom the offence was committed the harm of the offence is of a minor nature.

Public Moral and Order Offences; Pornography

The next section of offences, dealing with exhibitionism (§ 183), public disturbance (§ 183a), pornography (§§ 184 to 184c) and unlawful prostitution (§§ 184 d to e) is less a *sexual* offence category, but rather a collection of *public order* offences connected with the expression of different forms of sexuality. Note that exhibitionism can only be committed by a male offender, which is somewhat questionable in purely doctrinal terms, but probably empirically justified by the very low occurrence rate in females; however, § 183(4) clarifies that females may commit exhibitionist acts under other provisions and that the treatment option under § 183(3) shall also apply to those. Furthermore, the completion of the offence will depend on the reaction of the victim who perceives the activity: if instead of being disgusted or shocked, the victim finds the act comical, does not attribute any sexual connotations to it or has pity with the offender, § 183 will not be made out;[9] attempts are not punishable. § 183a penalises, as it were, random acts of exhibitionism, etc not aimed at an individual victim, yet still causing annoyance with individual people. The protection is thus not aimed at the public moral sphere, but at the right of individuals not to have to be unwillingly confronted with sexual activity.[10]

§ 183 Exhibitionism

(1) A man who annoys another person by an exhibitionist act shall be liable to imprisonment of not more than one year or a fine.
(2) The offence shall only be prosecuted upon request unless the prosecuting authority considers propio motu that prosecution is required out of special public interest.
(3) The court may suspend the sentence if there is reason to believe that the offender will only cease to commit exhibitionist acts after lengthy medical treatment.
(4) Subsection (3) above shall also apply if a man or a woman is convicted because of an exhibitionist act

   1. under another provision which imposes a maximum term of imprisonment of no more than one year; or
   2. under § 174(2) No 1 or § 176(3) No 1.

§ 183a Causing a public disturbance

Whosoever in public engages in sexual activity and thereby intentionally or knowingly creates a disturbance shall be liable to imprisonment of not more than one year or a fine unless the act is punishable under § 183.

A far more serious offence is the distribution of pornography. §§ 184 to 184c divide and stagger the liability, starting with the basic offence of § 184 over pornography depicting violence and sodomy in § 184b, to child pornography in § 184c, and finally the distribution by means of mass media in § 184d. Note that § 184c(2) and (4) criminalise the possession of child pornography only if the materials reproduce an actual or realistic activity, which excludes certain forms of comics, drawings, writings, etc. The reason for this restriction is said to be that in those cases there is typically no concern that an actual child abuse occurred in the

[9] BGH NJW 1970, 1855.
[10] See BGHSt 11, 284 for the previous version; for the current law see Sch/Sch-Lenckner/Perron/Eisele, § 183a, Mn. 1.

preparation of those materials. The measure of what is realistic is whether an ordinary average observer could safely exclude that the material was based on actual events—if he or she cannot, liability accrues. In the age of computer animated design, this provision will have to be interpreted with great care.[11]

§ 184 Distribution of pornography

(1) Whosoever with regard to pornographic written materials (§ 11(3))

1. offers, gives or makes them accessible to a person under eighteen years of age;
2. displays, presents or otherwise makes them accessible at a place accessible to persons under eighteen years of age, or which can be viewed by them;
3. offers or gives them to another in retail trade outside the business premises, in kiosks or other sales areas which the customer usually does not enter, through a mail-order business or in commercial lending libraries or reading circles;
3a. offers or gives them to another by means of commercial rental or comparable commercial supply for use, except for shops which are not accessible to persons under eighteen years of age and which cannot be viewed by them;
4. undertakes to import them by means of a mail-order business;
5. publicly offers, announces, or commends them at a place accessible to persons under eighteen years of age or which can be viewed by them, or through dissemination of written materials outside business transactions through the usual trade outlets;
6. allows another to obtain them without having been requested to do so;
7. shows them at a public film showing for an entry fee intended entirely or predominantly for this showing;
8. produces, obtains, supplies, stocks, or undertakes to import them in order to use them or copies made from them within the meaning of Nos 1 to 7 above or to facilitate such use by another; or
9. undertakes to export them in order to disseminate them or copies made from them abroad in violation of foreign penal provisions or to make them publicly accessible or to facilitate such use,

shall be liable to imprisonment of not more than one year or a fine.

(2) Subsection (1) No 1 above shall not apply if the offender is the person in charge of the care of the person, unless that person grossly violates his duty of education by offering, giving, or making them available. Subsection (1) No 3a above shall not apply if the act takes place in business transactions with commercial borrowers.

§ 184a Distribution of pornography depicting violence or sodomy

Whosoever

1. disseminates;
2. publicly displays, presents, or otherwise makes accessible; or
3. produces, obtains, supplies, stocks, offers, announces, commends, or undertakes to import or export, in order to use them or copies made from them within the meaning of Nos 1 or 2 above or facilitates such use by another,

[11] BGHSt 43, 369 and Sch/Sch-Lenckner/Perron/Eisele, § 184b, Mn. 11.

pornographic written materials (§ 11(3)) that have as their object acts of violence or sexual acts of persons with animals shall be liable to imprisonment of not more than three years or a fine.

§ 184b Distribution, acquisition and possession of child pornography

(1) Whosoever

   1. disseminates;
   2. publicly displays, presents, or otherwise makes accessible; or
   3. produces, obtains, supplies, stocks, offers, announces, commends, or undertakes to import or export in order to use them or copies made from them within the meaning of Nos 1 or 2 above or facilitates such use by another

   pornographic written materials (§ 11(3)) related to the sexual abuse of children (§§ 176 to 176b) (child pornography) shall be liable to imprisonment from three months to five years.
(2) Whosoever undertakes to obtain possession for another of child pornography reproducing an actual or realistic activity shall incur the same penalty.
(3) In cases under subsection (1) or subsection (2) above the penalty shall be imprisonment of six months to ten years if the offender acts on a commercial basis or as a member of a gang whose purpose is the continued commission of such offences and the child pornography reproduces an actual or realistic activity.
(4) Whosoever undertakes to obtain possession of child pornography reproducing an actual or realistic activity shall be liable to imprisonment of not more than two years or a fine. Whosoever possesses the written materials set forth in the 1st sentence shall incur the same penalty.
(5) Subsections (2) and (4) above shall not apply to acts that exclusively serve the fulfilment of lawful official or professional duties.
(6) In cases under subsection (3) above § 73d shall apply. Objects to which an offence under subsection (2) or (4) above relates shall be subject to a deprivation order. § 74a shall apply.

§ 184c Distribution of pornographic performances by broadcasting, media services or telecommunications services

Whosoever disseminates pornographic performances via broadcast, media services, or telecommunications services shall be liable pursuant to §§ 184 to 184b. In cases under § 184(1) the 1st sentence above shall not apply to dissemination via media services or telecommunications services if it is ensured by technical or other measures that the pornographic performance is not accessible to persons under eighteen years of age.

Unlawful Prostitution

The fact that the views of society have changed as far as the working environment of prostitutes is concerned does not mean that its views on the moral desirability of the institution as such have. In fact, while many people avail themselves of the services of prostitutes, the overall attitude still appears to be that it is an immoral activity and should not be allowed to go on unchecked. Yet one should take care to understand that the aim of §§ 184d to e is the protection from the undesirable side-effects of prostitution, such as kerb-crawling, degradation of residential neighbourhoods because of the nature of the trade and its attendant circumstances, etc, which one might almost describe as a legal NIMBY[12] scenario. In the case of § 184e, it is even more clearly the protection of young and impressionable persons from these factors which would be nigh unavoidable if prostitution were allowed to be practiced openly near schools or private dwellings, etc if the actual form of its exercise is likely to have a corrupting effect on the young person. A discreet escort service, for example, may not fulfil these criteria.[13]

§ 184d Unlawful prostitution

Whosoever persistently contravenes a prohibition enacted by ordinance against engaging in prostitution in particular places at all or during particular times of the day, shall be liable to imprisonment of not more than six months or a fine of not more than one hundred and eighty daily units.

§ 184e Prostitution likely to corrupt juveniles

Whosoever engages in prostitution

1. in the vicinity of a school or other locality which is intended to be visited by persons under eighteen years of age; or
2. in a house in which persons under eighteen years of age live,

in a way which is likely to morally corrupt these persons, shall be liable to imprisonment of not more than one year or a fine.

Human Trafficking

Not situated within the chapter on sexual offences in the Code's Special Part is the offence of human trafficking for sexual exploitation, because the legislature apparently considered that the element of personal freedom of movement was the defining aspect; that is a questionable view given similarly exploitative circumstances that are the basis for offences within the chapter on sexual offences proper.[14] The provision is self-explanatory. § 233a is an ancillary provision that penalises typical support and assistance activities without which human trafficking rings could not operate.

---

[12] NIMBY = Not In My BackYard.
[13] Sch/Sch-Lenckner/Perron/Eisele, § 184d, Mn. 1.
[14] This criticism is shared by Sch/Sch-Eisele, § 232, Mn. 7.

§ 232 Human trafficking for the purpose of sexual exploitation

(1) Whosoever exploits another person's predicament or helplessness arising from being in a foreign country in order to induce them to engage in or continue to engage in prostitution, to engage in exploitative sexual activity with or in the presence of the offender or a third person or to suffer sexual acts on his own person by the offender or a third person shall be liable to imprisonment from six months to ten years. Whosoever induces a person under twenty-one years of age to engage in or continue to engage in prostitution or any of the sexual activity see above mentioned in the 1st sentence above shall incur the same penalty.

(2) The attempt shall be punishable.

(3) The penalty shall be imprisonment from one to ten years if

 1. the victim is a child (§ 176(1));
 2. the offender through the act seriously physically abuses the victim or places the victim in danger of death; or
 3. the offender commits the offence on a commercial basis or as a member of a gang whose purpose is the continued commission of such offences.

(4) The penalty under subsection (3) above shall be imposed on any person who

 1. induces another person by force, threat of serious harm or by deception to engage in or continue to engage in prostitution or any of the sexual activity see above mentioned in subsection (1) 1st sentence above or
 2. gains physical control of another person by force, threat of serious harm or deception to induce them to engage in or continue to engage in prostitution or any of the sexual activity see above mentioned in subsection (1) 1st sentence above.

(5) In less serious cases under subsection (1) above the penalty shall be imprisonment from three months to five years, in less serious cases under subsections (3) and (4) above imprisonment from six months to five years.

§ 233a Assisting in human trafficking

(1) Whosoever assists in human trafficking under § 232 or § 233 by recruiting, transporting, referring, harbouring or sheltering another person shall be liable to imprisonment from three months to five years.

(2) The penalty shall be imprisonment from six months to ten years if

 1. the victim is a child (§ 176(1));
 2. the offender through the act seriously physically abuses the victim or places the victim in danger of death; or
 3. the offender commits the offence on a commercial basis or as a member of a gang whose purpose is the continued commission of such offences.

(3) The attempt shall be punishable.

Stalking

Based on a number of occurrences in recent times, Parliament introduced a stalking offence, because the behaviour involved in stalking could not be adequately caught under other provisions, and these did not fully address the specific harm connected with being stalked. The offence is not as such a sexual offence, but part of its application will be in the context of stalking for sexual purposes.

§ 238 Stalking

(1) Whosoever unlawfully stalks a person by

1. seeking his proximity,
2. trying to establish contact with him by means of telecommunications or other means of communication or through third persons,
3. abusing his personal data for the purpose of ordering goods or services for him or causing third persons to make contact with him,
4. threatening him or a person close to him with loss of life or limb, damage to health or deprivation of freedom, or
5. committing similar acts

and thereby seriously infringes his lifestyle shall be liable to imprisonment of not more than three years or a fine.

(2) The penalty shall be three months to five years if the offender places the victim, a relative of or another person close to the victim in danger of death or serious injury.
(3) If the offender causes the death of the victim, a relative of or another person close to the victim the penalty shall be imprisonment from one to ten years.
(4) Cases under subsection (1) above may only be prosecuted upon request unless the prosecuting authority considers propio motu that prosecution is required because of special public interest.

Forced Marriages

Against the background of a spate of media reports and general indignation in most sectors of society about the practice in some ethnicities represented in the population of Germany, mainly from the Turkish and Kurdish backgrounds, Parliament, apart from other sexuality-related issues, outlawed forced marriages in the 37th Criminal Law (Amendment) Act 2005 and made them an aggravating factor within the general provision of § 240. Forcing a woman to marry against her will is one of the most blatant violations of her right to sexual self-determination, and for this reason a provision solely dedicated to forced marriage as an offence in its own right would have been a more appropriate choice.[15]

---

[15] See also Sch/Sch-Eser, § 240, Mn. 38.

§ 240 Using threats or force to cause a person to do, suffer or omit an act

(1) Whosoever unlawfully with force or threat of serious harm causes a person to commit, suffer or omit an act shall be liable to imprisonment of not more than three years or a fine.
(2) The act shall be unlawful if the use of force or the threat of harm is deemed inappropriate for the purpose of achieving the desired outcome.
(3) The attempt shall be punishable.
(4) In especially serious cases the penalty shall be imprisonment from six months to five years. An especially serious case typically occurs if the offender

    1. causes another person to engage in sexual activity or to enter into marriage;
    2. causes a pregnant woman to terminate the pregnancy; or
    3. abuses his powers or position as a public official.

11

Property Offences

Overview

When we talk about property offences in the context of German criminal law, we need to make a distinction between offences against property in the meaning of '*Eigentum*', ie title to chattels and land, and property in the meaning of '*Vermögen*', ie the assets of a person, which includes *Eigentum* and non-tangible assets such as choses in action, etc. *Vermögen* is thus the wider concept. The category of *Eigentum* is based on a legal criterion, that of *Vermögen* on a combined legal-economic model. One also needs to understand that the offender, of course, cannot obtain *title* by the mere act of stealing—he may by deception—but merely gains possession or the factual opportunity to dispose of the assets, and thus the offences under this heading might be more appropriately entitled 'offences against the right to free possession and enjoyment',[1] but the current practice conveys the same meaning and one should not fuss about labels unnecessarily.[2]

A further fundamental fact is that German law does not use a general term such as 'appropriation', but distinguishes between 'taking away' (*Wegnahme*) and getting the victim to 'dispose of' (*Verfügung*) the protected goods. Taking away means breaking the victim's custody, which is both a narrower and wider concept than possession under civil law (*Besitz*),[3] over a chattel against or without her consent, whilst getting her to dispose of the chattel can be done either by tricking her into parting with it, or by making her do so by threats, as in blackmail. Only the first version can be applied in theft, so that under German law results such as in *Hinks*[4] are excluded. Theft, then, means something different in English and German law, if *Hinks* is to stand. That conclusion must, however, be kept apart from the question of *when* we can talk about *Wegnahme* and when about *Verfügung*, which is not always easy to tell in each individual case. An oft-discussed case in point is that of self-service fuel stations: if D fills up his car with the intention of making off without payment, is he taking the fuel away under § 242, because V, the owner of the station, would not consent to him using the pump if

---

[1] See similarly Sch/Sch-Eser, § 242, Mn. 1–2.
[2] The title suggested might, eg lead to the inclusion of criminal trespass under § 123, which is not as such a property offence.
[3] Sch/Sch-Eser, § 242, Mn. 31.
[4] [2000] Cr App R 1.

he knew of D's intentions, or is he merely appropriating foreign property under § 246? Or is he defrauding V under § 263 because V only lets him use it because all customers make an implied representation that they are going to pay when they use the pump? Can one rely on V's purely internal mental reservations or is he bound by the external fact that he has made it possible for everyone to use the pumps? Does it matter whether he actually observes D while the latter is fuelling up? Depending on the individual circumstances, any of the provisions may apply. In the last scenario, we may have at least an attempted fraud, if D realises that V, who sees him, may be letting him use the pump in the expectation that he will pay like anyone else. If V sees D coming and because he has had trouble with him before tells him to go away, it may be theft if D nevertheless uses the pump and V cannot interfere because, to create an improbable example, he is tied to a wheel-chair after an accident and cannot put up any real resistance. If none of these apply, D may, according to some, acquire title to the fuel by filling it into the tank of his car and, therefore, if he makes off with it, may no longer fulfil the element of 'property belonging to someone else'. This is also a good example of the fact that in property offences in particular, issues of civil law play a large role in defining the normative elements of the *Tatbestand*.[5]

The classic[6] law of property offences is divided into Chapter 19 on theft and related offences, Chapter 20 on robbery and blackmail, Chapter 21 on assistance after the fact and handling stolen goods and Chapter 22 on fraud and embezzlement. We will look at a number of the offences in these chapters in turn.

Theft and Unlawful Appropriation

The basic offence is laid out in § 242:

§ 242 Theft

(1) Whosoever takes chattels belonging to another away from another with the intention of unlawfully appropriating them for himself or a third person shall be liable to imprisonment of not more than five years or a fine.
(2) The attempt shall be punishable.

Theft under § 242 only applies to chattels. One cannot take away land, although, of course, one can defraud a victim out of its possession or even title. V's consent to D's taking possession of the chattel acts as a factor negating the *actus reus*, not as a defence in the proper meaning. D must have the *intention* to appropriate (*Zueignungsabsicht*) the chattel unlawfully, which means he must intend to treat it

---

[5] See on the discussion with further references Sch/Sch-Eser, § 246, Mn. 7.

[6] There are, of course, numerous offences that impact on issues of property, either directly or indirectly, such as in insolvency offences, bribery, etc, yet the core crimes are found in the Chapters of the Criminal Code mentioned in this chapter.

as if he were the rightful owner, who has the full power to dispose of any chattel as he sees fit, without actually having the right to do so. Traditionally, this intention is divided into two subcategories, that of intending V's *Enteignung*, ie the exclusion of the previous owner's control, and intending the *Aneignung*, the establishment of D's own permanent control over the chattel. The second subcategory is the one which distinguishes theft from the merely unlawful use of the chattel (*furtum usus*), which is, with a few exceptions such as, for example, taking a motor-vehicle under § 248b[7] and unlawful use of pawns under § 290,[8] not an offence.

The offence of theft has a number of derivative offences in the wider meaning, for example, § 243:

§ 243 Aggravated theft

(1) In especially serious cases of theft the penalty shall be imprisonment from three months to ten years. An especially serious case typically occurs if the offender

1. for the purpose of the commission of the offence breaks into or enters a building, official or business premises or another enclosed space or intrudes by using a false key or other tool not typically used for gaining access or hides in the room;

---

[7] See for a similar problem in English law the recent case of *Mitchell* [2008] All ER (D) 109 (Apr): D was charged with robbery. He had been one of four men who had crashed their vehicle after being pursued by police officers, and had then approached V, who had been sitting in her husband's car, smashed the windows of her car, pulled her out, and had then driven off with the vehicle, which they subsequently abandoned. The prosecution relied on s 6(1) of the Theft Act 1968. There was evidence that after abandoning the first car, D and others had taken a red car which was later abandoned, and that they had taken another car, which they had later burnt. The judge found that the taking, using and abandoning of the vehicle was sufficient evidence capable of amounting to an intention to dispose of property regardless of owner's rights pursuant to s 6(1) of the Act. It was conceded by the prosecution that the red vehicle, which had been taken after the first vehicle, had not been stolen. In response to a question about the difference between that vehicle and the vehicle from which the victim had been ejected, counsel submitted that in the latter case, the distinguishing feature was that the victim had been removed with force, hence showing an intention by D to treat the vehicle as his. D was convicted and appealed. The appeal was successful. The Court of Appeal held that the purpose of s 6 was not to widen the requirement pursuant to s 1 to permanently deprive the other of property substantially. It provided a broader definition of that intention to deal with a small number of difficult cases which arose when, even if there was no intention permanently to deprive, nevertheless, something equivalent that could be obtained through the intention to treat the thing as one's own and to dispose of the owner's right. S 6(1) was not intended to cut down the definition of theft in s 1(1) of the 1968 Act. Accordingly, not every conversion amounted to theft. If that were the case, it would mean, eg that every case of taking a vehicle without authority contrary to s 12 of the Act would amount to a case of theft. Theft had to be present to establish an offence of robbery. Theft required an intention permanently to deprive the owner of property or an intention under s 6(1) of the Act. In the instant case, the facts did not support a case of theft or of robbery to go before the jury. The victim's vehicle had plainly been taken for the purpose of use as a getaway car. There had been nothing about its use or subsequent abandonment to suggest otherwise. The obvious prima facie inference to be drawn was that the defendant had needed another conveyance. The fact that the taking of the two other vehicles could not be prosecuted as a case of theft demonstrated that the taking of the victim's car could not be regarded as a case of theft or robbery. None of the authorities extended the scope of s 6 to a case, however violent, of taking a car for its brief use before abandoning it.

[8] '§ 290 Unlawful use of pawns

Public pawnbrokers who make unauthorised use of the chattels which they have taken as a pawn shall be liable to imprisonment of not more than one year or a fine.'

2. steals property which is especially protected by a sealed container or other protective equipment;
3. steals on a commercial basis;
4. steals property which is dedicated to religious worship or used for religious veneration from a church or other building or space used for the practice of religion;
5. steals property of significance for science, art or history or for technical development which is located in a generally accessible collection or is publicly exhibited;
6. steals by exploiting the helplessness of another person, an accident or a common danger; or
7. steals a firearm for the acquisition of which a licence is required under the Weapons Act, a machine gun, a submachine gun, a fully or semi-automatic rifle or a military weapon containing an explosive within the meaning of the Weapons of War (Control) Act or an explosive.

(2) In cases under subsection (1) 2nd sentence Nos 1 to 6 above an especially serious case shall be excluded if the property is of minor value.

§ 243 contains a non-exhaustive list of examples of aggravated cases of theft, such as breaking and entering; these examples are, however, not proper qualifications of the *Tatbestand* of theft itself, but typified examples (*Regelbeispiele*) of sentencing factors that make a theft into an aggravated case. Nevertheless, they are treated similarly to offence elements as far as the knowledge of the offender is concerned; this is a function of the general principle of blameworthiness (*Schuldprinzip*) that would forbid punishing D with an increased sentence unless he or she was aware of the factors that made his or her conduct more serious than the average case. The character of these typifications as sentencing factors also has an impact on the attempt liability if the theft has been completed, but the sentencing factor only attempted, ie D wants to break into V's house to steal a precious Ming vase by breaking down the door, but finds the door open. Because the breaking and entering is not a proper offence element, using it as one is prohibited by the ban on analogy, so the fact that D intended to break down the door may only serve as an independent indicator that the case is an aggravated one.[9] No problem exists, however, if D breaks down the door and then only gets to the attempt stage of taking away the vase, because V catches him in the act, for example: the sentencing factor has been fulfilled and the attempt is thus an aggravated one.

Other qualifications are § 244 and its sister provision, § 244a:

§ 244 Carrying weapons; acting as a member of a gang; burglary of private homes

(1) Whosoever

1. commits a theft during which he or another accomplice

   a) see above carries a weapon or another dangerous instrument;
   b) otherwise carries an instrument or means in order to prevent or overcome the resistance of another person by force or threat of force;

---

[9] See on the discussion Sch/Sch-Eser, § 243, Mn. 44.

2. steals as a member of a gang whose purpose is the continued commission of robbery or theft under participation of another member of the gang; or
3. commits a theft for the commission of which he breaks into or enters a dwelling or intrudes by using a false key or other tool not typically used for gaining access or hides in the dwelling

shall be liable to imprisonment from six months to ten years.
(2) The attempt shall be punishable.
(3) In cases under subsection (1) No 2 above, § 43a and § 73d shall apply.

§ 244a Aggravated gang theft

(1) Whosoever commits theft under the conditions listed in § 243 (1) 2nd sentence or in cases under § 244(1) Nos 1 or 3 as a member of a gang whose purpose is the continued commission of robbery or theft under participation of another member of the gang shall be liable to imprisonment from one to ten years.
(2) In less serious cases the penalty shall be imprisonment from six months to five years.
(3) § 43a and § 73d shall apply.

§ 244, in contrast to § 243, provides a real qualification of § 242. A hybrid provision is § 244a on aggravated gang theft, which makes reference to the *Regelbeispiele* of § 243; however, because of the reference in § 244a, some commentators have argued that they have become proper qualifications and lost their character as mere sentencing factors.[10] See also § 252 on theft in connection with the use of force, etc below, where the rules on robbery are made applicable.

§§ 247 and 248a contain conditions on the prosecution of less serious cases of theft, either because the victim was a relative, etc or because the value of the stolen object was negligible. Generally, it is not merely the financial value of the object that determines the applicability of § 248a, yet the courts appear to be developing tariffs nonetheless, and currently the borderline seems to hover around €50.[11]

§ 247 Theft from relatives or persons living in the same home

If a relative, the guardian or the carer of the offender is the victim of the theft or if the victim lives in the same household as the offender the offence may only be prosecuted upon request.

§ 248a Theft and unlawful appropriation of objects or minor value

Theft and unlawful appropriation of property of minor value may only be prosecuted upon request in cases under § 242 and § 246, unless the prosecuting authority considers propio motu that prosecution is required because of special public interest.

§ 248b establishes liability for taking a motor vehicle without the necessary intent of permanent appropriation:

---

[10] Sch/Sch-Eser, § 244a, Mn. 4.
[11] Sch/Sch-Eser, § 248a, Mn. 7–10.

§ 248b Unlawful taking of a motor-vehicle or bicycle

(1) Whosoever uses a motor-vehicle or a bicycle against the will of the person authorised to use it shall be liable to imprisonment of not more than three years or a fine unless the act is subject to a more severe penalty under other provisions.
(2) The attempt shall be punishable.
(3) The offence may only be prosecuted upon request.
(4) Motor-vehicles within the meaning of this provision are vehicles which are driven by machine power; this applies to terrestrial motor-vehicles only to the extent that they are not rail-bound vehicles.

Because theft only applies to chattels, the 'stealing' of electrical energy could not be subsumed under § 242, which made a special provision necessary to cover this scenario, § 248c:

§ 248c Theft of electrical energy

(1) Whosoever taps the electrical energy of another from an electrical facility or installation by means of a conductor which is not intended for the regular withdrawal of energy from the facility or installation, shall, if the offence was committed with the intent of appropriating the electrical energy for himself or a third person, be liable to imprisonment of not more than five years or a fine.
(2) The attempt shall be punishable.
(3) § 247 and § 248a shall apply mutatis mutandis.
(4) If the offence under subsection (1) above is committed with the intent of unlawfully inflicting damage on another the penalty shall be imprisonment of not more than two years or a fine. The offence may only be prosecuted upon request.

Theft under § 242, as we saw, requires the breaking of V's custody. Not so for § 246, which is related to unlawful appropriation:

§ 246 Unlawful appropriation

(1) Whosoever unlawfully appropriates chattels belonging to another for himself or a third person shall be liable to imprisonment of not more than three years or a fine unless the offence is subject to a more severe penalty under other provisions.
(2) If in cases under subsection (1) above the property was entrusted to the offender the penalty shall be imprisonment of not more than five years or a fine.
(3) The attempt shall be punishable.

§ 246 catches cases where D factually appropriates chattels without breaking V's custody, for example, if V has lent D his car for the weekend and D does not give it back, rather she goes on to sell it to T.

Robbery and Blackmail

§§ 249 to 255 deal with the offences of robbery and blackmail. Whereas at first glance it would appear that robbery is merely another qualification of theft, ie theft by force or use of threats, this is not the case. Robbery has long been recognised as a separate and distinct offence,[12] which is supported by § 252. Its character as such is that of a theft combined with elements of force; the protected interest, however, is not just the property of V, but also her personal freedom. §§ 249 to 251 provide for different forms of robbery, and § 252 equates a theft where D uses force not to *obtain* possession, but to *retain* it, with robbery:

§ 249 Robbery

(1) Whosoever, by force against a person or threats of imminent danger to life or limb, takes chattels belonging to another from another with the intent of appropriating the property for himself or a third person, shall be liable to imprisonment of not less than one year.

(2) In less serious cases the penalty shall be imprisonment from six months to five years.

§ 250 Aggravated robbery

(1) The penalty shall be imprisonment of not less than three years if

    1. the offender or another accomplice to the robbery

        (a) carries a weapon or other dangerous instrument;
        (b) otherwise carries an instrument or means in order to prevent or overcome the resistance of another person by force or threat force;
        (c) by the act places another person in danger of serious injury; or

    2. the offender commits the robbery as a member of a gang whose purpose is the continued commission of robbery or theft under participation of another member of the gang.

(2) The penalty shall be imprisonment of not less than five years if the offender or another accomplice to the robbery

    1. uses a weapon or other dangerous instrument during the commission of the offence;
    2. carries a weapon in cases under subsection (1) No 2 above; or
    3. during or by the offence

        (a) seriously physically abuses another person; or
        (b) places another person in danger of death.

(3) In less serious cases under subsections (1) and (2) above the penalty shall be imprisonment from one to ten years.

§ 251 Robbery causing death

If by the robbery (§ 249 and § 250) the offender at least by gross negligence causes the death of another person the penalty shall be imprisonment for life or not less than ten years.

---

[12] BGH NJW 1968, 1292.

§ 252 Theft and use of force to retain stolen goods

Whosoever when caught in the act during the commission of a theft uses force against a person or threats of imminent danger to life and limb in order to retain possession of the stolen property shall be liable to the same penalty as a robber.

Robbery in all its form requires the use of force or threats *as a means* in order to make the taking away of a chattel, ie property in the sense of *Eigentum* possible. That is why § 252 is an important extension of the offence of theft, because in that situation D is using it only to ensure that he keeps possession of the already stolen object.

Blackmail in § 253 is an offence that combines the offence of compulsion under § 240 with damage to property in the sense of *Vermögen*. The basic offence has a relatively low sentencing scale, but as we can see from § 255, it is equated with robbery if the means of robbery are employed which raises the minimum sentence to one year and opens up the range to the maximum sentence of 15 years.

§ 253 Blackmail

(1) Whosoever unlawfully with force or threat of serious harm causes a person to commit, suffer or omit an act and thereby causes damage to the assets of that person or of another in order to enrich himself or a third person unlawfully shall be liable to imprisonment of not more than five years or a fine.
(2) The act shall be unlawful if the use of force or the threat of harm is deemed inappropriate to the purpose of achieving the desired outcome.
(3) The attempt shall be punishable.
(4) In especially serious cases the penalty shall be imprisonment of not less than one year. An especially serious case typically occurs if the offender acts on a commercial basis or as a member of a gang whose purpose is the continued commission of blackmail.

. . .

§ 255 Blackmail and use of force or threats against life or limb

If the blackmail is committed by using force against a person or threats of imminent danger to life or limb the offender shall be liable to the same penalty as a robber.

This does, of course, raise the question of how to delineate robbery from blackmail in those cases. The answer is that conceptually for § 255 only *vis compulsiva* can apply.[13] Generally, any use of force that robs the victim of the choice to decide whether or not to part with the goods will more likely be seen as robbery than as blackmail, although the distinction can be difficult in the individual case and the courts tend to view the mere acceptance of D's actions by V (*Duldung*) as sufficient, instead of a *Verfügung* as required by the prevailing opinion in academic commentary.[14] This leads to undesirable conceptual overlaps.

[13] Sch/Sch-Eser, § 255, Mn. 2.
[14] Sch/Sch-Eser, § 253, Mn. 8–8a.

Assistance after the Fact and Handling Stolen Goods

§ 257 on assistance after the fact and § 259 on handling stolen goods are as such both support or ancillary offences to a previous property offence. Both require that D was not already an accomplice to the previous offence:

§ 257 Assistance after the fact

(1) Whosoever renders assistance to another who has committed an unlawful act, with the intent of securing for him the benefits of that act, shall be liable to imprisonment of not more than five years or a fine.

(2) The penalty must not be more severe than that for the act.

(3) Whosoever is liable as an accomplice to the act shall not be liable for assistance after the fact. This shall not apply to a person who abets another person who did not take part in the act to provide assistance after the fact.

(4) An offence of assistance after the fact may only be prosecuted upon request, authorisation or a request by the foreign state if the offender could only be prosecuted upon request, authorisation or a request by the foreign state if he had been a principal or secondary participant to the act. § 248 shall apply mutatis mutandis.

. . .

§ 259 Handling stolen goods

(1) Whosoever in order to enrich himself or a third person, buys, otherwise procures for himself or a third person, disposes of, or assists in disposing of property that another has stolen or otherwise acquired by an unlawful act directed against the property of another shall be liable to imprisonment of not more than five years or a fine.

(2) § 247 and § 248a shall apply mutatis mutandis.

(3) The attempt shall be punishable.

§ 260 and § 261a take the handling to a more serious level of punishment if it is done commercially or as a member of a gang:

§ 260 Handling on a commercial basis or as a member of a gang

(1) Whosoever handles stolen goods

1. on a commercial basis; or
2. as a member of a gang whose purpose is the continued commission of robbery, theft or handling stolen goods

shall be liable to imprisonment from six months to ten years.

(2) The attempt shall be punishable.

(3) In cases under subsection (1) No 2 above, § 43a and §73d shall apply. § 73d shall also apply in cases under subsection (1) No 1 above.

§ 260a Commercial handling as a member of a gang

(1) Whosoever on a commercial basis handles stolen goods as a member of a gang, whose purpose is the continued commission of robbery, theft or handling stolen goods shall be liable to imprisonment from one to ten years.

(2) In less serious cases the penalty shall be imprisonment from six months to five years.

(3) § 43a and §73d shall apply.

A specific form of assistance after the fact or handling in the wider sense is the offence of money laundering under § 261, which is strictly speaking not a property offence, but may include them as previous offences, and is included here for completeness's sake:

§ 261 Money laundering; hiding unlawfully obtained financial benefits

(1) Whosoever hides an object which is a proceed of an unlawful act listed in the 2nd sentence below, conceals its origin or obstructs or endangers the investigation of its origin, its being found, its confiscation, its deprivation or its being officially secured shall be liable to imprisonment from three months to five years. Unlawful acts within the meaning of the 1st sentence shall be

1. felonies;
2. misdemeanours under

   (a) § 332(1), also in conjunction with subsection (3), and § 334;
   (b) § 29(1) 1st sentence No 1 of the Drugs Act and § 29(1) No 1 of the Drug Precursors (Control) Act;

3. misdemeanours under § 373 and under § 374(2) of the Fiscal Code, and also in conjunction with § 12(1) of the Common Market Organisations and Direct Payments (Implementation) Act;
4. misdemeanours

   (a) under § 152a, § 181a, § 232(1) and (2), § 233(1) and (2), § 233a, § 242, § 246, § 253, § 259, §§ 263 to 264, § 266, § 267, § 269, § 284, § 326(1), (2) and (4), and § 328(1), (2) and (4);
   (b) under § 96 of the Residence Act and § 84 of the Asylum Procedure Act and § 370 of the Fiscal Code

   which were committed on a commercial basis or by a member of a gang whose purpose is the continued commission of such offences; and

5. misdemeanours under § 129 and § 129a(3) and (5), all of which also in conjunction with § 129b(1), as well as misdemeanours committed by a member of a criminal or terrorist organisation (§ 129 and § 129a, all of which also in conjunction with § 129b(1)).

The 1st sentence shall apply in cases of tax evasion committed on a commercial basis or as a gang under § 370 of the Fiscal Code, to expenditure saved by virtue of the tax evasion, of unlawfully acquired tax repayments and allowances, and in cases under the 2nd sentence no 3 the 1st sentence shall also apply to an object in relation to which fiscal charges have been evaded.

(2) Whosoever

1. procures an object indicated in subsection (1) above for himself or a third person; or
2. keeps an object indicated in subsection (1) above in his custody or uses it for himself or a third person if he knew the origin of the object at the time of obtaining possession of it

shall incur the same penalty.

(3) The attempt shall be punishable.
(4) In especially serious cases the penalty shall be imprisonment from six months to ten years. An especially serious case typically occurs if the offender acts on a commercial basis or as a member of a gang whose purpose is the continued commission of money laundering.
(5) Whosoever, in cases under subsections (1) or (2) above is, through gross negligence, unaware of the fact that the object is a proceed from an unlawful act named in subsection (1) above shall be liable to imprisonment of not more than two years or a fine.
(6) The act shall not be punishable under subsection (2) above if a third person previously acquired the object without having thereby committed an offence.
(7) Objects to which the offence relates may be subject to a deprivation order. § 74a shall apply. § 43a and § 73d shall apply if the offender acts as a member of a gang whose purpose is the continued commission of money laundering. § 73d shall also apply if the offender acts on a commercial basis.
(8) Objects which are proceeds from an offence listed in subsection (1) above committed abroad shall be equivalent to the objects indicated in subsections (1), (2) and (5) above if the offence is also punishable at the place of its commission.
(9) Whosoever

1. voluntarily reports the offence to the competent public authority or voluntarily causes such a report to be made, unless the act had already been discovered in whole or in part at the time and the offender knew this or could reasonably have known and
2. in cases under subsections (1) or (2) above under the conditions named in No 1 above causes the object to which the offence relates to be officially secured

shall not be liable under subsections (1) to (5) above.
Whosoever is liable because of his participation in the antecedent act shall not be liable under subsections (1) to (5) above, either.
(10) The court in its discretion may mitigate the sentence (§ 49(2)) in cases under subsections (1) to (5) above or order a discharge under these provisions if the offender through voluntary disclosure of his knowledge has substantially contributed to the discovery of the offence beyond his own contribution thereto, or of an unlawful act of another named in subsection (1) above.

Fraud and Embezzlement

§§ 263 to 265b cover different forms of fraud, the basic offence being § 263, as well as computer fraud, subsidy fraud, capital investment fraud and insurance fraud and obtaining credit by deception. German law has so far resisted the temptation that the law of England and Wales has succumbed to with the Fraud Act 2006 of omitting the requirement of causing damage to V's assets and making fraud an inchoate offence. In structure and doctrine, the law in Germany is therefore still more akin to that of England and Wales until 2007.

§ 263 Fraud

(1) Whosoever with the intent of obtaining for himself or a third person an unlawful material benefit damages the property of another by causing or maintaining an error by pretending false facts or by distorting or suppressing true facts shall be liable to imprisonment of not more than five years or a fine.
(2) The attempt shall be punishable.
(3) In especially serious cases the penalty shall be imprisonment from six months to ten years. An especially serious case typically occurs if the offender

    1. acts on a commercial basis or as a member of a gang whose purpose is the continued commission of forgery or fraud;
    2. causes a major financial loss of or acts with the intent of placing a large number of persons in danger of financial loss by the continued commission of offences of fraud;
    3. places another person in financial hardship;
    4. abuses his powers or his position as a public official; or
    5. pretends that an insured event has happened after he or another have for this purpose set fire to an object of significant value or destroyed it, in whole or in part, through setting fire to it or caused the sinking or beaching of a ship.

(4) § 243(2), § 247 and § 248a shall apply mutatis mutandis.
(5) Whosoever on a commercial basis commits fraud as a member of a gang, whose purpose is the continued commission of offences under §§ 263 to 264 or §§ 267 to 269 shall be liable to imprisonment from one to ten years, in less serious cases to imprisonment from six months to five years.
(6) The court may make a supervision order (§ 68(1)).
(7) § 43a and 73d shall apply if the offender acts as a member of a gang whose purpose is the continued commission of offences under §§ 263 to 264 or §§ 267 to 269. § 73d shall also apply if the offender acts on a commercial basis.

§ 263a Computer fraud

(1) Whosoever with the intent of obtaining for himself or a third person an unlawful material benefit damages the property of another by influencing the result of a data processing operation through incorrect configuration of a program, use of incorrect or incomplete data, unauthorised use of data or other unauthorised influence on the course of the processing shall be liable to imprisonment of not more than five years or a fine.
(2) § 263(2) to (7) shall apply mutatis mutandis.
(3) Whosoever prepares an offence under subsection (1) above by writing computer programs the purpose of which is to commit such an act, or procures them for himself or another, offers them for sale, or holds or supplies them to another shall be liable to imprisonment of not more than three years or a fine.
(4) In cases under subsection (3) above § 149(2) and (3) shall apply mutatis mutandis.

§ 264 Subsidy fraud

(1) Whosoever

    1. makes incorrect or incomplete statements about facts relevant for granting a subsidy to himself or another that are advantageous for himself or the other, to a

public authority competent to approve a subsidy or to another agency or person which is involved in the subsidy procedure (subsidy giver);

2. uses an object or monetary benefit the use of which is restricted by law or by the subsidy giver in relation to a subsidy contrary to that restriction;
3. withholds, contrary to the law relating to grants of subsidies, information about facts relevant to the subsidy from the subsidy giver; or
4. uses a certificate of subsidy entitlement or about facts relevant to a subsidy, which was acquired through incorrect or incomplete statements in subsidy proceedings,

shall be liable to imprisonment of not more than five years or a fine.

(2) In especially serious cases the penalty shall be imprisonment from six months to ten years. An especially serious case typically occurs if the offender

1. acquires, out of gross self-seeking or by using counterfeit or falsified documentation, an unjustified large subsidy for himself or another;
2. abuses his powers or his position as a public official; or
3. uses the assistance of a public official who abuses his powers or his position.

(3) § 263(5) shall apply mutatis mutandis.
(4) Whosoever acts in gross negligence in cases under subsection (1) Nos 1 to 3 above shall be liable to imprisonment of not more than three years or a fine.
(5) Whosoever voluntarily prevents the granting of a subsidy on the basis of the offence shall not be liable pursuant to subsections (1) and (4) above. If the subsidy is not granted regardless of the contribution of the offender he shall be exempt from liability if he voluntarily and earnestly makes efforts to prevent the subsidy from being granted.
(6) In addition to a sentence of imprisonment of at least one year for an offence under subsections (1) to (3) above the court may order the loss of the ability to hold public office, to vote and see above be elected in public elections (§ 45(2) and (5)). Objects to which the offence relates may be subject to a deprivation order; § 74a shall apply.
(7) A subsidy for the purposes of this provision shall mean

1. a benefit from public funds under Federal or state law for businesses or enterprises, which at least in part

   a) is granted without market-related consideration; and
   b) is intended for the promotion of the economy;

2. a benefit from public funds under the law of the European Communities which is granted at least in part without market-related consideration.

A public enterprise shall also be deemed to be a business or enterprise within the meaning of the 1st sentence No 1 above.

(8) Facts shall be relevant to a subsidy within the meaning of subsection (1) above

1. if they are designated as being relevant to a subsidy by law or by the subsidy giver on the basis of a law; or
2. if the approval, grant, reclaiming, renewal or continuation or a subsidy depends on them for reasons of law.

§ 264a Capital investment fraud

(1) Whosoever in connection with

1. the sale of securities, subscription rights or shares intended to grant participation in the yield of an enterprise; or
2. an offer to increase the capital investment in such shares,

makes incorrect favourable statements or keeps unfavourable facts secret in prospectuses or in representations or surveys about the net assets to a considerable number of persons in relation to circumstances relevant to the decision about acquisition or increase, shall be liable to imprisonment of not more than three years or a fine.
(2) Subsection (1) above shall apply mutatis mutandis if the act is related to shares in assets which an enterprise administers in its own name but for the account of a third party.
(3) Whosoever voluntarily prevents the benefit contingent upon the acquisition or the increase from accruing shall not be liable pursuant to subsections (1) and (2) above. If the benefit does not accrue regardless of the contribution of the offender he shall be exempt from liability if he voluntarily and earnestly makes efforts to prevent the benefit from accruing.

§ 265 Insurance fraud

(1) Whosoever damages, destroys, impairs the usefulness of, disposes of or supplies to another an object which is insured against destruction, damage, impairment of use, loss or theft in order to obtain for himself or a third party a payment from the insurance shall be liable to imprisonment of not more than three years or a fine unless the offence is punishable under § 263.
(2) The attempt shall be punishable.

. . .

§ 265b Obtaining credit by deception

(1) Whosoever, in connection with an application for or for a continuance of credit or modification of the terms of credit for a business or enterprise or for a fictitious business or enterprise

1. (a) submits incorrect or incomplete documentation, in particular, calculations of balance, profit and loss, summaries of assets and liabilities or appraisal reports; or
   (b) makes incorrect or incomplete written statements,

about financial circumstances that are favourable to the credit applicant and relevant to the decision on such an application, to a business or enterprise; or
2. does not inform a business or enterprise in the submission about any deterioration in the financial circumstances represented in the documentation or statements that are relevant to the decision on such an application,

shall be liable to imprisonment of not more than three years or a fine.
(2) Whosoever voluntarily prevents the creditor from providing the credit applied for shall not be liable pursuant to subsection (1) above. If the credit is not provided regardless of the contribution of the offender he shall be exempt from liability if he voluntarily and earnestly makes efforts to prevent the credit from being provided.

(3) Within the meaning of subsection (1) above

1. businesses and enterprises shall be those which require by their nature and size, but regardless of their purpose, a properly organised operation applying the appropriate commercial customs, rules and standards;
2. credits shall be money loans of all kinds, acceptance credits, the acquisition for payment or the deferment of monetary claims, the discounting of promissory notes and cheques and the assumption of sureties, guarantees and other warranties.

Because of the problem that one cannot as such deceive machines and other facilities, a special provision was required that covered their fraudulent manipulation:

§ 265a Obtaining services by deception

(1) Whosoever obtains the service of a machine or a telecommunications network serving public purposes or uses a means of transportation or obtains entrance to an event or institution by deception with the intent of not paying for them shall be liable to imprisonment of not more than one year or a fine unless the act is punishable under other provisions with a more severe penalty.
(2) The attempt shall be punishable.
(3) § 247 and § 248a shall apply mutatis mutandis.

The final offences to be examined in this chapter are § 266 on embezzlement and § 266b on misuse of credit cards. § 266 has two alternatives: the abuse of power (*Missbrauch*) to make binding agreements for another; and the violation of a duty of trust (*Treubruch*) to safeguard another's property interests in the sense of *Vermögen*. The prevailing opinion in the jurisprudence and academic commentary appears to treat the *Missbrauch* as a special case of *Treubruch*, especially with regard to the question of the responsibility for another's property interests, which under the mere wording of the provision does not clearly apply to both alternatives;[15] this is, however, controversial.

§ 266 Embezzlement and abuse of trust

(1) Whosoever abuses the power accorded him by statute, by commission of a public authority or legal transaction to dispose of assets of another or to make binding agreements for another, or violates his duty to safeguard the property interests of another incumbent upon him by reason of statute, commission of a public authority, legal transaction or fiduciary relationship, and thereby causes damage to the person, whose property interests he was responsible for, shall be liable to imprisonment of not more than five years or a fine.
(2) § 243(2), § 247, § 248a and § 263(3) shall apply mutatis mutandis.

§ 266b is a special case of duty of care encountered in the ubiquitous use of credit cards, where fraud is inapplicable because of the lack of an act of deception, and § 266 is not triggered because the holder of the credit card has been given

---

[15] Sch/Sch-Eser, § 266, Mn. 2 with references and the dissenting view of *Eser*.

the power to make binding agreements in his or her own—not the issuer's—interests.[16]

§ 266b Misuse of cheque and credit cards

(1) Whosoever abuses the possibility accorded him through delivery of a cheque or credit card of obliging the issuer to make a payment and thereby causes damage to the issuer shall be liable to imprisonment of not more than three years or a fine.
(2) § 248a shall apply mutatis mutandis.

[16] Sch/Sch-Eser, § 266b, Mn. 1.

INDEX

Index

Index

Index

Index